Working Women

Working Women
Stories of Strife, Struggle and Survival

Edited by

Kogi Naidoo and Fay Patel

Los Angeles • London • New Delhi • Singapore • Washington DC
www.sagepublications.com

First published in 2009 by

 SAGE Publications India Pvt Ltd
B1/I-1 Mohan Cooperative Industrial Area
Mathura Road, New Delhi 110 044, India
www.sagepub.in

SAGE Publications Inc
2455 Teller Road
Thousand Oaks
California 91320, USA

SAGE Publications Ltd
1 Oliver's Yard, 55 City Road
London EC1Y 1SP, United Kingdom

SAGE Publications Asia-Pacific Pte Ltd
33 Pekin Street
#02-01 Far East Square
Singapore 048763

Published by Vivek Mehra for SAGE Publications India Pvt Ltd, typeset in 10/13 pt Aldine401 BT by Star Compugraphics Private Limited, Delhi and printed at Chaman Enterprises, New Delhi.

Library of Congress Cataloging-in-Publication Data

Working woman: stories of strife, struggle, and survival/edited by Kogi Naidoo and Fay Patel.

    p. cm.

Includes bibliographical references.

    1. Women—Employment. 2. Women—Psychology. 3. Women—History. I. Naidoo, K., 1956– II. Patel, Fay.

HD6053.W6775	331.4—dc22	2009	2008048188

ISBN: 978-81-7829-922-8 (HB)

The SAGE Team: Rekha Natarajan, Sushmita Banerjee, Anju Saxena and Trinankur Banerjee

We dedicate this book to all those women who experience pain and suffering everyday but who cannot have their voices heard and are never seen. Let us not forget them.

This book is also dedicated to our parents, to the men in our lives and to our children who supported us in our personal and professional growth and development through the many struggles in our lives. Their love and encouragement gave us strength to tell our stories through other voices.

∽∾

I am grateful to my husband and partner, Siva Naidoo, and our children, Kami and Des, for their belief in me and their ongoing support. It has made all the hard work, struggles and strife worthwhile.

Kogi Naidoo

∽∾

I am indebted to my husband Feisal Patel and to our son Farhaan for their patience and endurance over the past 20 years as we struggled through life's many challenges. Each one of us gave up so many of our own dreams to support the other. However, we were always blessed by the grace of God and our love endured through time and distance. Most of all, our spirit remained strong because of our faith in God and humanity.

Fay (Feiziya) Patel

∽∾

Contents

Foreword

This book makes a valuable contribution of making explicit the connections between success, struggles and strife of women venturing into different work-spaces. Sometimes some studies that favour a particular viewpoint become judgemental and may even be ethnocentric, thereby disempowering or silencing alternative perspectives. This book attempts to address this problem by supporting the feminist goal of making the different voices of women heard without exploiting, distorting or trivialising their experiences. It is premised on the 'important assumption that women in specific contexts are best suited to help develop presentations of their lives and that contexts are located in specific structures and historical and material moments' (Olesen 2000: 235). The book is an interesting collection of papers with different formats—some staying within and some flowing across the academic boundaries—blurring what is academic and what is non-academic.

A key strength of this book lies in bringing together the diverse perspectives of women from very different social and cultural backgrounds. These are stories of women who have achieved success within their own contexts, and which reflect the struggles, strife and loss that women experience in order to succeed. Each chapter unfolds a different dimension of success and the associated struggles. Each form of success is equally worthwhile and challenging. Juxtaposing perspectives of women from such different walks of life has a powerful effect of creating a unified *we*. Several common themes emerge from the diverse experiences of women reported in this book, such as competing commitments in their various roles, exploitation at work, a sense of isolation, loss of health, impact on family and challenges associated with maintaining their confidence and dignity in difficult circumstances. Despite these common themes, the unified *we* that is promoted in this book is not a single *we*, in other words, it does not simplify or essentialise women's experience. Rather, it is a fluid *we* that is more encompassing, more uncertain, more empathetic to the cultural and contextual nature of the successes, struggles and strife encountered by these women. An excellent example of this is an insightful reflection from Thenjiwe Magwaza where she deconstructs the Western notion of a 'balanced life' to contest its viability and desirability in all contexts.

The diversity of forms of success and struggles, strategies for overcoming various challenges and perspectives on morality and spirituality, as represented by different women in this book is impressive. On the one hand, it allowed me to bond with the authors and the participants whose perspectives are represented in different chapters. I could resonate with the many themes represented here, such as the isolation and struggles of academic life, loss of health, loss of relationships and a sense of failing to meet everyone's expectations. On the other hand, it had the powerful effect of helping me see through many different lenses. Each chapter highlights a different notion of success, empowerment, financial independence, emancipation, fulfilment, loss, grief, dignity and hidden costs of success. Vivid descriptions of diverse dilemmas, struggles and losses that these women went through in their pursuits of fulfilment forced me to question the artificiality of several dichotomies: among them, success and failure, good and bad, moral and immoral, and ethical and unethical.

What might success mean to a single mother? How might someone with a physical disability define success? How are women being exploited within different professions? How little time are women able to give themselves in their attempts to meet the demands of their various roles? What are some strategies that worked for these women in different circumstances? These are all very important questions addressed from multiple angles in this book.

The simplicity of representational styles adopted in different chapters makes it an easy read. It has the potential to provide a genuine feel for the struggles, dilemmas, value decisions, trade-offs that the women had to go through in achieving their independence. The book will appeal to many women from different walks of life. In particular, women's clubs, support groups and working women internationally will be able to identify with the stories in the book and will find the book an inspirational collection. Even though this book may not fall within the traditional boundaries of 'academic' work, the breadth of perspectives represented here and the authenticity and credibility of various accounts makes it a good resource for anyone venturing into feminist studies, cultural studies and organisational communication culture.

Harsh Suri
Centre for the Advancement of Learning and Teaching
Monash University, Melbourne

REFERENCE

Olesen, V.L. 2000. 'Feminisms and Qualitative Research at and into the Millennium', in N.K. Denzin and Y.S. Lincoln (eds), *Handbook of Qualitative Research*, 2nd edition, pp. 215–255. Thousand Oaks: Sage.

Preface

The contributors of this volume share various accounts of women's struggles of life and destiny, disability, divorce, abuse, family dysfunction and violence, racism, religious commitments, barriers of caste and class to name a few. Women's struggles are not yet over. How women overcome these barriers are experiences and stories that only women (and few men) know, appreciate and understand.

The purpose of inviting women to tell their stories of struggle through this book was to allow them a space to inform and educate those of us who are more privileged and advantaged. We provided an open forum to women and men to share their stories about women's struggles. Men who align themselves with women's struggles and support them may fall into the feminist category of 'male feminists and pro feminist men', according to Wood (2005: 302). Whatever aspects of feminism men may choose to support, it is important to note that there are men who believe that women deserve better.

The idea for the book was conceptualised out of our own experiences. We know what it means to be born into a society that is oppressed and confined to the dark, black spaces of the land; to be of different ('the wrong') skin colour; to be women who are even today classified according to language, race and ethnicity; and to be denied access and opportunity because of language, race, gender and ethnicity. And yet, as women who have experienced the effects of colonisation, Apartheid and Afrikaner nationalism, we continue to be chained to our past, to be conditioned into accepting the unreasonable demands of institutional and other authority while making feeble attempts to counter the oppression, only to find solace in our cultural, religious and historical roots. We remain 'educated' slaves who succumb to Western ideals and agendas.

With regard to writing styles, contributors have used multidisciplinary approaches in their writings. We hope that this book provides deep insights into women's diverse cultural perspectives and their significant contributions to the workplace. This book follows the trend of the 'Women Writing Women' series where a forum is provided for a 'variety of women's voices, allowing women to speak for and about themselves in ways that have often been excluded from academic discourse' (Hart, Weathermon and Armitage 2006: 3). All the contributors have adopted distinct styles and approaches to tell their stories and to share their knowledge and insights. While we wanted to maintain a consistency in style and approach, we the contributors were encouraged to use their preferred writing styles. What our book demonstrates is that by providing a diverse range of opportunities for women to tell their stories encouraged more women to come forward and to tell their stories without the constraints of specific writing styles being imposed on them.

Many of the contributors to this book raise issues of defining women's work, workspaces and of the need to balance work with their roles such as mothers, daughters and wives. We began by inviting professional women to contribute to this text and found that this excluded other women. What about women who did not belong in the 'professional' category? So we extended the invitation to all women. What physical space could be regarded as 'legitimate working space' was another question that was raised. Further down the line we found that we had to make the book more inclusive of women who worked within the home and from home, as well as women and men who worked in women's and/or men's traditional spaces. We also received an enquiry from a male author as to whether the book was intended for women by women only. We then extended the invitation to men who appreciate and understand women's struggles.

The underlying goal of the book is to identify the struggles of women who are marginalised, and who continue their fight for survival, recognition, respect and dignity. The book is organised according to the broad themes outlined in the 21st century in the call for submissions and includes new emerging themes. Part One includes stories related to struggles in the workplace, while Part Two focuses specifically on exploitation and strategies for survival in the workplace. Part Three of the book moves on to stories and struggles about health and wellness and Part Four reveals the interconnectedness of spirituality and religion to women's resolve to withstand injustices. While cultural identities and spiritual immersion were not highlighted under the broad categories, these emerged as significant themes. A deep spirituality and religious conviction guided many women through their struggles, particularly when they experienced conflict as a result of their multiple cultural identities in the workplace. Part Four takes us on a spirited journey that demonstrates how women triumph in the face of adversity. Part Five introduces us to women's strong resolve and resilience in overcoming obstacles. The hope and positive energy that one derives from these stories brings to bear on our own realities: that there are many women less fortunate than we are. In Part Six the concluding chapter pulls together the threads that spin webs around the freedoms of women everywhere and that keep them entwined in endless knots only because the richness and the significance of their cultural knowledge, identities and perspectives remain unrecognised in the workplace.

Readers will not only be educated and informed about women's struggles, but also be able to critically analyse policies and practices that create barriers, ostracise and marginalise them. Our book brings hope and encouragement to women struggling against all odds to care for themselves and their families while meeting the demands of their work and life in general.

This text is a humble attempt to add to the already vast literature on women's ways of knowing and their contributions to their personal and professional lives. We also hope that reading clubs and women's groups would use this book as a point of departure to encourage women to share their unique contributions to the social development of their communities. This book is directed at a wide readership that includes multiple fields of interest including organisational culture in the global workplace. Fields of interest may include, for example, contexts related to human resource management, organisational culture and communication, international communication, development communication, women's and gender studies, sociology and cultural studies, governmental and non-governmental organisations. The book would also appeal to communities that live and work in a developing context and those who would like to have an insight into women's struggles in a developing context. Contributors originate from New Zealand, Australia, United Kingdom, United States of America, South Africa, Canada and India, and identify with multiple histories. Sadly, this book mirrors our current reality, however much we wish to deny it.

It is time that women reclaim their right to respect and dignity, and to fair space in the workplace. The right to participate in a free and fair democracy must be equivalent not only to the right to be employed in a range of workplaces on an equitable level. More importantly, workplaces must integrate women's cultural perspectives and approaches so that women can participate in an environment that respects their knowledge. It is important that democracies empower women by integrating policies and practices that support and nurture women's cultural identities and perspectives in their place of work.

REFERENCES

Hart, P., K. Weathermon and S. Armitage. 2006. *Women Writing Women: The Frontier Reader*. Lincoln, Nebaska: University of Nebraska Press.

Wood, J. 2005. *Gendered Lives: Communication, Gender and Culture*. 6th edition. Canada: Wadsworth, Thomson Learning, Inc.

Acknowledgements

Editing a book such as this is no easy feat when you consider the challenges of working across time and space coordinating with the authors and the publisher spread across seven countries. However, the asynchronous nature of new communication technologies such as the Internet and e-mail made this enormous undertaking look easy as we worked harmoniously in a mutually respectful manner.

We would like to thank all contributing authors without whom this book would not have become a reality. Thank you for sharing your stories and ideas. We are indebted to you for the warm support and encouragement through the three year process of gathering the material and working with our publisher. Your patience and kind words were especially heart-warming. Many of you generously showered compliments and blessings which certainly kept us motivated. Working with a wonderful team of authors made this a treasured experience.

A special thanks to Subash and Shivani, children of Sheila Chirkut, who gave their permission to publish their mother's work posthumously so that her dedication to women's struggles will be remembered forever. Sheila sacrificed her own career goals in order to educate her children first.

We are grateful to Dr Harsh Suri for agreeing to write the Foreword. Harsh has also survived several personal and professional challenges of her own.

Our sincere appreciation goes to Dr Sugata Ghosh and Ashok R. Chandran and to SAGE Publications for their confidence in our abilities to produce this book. We are also grateful to Rekha Natarajan for her editorial assistance, advice and recommendations on improving the quality and style of the text. We thank Sushmita Banerjee and the team of editors for their gentle prodding to keep us on track during the final stages of preparation.

We treaded carefully through our own challenges which life threw at us over the three years. We both commuted across three countries (Canada, New Zealand and Australia) to get from home to work. We cherished our hours and days with our spouses and children who also sacrificed so much. Our spouses went through incredible health issues on their own as they shared this dream in completing an important project—our first book. These two men in our lives are exceptional human beings who themselves broke through barriers of gender, race and culture to allow us to fulfil our life's ambition. Both men are gentle, loving souls who have always stood by our side. If more men were like the men in our lives, we would achieve a harmonious balance in the home and the workplace as well in the spaces in between.

We also thank all our friends and colleagues who offered their valuable advice over countless cups of coffee and many corridor chats.

Kogi Naidoo
Fay Patel

PART ONE
Struggles in the Workplace

Women experience pressures in a number of contexts: cultural, domestic, work and professional. Despite women professionals having the requisite qualifications and experience, they are continually undermined, undervalued, unsupported and marginalised. The stories from our contributing authors reflect their personal struggles in the workplace. Women find themselves in situations which they do not recognise as unfair and unjust. Many remain trapped and finally succumb.

The stories in Part One of the book bear testimony to the struggles that women face in the workplace.

Thenjiwe Magwaza interrogates the Western concept of 'balancing work and life'—not about how to balance but questioning the need to comply with Western norms of balance. There are tensions between the women's personal identities and work roles. Which balance is more important—the externally driven balance or the internal balance? Heide Kaminski projects the dilemmas of a single mother in America and candidly addresses some of the highpoints of her struggle. Millicent Daweti analyses and questions the 'meaning of self' in relation to the number of cultural roles that women experience from childhood to maturity. Maureen Lewis raises pertinent questions about the rightful place of migrant women in the workplace.

1

Experiences of a Black South African Woman

Thenjiwe Magwaza

INTRODUCTION AND BACKGROUND

A number of international land South African[1] based studies have been conducted on either the state of women at work or on the reciprocal effects of workplace on family life. The considerable growth in the number of women in formal employment over the past five decades has caused enormous concern about their ability to fulfil their roles as mothers, that is essential for the survival of the human race. This concern has generated these kinds of studies and other kinds of literature. Since the early 1980s[2] writing on women and work pointed out that there is a need that studies go beyond an empirical overview and analysis of women's work, to focus on providing an inside view of what women themselves have to say about the opposing demands of employment and family life. It is reassuring to see that contemporary studies on women at work do not solely focus on 'typical female' reproductive tasks.

In this chapter, I reflect on my experiences in the domains of work and family,[3] and how the two form for me an inseparable continuum. As I continuously operate in the two spheres, I find that the requirements of my formal work enjoy the upper hand, while my family and my cultural group[4] all intertwine in constructing my life. I question here the usefulness of the often imparted advice to balance work and family life, and rather argue that women often have to opt for an unbalanced scale. I reflect on how I perceive and respond to the often conflicting obligations of family, cultural group and office duties. I would like to believe that most Black South African professional women could find resonance with the experiences[5] that I have outlined here. However, I do not attempt to imply that my experiences generally reflect those of other Black women workers, whether in academic or in other fields.

Equally, though sceptical about Bayraktar and Salman's (2003) findings, I need to note that women have different work-family experiences. Bayraktar and Salman's study asserts that highly educated professional women report nil to minimum negative effects of their work on their family and social life. The personal experience I draw on portrays a totally different reality. I also reflect on utterances and behaviours related to work-family domains made by colleagues, friends and family, which I have found remarkable. Although they may not have meant any harm, they however indicate deep seated beliefs and stereotyped expectations on working women, hence my reference to them. In the course of time I have observed that my responses to such utterances have proven ineffective, as people continue with similar behaviours or statements. The utterances and behaviours point to the crude reality that most of women's work continues to remain invisible, not only to family members, but also at the workplace and to policymakers. On the whole, although this is an opportunity to share a part of my life story, it is an outlet for my frustrations and a statement of realities in the binominal of my work-family life. In line with Stanley and Wise (1983); Hill-Collins (1990); Morwenna (1995) and Mann (2001) who assert that what happens in our daily lives matters equally as what goes on in the mainstream, this essay looks 'back into the personal' as it reflects on certain aspects of my life, re-evaluates them and regards them as an information source.

We have learnt more about the difficulties than successes of managing work and family. For instance, Ruddick (1994) and Bobel (2001) make reference to the paradoxes facing those who adopt traditional definitions of motherhood, as most women search for ways to balance family life with pursuits outside the home. This and other literatures (Granrose and Kaplan 1996; Dex and Scheibl 2001 and Hattery 2001) note the tensions, contradictions and limitations that contemporary working women face, and in turn advice on strategies that could be adopted by both employers and employees to assist in balancing the two domains. Glossop (1998: 3) observes, 'work and family has been characterised most often as a "balancing act" involving "trade-offs" between competing and divided interests.' Robert Glossop's analysis points out how societies have strived to largely maintain artificial boundaries between the two spheres. Reflecting on this list of literature poses a number of questions in my mind, that is, why should women strive to *balance* family and work responsibilities? What is wrong about not balancing or working towards a balance? To whose benefit is the ideal *balance*? What is wrong about making choices that do not aim at *striking a balance*?

Social, cultural and work expectations and boundaries tend to create and emphasise the two domains: family and work, as contradictory, and a problem for those involved in them, hence the need to achieve parity. I reflect on the challenges of my efforts in trying to *strike the balance* as I strive to satisfy all parties involved in my work-personal life. I argue for the recognition of a scale that may not be balanced but is functional for women. I have found that striving towards gratifying all parties brings unnecessary pressure, leads to depression and in turn has negative effects on everyone.

What has influenced this narration is, first and foremost personal experiences and struggles as I make attempts to define my role, identity and choices both in my personal life and career. I draw from Stephanie Vermeulen's work (2004) which is not only inspirational but also a strong contemporary wake-up call for the female folk. She writes about how, in all cultures, girls are still emotionally programmed to become good wives and mothers, and are preached about the need to sacrifice themselves for husbands and children. I find resonance with this discussion and am struck by how it gets extended to include expectations with regard to women in the workplace. In addition to the office work, my traditional role of being a Zulu woman is not fully relinquished. I find that a number of my identities and duties are at play at the same time: mother, daughter, daughter-in-law, sister, aunt, guardian, a daughter in my place of birth[6] at Inanda where parents live and wife. All are interdependent categories, not only making up who I am, but exerting enormous pressure to respond to such expectations. Due to the South African cultural history, demands of these categories become intense for Black women in particular. Professional women—perceived to be earning healthy salaries—are expected to pull out of poverty, family members and other people with whom they come into contact. Such a cultural tenet forms an extension of the concept and practice of 'patronage', widely applied in all eras in developing countries of the world, according to which a person who possesses wealth is obliged to provide for the less fortunate, who in turn, offer 'gratuitous' service and devotion and serve as a shield against the nefarious workings of witchcraft. This expectation has been elevated into a socio-cultural practice, and Black women must fulfil it as part of their 'multi-mother' role. I have observed that this is not the case with other South African social groups. In a study[7] conducted on Black and White mothers of Durban, South Africa, I detail some of the existing general perceptions about mothering practices and motherhood held by the two social groups.

At the turn of the 20th century, the role of a Zulu woman was mainly within the confines of the home. This state of affairs carried on during the Industrial Revolution era and into a period of mass exodus of men from rural areas to cities in search of employment. The woman was expected mainly to give birth and look after the children and the family[8] through her gender defined domestic roles. On the whole, traditionally the Zulu woman was expected to be of service to the family within the domain of the home; they would collect firewood, fetch water, engage in small scale subsistence farming, clean the household and prepare food for the family. These duties were referred to as makoti[9] duties. In the absence of her husband who would be staying for longer periods of time at an urban place of work, her role included making and taking decisions within the household, however, doing so in consultation with a male figure (husband's father, brother or uncle). The mother-in-law also played a role in this factor.

In contemporary times, as most women are active in formal work activities outside the home, the traditional role of a Zulu married woman should be altered by demands of a different set-up. However, reality spells a different scenario as both the family and community at large expect married women to continue to carry out her makoti duties. Attempting not to disappoint family and community members and in turn strain relations, it is common for women to carry out the set expected duties during afternoons and at weekends. Although the traditional setting and aligned married women's gender duties were convenient for a rural environment and a woman not involved in formal work outside the home, a number of these duties have been transferred to non-traditional and non-rural settings.

WHOSE MOTHER AM I?

I use the term 'multi-mother', given the strong feelings I have about the expectations of a number of people in my family and place of employment. The expectations range from varied levels of anticipation, to demands that I provide finance, food, clothing and see to other subsistence needs. Although this statement may seem on the surface not enough to qualify my assumption that I am regarded as a mother, I have, on a number of occasions, felt that requests made on me, consciously or unconsciously, infer that I assume a mothering role. Or, could it be that I am perceived as a father figure, a provider? I get engrossed and confused as to which parent figure I am expected to represent. On the whole, I find myself having to take on parenting duties, albeit in varying degrees, for my biological and adopted daughters, for my widowed father-in-law, husband, husband's siblings, members of a northern Durban community where I volunteer as a periodical caregiver to Acquired Immune Deficiency Syndrome (AIDS) patients and even for my students. Such extended mothering duties have effects not only on me as an expected provider, but on each of these people. The diverse roles I am expected to play as 'multi-mother', provider, counsellor and social worker, cause a strain that leads to disgruntles. It is common to notice each of the beneficiaries complaining about being neglected, not given enough time, ignored and even not loved anymore.

I find it necessary to reflect on this subject in order to get researchers on motherhood to consider 'extended mothering' or a similar concept in their discourse. Often, we hear about the rewards of mothering, but little is said about the costs, or what are the demands of what I refer to as 'multiple motherhood' or 'extended mothering'. Women and mothers are expected to serve unconditionally and feel obligated to respond affirmatively to all requests, irrespective of their reasonableness. Intertwined with these expectations is what women avoid discussing, which is the heavy emotional and economic price they pay as 'extended mothers'. The fear of being labelled unreasonable and selfish, as Vermeulen (2004) rightly notes, overcomes women's ability to be self-considerate. This in turn leads to actions of self-sacrifice. Notions of the goodness of motherhood tend to be stressed to the point of becoming oppressive to women (Gerson 1985).

Reflecting on some of my extended mothering experiences, in particular the relationship I have with volunteer caregivers for AIDS patients of a Durban community, I realise that poverty has a role in intensifying and fulfilling this function. I have found that in this community, poverty and unemployment push people to reformulate relations that are essentially professional in nature into parenting relations. Though fully aware as a Zulu person, of the significance of the bond that develops when people learn that they share a family name, I find that people who lack basic resources become obsessed about such relations. Their socio-economic conditions compel them not only to overstate such relations, but to look on them as alternate sources of help in their plight. Having learned of my career and assuming affluence, on several occasions I have found needy people making serious attempts to investigate at length any possibility that I might be related to them. Besides the family name I use to identify myself, questions are asked about my clan names, about mine and my mother's maiden names, and even about my grandparents. Such extreme interest in my background has never been experienced so deeply by me, and has been a surprising revelation of the strength of the Zulu tradition. With such insistent family tree research, the possibilities of established 'relations' are enhanced, and consequently factual stories about poverty and requests that I provide come into the picture. Although, at times, I find this situation strenuous, I have learned not only to embrace my 'multi-mother' identity, but to regard it as part of my work. I want to believe that my socio-cultural upbringing has a great influence in my choice to adopt this attitude.

SOCIAL AND CULTURAL INFLUENCES

The society is torn between traditional expectations on women, and their recently achieved assertiveness and capabilities in various roles. Although the benefits of women at work are there for all to see, there persists some reluctance towards completely freeing them to pursue their careers and accepting that their successes involve some curtailments on both social and family availability. There seems to be an unwritten but vigorous accord about what women can and should do, influenced by cultural ideologies based on traditional behaviour. For instance, women are strongly encouraged to mother children in accordance with laid down models, even if, those models are not clearly defined. It should be noted that pressures, expectations and the manner in which they are dealt with may vary from one family to the next, even within an urban Zulu family. Albertina Sisulu in Erasmus–Kritzinger (2003) rightly admonishes that 'women in this country should not be viewed as a homogenous entity.'[10]

Historically, most women have been involved in productive enterprises while also nurturing their children,[11] Statistics South Africa (2000, 2001 and 2002) report that Black women have formed a higher labour force rate than their White, Indian and Coloured counterparts. Despite this fact, the verbal utterances I hear strongly suggest that, although I have academic career obligations, I am still a Black Zulu woman expected to fulfil my socio-cultural roles. Much of this talk is delivered in unconscious modes, by both perpetrators and fellow woman victims. In the past I have had to work hard to demonstrate that my higher education has not changed my Zuluness, and that I continue to uphold my cultural group's values and to perform my expected duties to the best of my abilities. Six years ago, on realising that my efforts in this direction were not enthusiastically appreciated, I decided to do only what I felt was strictly possible, thus ditching the pains of 'balancing the scales'. It was a liberating decision which I hold reflects the nature of duties and roles women play, that is, as they are not at par, parity is impossible. These struggles have existed even within the feminist movement. Writing in the 1980s, Barbara Wishart,[12] a lesbian feminist who chose to have a child and to breastfeed, questions the stereotypical feminist stances of her time, that were loathe to the coexistence of all the choices she had made.

PUZZLES OF THE ACADEMIA

Universities are supposed to be institutions where cutting edge scientific knowledge is acquired and developed. The transmission of such

knowledge is the aim of such institutions, which further have the
task of stimulating research, so that science may be advanced in all its
facets. I found out, however, that the transmission process is taken
for granted, in an academic atmosphere characterised by an extremely
individualistic ethos, where one is thrown into the deep end and told to
swim, whether one knows how to or not. I felt this acutely as a young
academic and as a woman. Appointment interviews only deal with one's
familiarity with the academic discipline. Once a person is appointed,
there are no mentoring programmes (for either sex) about the important
aspects of academic work; no talks or discussions or training courses to
highlight, for example, the differences between teaching and lecturing;
the requirements of research and publications to advance knowledge
in a particular subject (the 'publish or perish' philosophy); the skills
required for the promotion of students' and staff's research programmes and ethos; the administrative duties of individuals, departments
and so forth. An academic who takes the work seriously is initially compelled to spend evenings and weekends in the office, to the detriment
of family and social life. In this way, the academic tends to become a
recluse and lose sight of the very society to be served and helped by the
academic endeavour.

Challenges experienced by women in their socio-cultural life get re-
plicated in the domain of the office, albeit in slightly different formats.
Besides having to balance employment and family life, women often find
that they have to struggle to be taken seriously. Long standing traditions
in both the domains, place women at the very bottom of the hierarchy,
providing minimal access to positions of authority. In the rare cases
where women are in authority, there is scepticism about their abilities,
hence the constant trend to ignore them or to interfere in their work.
I have noticed a marked enthusiasm by several outsiders to interfere
with my duties and to stipulate certain management styles. Deborah
Rhode (2003) notes that the legacy of disregarding women leadership
is still frequent and their successes, or the difference they make, are not
flagged. Such disregard is an indication that women's work continues to
be undervalued and that conservative ideas about women continue
to be upheld, in spite of epochal shifts in official policies and weighty
pronouncements by the highest authorities in the land.

Besides the low regard for women and their social and intellectual contributions, the academic career path poses different challenges. With expectations that I strive to balance office and family duties, blending the two and getting both to work equally well is a mammoth task. There is little practical support to ensure that women in particular succeed in the academia. It is common for higher education institutions to expect women academics to succeed in their jobs by their own unguided efforts. There is a need for regularly monitored mentorship programmes, evaluated by all stakeholders, to realise maximum success of particularly women in the academia.

In 1999, on joining my institution, I was not assigned a mentor nor was the academic career path explained to me. Nine months on the job I stumbled across a notice requiring submission of publication records. As I did not relate to the notice, I ignored it. It was only a year later, after attending a conference, that some enlightenment about submission of publication records was brought home to me. Had I not been curious about Zambia and eager to visit Lusaka, where one of my cousins was born, it would have taken me much longer to be introduced to the concept of academic publications. It was at the Zambia conference that the mystery was laid bare. A year later, I managed to publish a journal article and thereafter thought it necessary to find a mentor. My first attempt in this direction was horrifying. Not only did the mentor fail to map out an academic path for me, but she jeered upon a research proposal I submitted and caustically criticised my very first attempt at publishing. I found this experience not only 'abusive', but it heavily dented my self-confidence and crippled my possibility of success. I vividly recall one of her lines of supposed 'encouragement': 'It is difficult being both a mother and an academic. Juggling around these jobs is hard.' On reflection, I am still puzzled about what this statement essentially meant. I continue to be both amazed and disappointed at another familiar assertion of my ex-mentor. I guess the displeasure also comes from noting that a number of other people have repeatedly sympathised with my previously disadvantaged background, condescendingly employing, without fault, the line: 'You have come a long way.' What strikes me is that the line gets accompanied by a sombre look, clearly indicative of the extent to which Blacks are pitied. The frequent use of this line is obviously loaded with inferred meaning: because you are Black you must have struggled all your life before joining the prestigious institution, and must therefore appreciate your current position or consider yourself lucky; your education and background are comparatively inferior and [supposed] inferiority and struggles beset you. Subsequently, because 'I have come a long way', I am often the subject of study, or could refer other South African and international scholars on any subject related to similar Blacks like me or who are generally struggling with—who knows what—but who have in any case 'come a long way'.

CONCLUSION

In this narration I have outlined my personal struggles in relation to the contrasting demands of home and office, the spheres in which I operate. The discussion has pointed out disturbing similarities and negative perceptions particularly about Black women, commonly held in both work and family domains. These realms mirror each other in curtailing women's advancement prospects. A further limitation outlined in this narration, is the view that the only outlets for women's work are family and office. Although these are the most visible aspects of women's involvement, their gainful employment in both the formal and informal sectors has been increasing in recent years. Furthermore, women tend to get involved in a large number of social projects that create a sense of community and make life possible, especially for those most seriously sidelined by the official branches of government, such as cultural enterprises and celebrations, assistance to the sick and the needy, care for children and old people, church and charitable initiatives, and the assistance to HIV/AIDS patients and orphan run homes.

Identifying what could be considered as women's work is problematic. Under the subtopic 'work', Budlender (2002: 5) reports that 'within each population group, a smaller proportion of women than men in the age group 15–65 years are employed, and a larger proportion are not economically active'. This statement reflects perceptions and attitudes about women's activities, as if only gainful employment is to be identified as 'work'. Women, as I have demonstrated, carry out many kinds of work, even though much of it is not recognised as 'gainful employment'. I have argued for the need to acknowledge the existence of other fields that make demands on women's time. Work, family, community and socio-cultural spheres do not only form part of women's lives but also need to be seen as an interconnected continuum that does not necessarily require 'balancing'.

Calls for efforts at balancing family and office duties emanate from the assumption that they are the only two domains existing in women's lives and are in competition, balking at the idea that women may be content with an unbalanced scale. As the possibility of an unbalanced scale is not accommodated, there is a danger for women to make compromises because they find themselves under pressure to fit in, either in the office culture or in the mores of their social group. In a study involving 10 countries, Nordenmark (2004) finds that, despite global gender equity advances, traditional ideologies held about men and women in relation to what constitutes work and the requirements thereof, continue to be at play.

I have raised questions about the reality of women's responsibilities versus the requirements imposed on them by traditional perceptions. Empirically based records of women's real experiences are necessary— where they relate about combining, not just balancing, family, social, community and employment roles. Subsequent to this, women's life decisions and choices, which may not be congruent with any of the expectations placed upon them, ought to be documented. South Africa needs a lot of studies similar to a study conducted by Granrose and Kaplan (1996), that would investigate and record women's decisions, choices and responses within their multiple roles. In addition to this, what women's experiences suggest to employing organisations will need examination in order to gain an insight on how women define and interpret their tasks. There is a need for organisational policies that are friendly and cognisant of the varied roles women play and try to accommodate them. Lisel Erasmus-Kritzinger, the compiler of *Inspirational Women at Work*, rightly notes the need that a profound difference is only possible if 'all women can make a difference in their own way, using their resources'[13] and being rightly acknowledged.

ACKNOWLEDGEMENTS

I with to acknowledge the South African National Research Foundation (NRF) and the University of KwaZulu-Natal for the resources made available for this project. Any opinions, findings and conclusions or recommendations expressed in this material are those of the author. The funding organisations do not have any liability in this regard. My gratitude also goes to Professor Canonici, my mentor, for his inputs on the final draft of the essay.

NOTES

1. Amongst these are, for example, the studies by Dex and Joshi (1999); Dex and Scheibl (2001); Hattery (2001); Basau and Altinay (2003) and essays in a book edited by Rhode (2003)—to mention a few conducted in the last decade. Also see, for example, Casale and Posel (2002); Erasmus-Kritzinger (2003) and Statistics South Africa (2003) amongst some of the works produced in the last five years.
2. See, for example Teresa Fogelberg's (1982) study on the Nanumba Women of Ghana.
3. I use the term *work* to refer to all my academic work, done in the confines of the office and outside. The term *family* is used to refer to my immediate family (my husband and daughters). In the Zulu (my ethnic group) community, the concept of family goes beyond one's immediate and extended family to include the entire clan into which one is born. The Zulu is the largest South African Black African ethnic group who live mainly in the province of KwaZulu-Natal.
4. Refers to my extended family and the social cultural group (Zulu) into which I was born and raised.
5. Muthuki (2004) had made this point in her MA dissertation. As one of the interviewees for her study, I give credit to her for provoking me to think analytically (and incidentally write this essay) about my work and family life.
6. Although I physically left the place more than 15 years ago, I still get called upon to assist in various ways by the church, organisations and individuals. All these facets form part of my life, what Garey (1999) calls a 'web of interconnections'.
7. See Magwaza (2003).
8. Family should be understood as a concept that includes both the nuclear and extended family.
9. *Makoti* is a Zulu language noun meaning bride. Bridal duties are generally expected to be more intense than wife or female gender duties, with the former implying a necessary obligation to dutifully serve in-law family members and relatives as an expression of being thankful for having been a chosen woman for wifehood.
10. In Erasmus-Kritzinger (2003: 11).

11. Folbre (1991); Jones (1987); Kessler-Harris (1981 and 1982) and Garey (1999) form part of the literature that reports on the history of women's participation in the paid labour force.
12. See Wishart (1984: 85–97).
13. Erasmus-Kritzinger (2003: 3). The book is a compilation of remarkable stories by South African women and a few others across the world.

REFERENCES

Basau, Anuradha and Eser Altinay. 2003. *Family and Work in Minority Ethnic Businesses*. Bristol: Policy Press.

Bayraktar, Meltem and Meryem Salman. 2003. 'The Impact of Family Life on Work Efficiency: A Study of Employed Women from Different Occupational Statuses in a Metropolitan Area in Turkey', *International Journal of Consumer Studies*, 27(1): 80–86.

Bobel, Chris. 2001. *The Paradox of Natural Mothering*. Philadelphia: Temple University Press.

Budlender, Debbie. 2002. *Women and Men in South Africa: Five Years On*. Pretoria, South Africa: Statistics South Africa.

Casale, Daniela and Dorrit Posel. 2002. 'The Continued Feminisation of the Labour Force in South Africa: An Analysis of Recent Data and Trends', *South African Journal of Economics*, 70(1): 156–184.

Dex, Shirley and Heather Joshi. 1999. 'Careers and Motherhood: Policies for Compatibility', *Cambridge Journal of Economics*, 23(5): 641–659.

Dex, Shirley and Fiona Scheibl. 2001. 'Flexible and Family-friendly Working Arrangements in UK-Based SMEs: Business Cases', *British Journal of Industrial Relations*, 39(3): 411–431.

Erasmus-Kritzinger, Lisel (ed.). 2003. *Inspirational Women at Work: 52 Personal and Life Experiences Shared to Empower, Encourage and Inspire*. Pretoria: Lapa Publishers.

Fogelberg, Teresa. 1982. *Nanumba Women: Working Bees or Idle Bums: Sexual Division of Labour, Ideology of Work, and Power Relations between Men and Women in Gole, a Village in Nanumba District, Northern Region, Ghana*. Leiden: Institute of Cultural and Social Studies.

Folbre, Nancy. 1991. 'The Unproductive Housewife: Her Evolution in Nineteenth-Century Economic Thought', *Signs*, 16(3): 463–484.

Glossop, Robert. 1998. *From the Kitchen Table to the Boardroom Table*. Canada: The Vanier Institute of Family.

Garey, Anita I. 1999. *Weaving Work and Motherhood*. Philadelphia: Temple University Press.

Granrose, Cheryl S. and Eileen E. Kaplan. 1996. *Work-Family Role Choices for Women in Their 20s and 30s*. Westport, Connecticut: Praeger Publishers.

Gerson, Kathleen. 1985. *Hard Choices: How Women Decide About Work, Career, and Motherhood*. Berkeley: University of California Press.

Hattery, Angela. 2001. *Women, Work and Family: Balancing and Weaving*. London: Sage Publications.

Hill-Collins, Patricia. 1990. *Black Feminist Thought: Knowledge, Consciousness and the Politics of Empowerment*. Boston: Unwin Hyman.

Jones, Jacqueline. 1987. 'Black Women, Work and the Family under Slavery', in Naomi Gerstel and Harriet Engel Gross (eds), *Families and Work*, pp. 84–110. Philadelphia: Temple University Press.

Kessler-Harris, Alice. 1981. *Women Have Always Worked: A Historical Overview*. Old Westbury, New York: Feminist Press.

———. 1982. *Out of Work: A History of Wage-Earning Women in the United States*. Oxford: Oxford University Press.

Magwaza, Thenjiwe. 2003. 'Perceptions and Experiences of Motherhood: A Study of Black and White Mothers of Durban, South Africa', *Jenda: A Journal of Culture and African. Women Studies*. Available online http://www.jendajournal.com/jenda/issue4/magwaza. html (downloaded 17 May 2006).

Mann, Patricia S. 2001. 'Review of Constituting Feminist Subjects' by Kathi Weeks, *Hypatia*, 16(2): 111–116.

Muthuki, Florence. 2004. 'Trends or Counter Trends? The Gender Identity Dilemma Facing Zulu Married Men and Women at the University of KwaZulu-Natal'. MA Dissertation, Durban: University of KwaZulu-Natal.

Morwenna, Griffiths. 1995. *Feminism and the Self: The Web of Identity*. London: Routledge.

Nordenmark, Mikael. 2004. 'Does Gender Ideology Explain Differences between Countries Regarding the Involvement of Women and of Men in Paid and Unpaid Work?', *International Journal of Social Welfare*, 13(3): 233–243.

Rhode, Deborah L. (ed.). 2003. *The Difference 'Difference' Make: Women and Leadership*. Stanford. California: Stanford Law and Politics.

Ruddick, Sarah. 1994. *Maternal Thinking*. Boston: Beacon Press.

Stanley, Liz and Sue Wise. 1983. ' "Back into the Personal" or Our Attempt to Construct "Feminist Research"', in G. Bowles and R.D. Klein (eds), *Theories of Women's Studies*, pp. 192–209. London: Routledge.

Statistics South Africa. 2000. *Employment Trends in Agriculture*. Joint Publication between Statistics South Africa and National Department of Agriculture. Pretoria: Statistics South Africa.

———. 2001. *Mean and Minimum Wages in South Africa, 1997*. Pretoria: Statistics South Africa.

———. 2002. *Calculating the Value of Unpaid Leave: A Discussion Document*. Pretoria: Statistics South Africa.

———. 2003. *Labour Force Study*. Pretoria: Statistics South Africa.

Vermeulen, Stephanie. 2004. *Stitched-Up: Who Fashions Women's Lives?* Johannesburg: Jacana Media.

Wishart, Barbara. 1984. 'Motherhood within Patriarchy: A Radical Feminist Perspective', in Barbara Wishart (ed.), *All Her Labours: Two Embroidering the Framework*, pp. 85–97. Sydney: Hale & Iremonger Pty Limited.

2

Single Motherhood in America: My Struggle

Heide Kaminski

I am a single mum. I am trying my best to be a good mum, a loyal employee, pay my bills, keep up the house, and in there somewhere, I am trying to pursue my dream of becoming a writer, as well as getting in a little 'me' time, as in 'Hey, world, I am still a woman with womanly needs!'

This is what my typical weekday looks like:

5:30 a.m.:	Get up, turn on the coffee pot, check e-mail on the computer, find writing opportunities, perhaps even write a thing or two or work on some moonlighting writing jobs. I do some newsletters and I write for a local newspaper on the side. I have got three books published and a lot of writing credits in anthologies.
6:15 a.m.:	Get my son, Tommy, out of bed. I generally get him dressed the night before on weekdays. Lunches and school bag are packed the night before. This way I can let him sleep as long as possible. Feed him breakfast, get myself ready.
6:30 a.m.:	Leave the house—no, I do not take more than five minutes to throw on some face-paint...
6:45 a.m.:	Arrive at work, kiss my son good-bye. I work in the Threes' room at the daycare, where he goes before and after school.
8:00 a.m.:	My son leaves for school.

Until noon:	I do my work. Teaching art, mostly. Change diapers or potty train, fix lunches and clean the kitchen after the little tykes are done eating. I have two co-workers and an average of 18 children in the room. We usually have a lot of fun together. That's a great incentive. The pay is extremely low. However, I work five minutes away from the school that my son—who has special needs (Attention Deficit Hyperactivity Disorder [ADHD])—attends. I can take off on short notice, occasionally run to his school and help intervene with problems (which have gone down dramatically since we changed the medications, thank God!).
Lunch break:	I take off to my male best friend's house. Boyfriend sounds so immature. He is male, and he is my best friend all around, so what do I call him?
1–4 p.m.:	Back to work: preparation for next day, finish up projects from current day (Threes needs some assistance with their art projects).
4:00 p.m.:	Tommy gets off the school bus, hopefully in a good mood.
4.00–5.30 p.m.:	I get off, depending on the number of children in the centre. Employees are sent home, in seniority order (allegedly…), as the child count goes down.
Arrive at home:	Check e-mail, feed Tommy a snack, feed cats, cry over bills and rejection letters from my mailbox, pray for a cheque or an acceptance, go online, seek opportunities to become rich as a writer. Or, lately, I have been taking on some acting gigs. I do not get money though, it's all for my portfolio…Tommy calls a friend—he has one nearby who he takes turns with, one evening their house, next one our house.

On weekends, I catch up on housecleaning, work on my newspaper assignments, the newsletters and write my heart out in the hopes of getting a break in a big magazine, and on Sundays I drive 45 minutes to teach at a Sunday school at the nearest Interfaith Centre.

We live in a duplex, the upstairs is currently vacant. When I moved in downstairs, I went across the lawn to introduce myself to the neighbours, a retired couple who has turned out to be quite a disgruntled pair. As soon as I mentioned my three children, two of them teenagers, I could see their eyebrows shoot up a few notches. Yes, I hang my laundry outside during nice weather, to save on electricity and yes, my house needs painting—my landlord's responsibility—but I am not the white trailer trash which these people obviously classify me as. My elder daughter now lives in her own apartment in another town nearby. My younger daughter just left for a year as an exchange student overseas. Both girls have graduated at the top of their class. Tommy is seven, too young to stay home alone, even though he wants me to go to the store without him sometimes. His dad currently works second shift, so Tommy rarely gets to see his father during the week. While I enjoyed my free time when he used to pick up Tommy in the evenings, this arrangement suited me fine. But, he is very irresponsible and while I don't undermine their contact, I prefer to keep it to a reduced time.

MY STORY

I am a rescuer. I even rescue people when I need rescuing myself. When I met my first husband, he had very low self-esteem. Mine, however, was lower. I had just, literally, escaped from a very physically violent relationship. So I rescued my first husband from his low self-esteem by providing him with someone below his level. As my confidence in myself grew, our relationship deteriorated. I was no longer what he needed, a damsel in distress, and he turned to first verbal and finally, physical violence. Ten years and two beautiful daughters later, I left.

I did OK by myself for a while, but then I met 'Hank.' While it was not really apparent at first, I know now that I must have felt drawn to him, because he needed to be rescued.

He was himself newly divorced, had just broken up with a totally crazy girlfriend (according to his side of the story, I never got to hear hers) and he was sleeping on a cot in his mother's laundry room. OK, so the signs of his need to be rescued were pretty obvious. What can

I say… love can blind you! Of course, he moved in with me quickly. After all, that was economically a good decision and my girls liked him; he was fun. Then I discovered that he had a little habit. It did not seem as dramatic as it was only an 'occasional' habit. Every Thursday he would drive to see his dealer and then he would hang out with his favourite pot-buddy until early dawn. He promised to keep the drug out of my sight, my house and away from my kids.

When I wanted to get my tubes tied, he walled up in an emotional moment. Between the two of us we had three girls, he wanted a boy. I insisted on being married for that, so all three girls got new dresses and together we eloped. I got pregnant immediately. Suddenly though fear set in. I was approaching 40, hence I was placed into the 'high-risk pregnancy' category. To top it off, my body began to rebel. 'Why are you putting me through this again?' it seemed to be asking me daily.

Getting pregnant at 40 is not something I recommend, unless this would be your first child. If you already have some, don't do it! When our son was born, much to my husband's delight, Tommy had no signs of Down syndrome as we had been told to be prepared for. However, even before my suspicions were confirmed—he was a stressful baby—Tommy has ADHD. He never wanted to sleep; he always wanted attention. I grew more and more tired. The plan of being a stay-at-home mother was quickly undermined by bills that demanded payment. So, I worked full-time and came home every night to also be a full-time mom and wife. My husband needed his beauty sleep more than I did, he claimed. After all, he made more money than I did. Welcome to Zombie Land. Too old to be a new mom in the first place, I was also too old to handle a special needs child without giving up something very precious: myself.

Tom's 'occasional' habit became a daily one. Along with that came the extended nightly outings without me. More and more frequently, he came home just in time to take a shower, change clothes and go to work. Of course, his withdrawal was solely my fault. After all, I was no longer fun. I had retained 20 pounds from the pregnancy (I was anorexic prior to the pregnancy… and Tom, well he had gained some 'sympathy' weight and also retained that after I gave birth. He was not anorexic prior to that…), thus I was no longer attractive to him. And my cooking was lousy, he claimed. Never mind that I gave up on fixing elaborate, well-balanced meals, as I never knew whether I would have appreciative diners sit down to it or had to reheat it at midnight or later. Never mind that I simply did not have enough money to buy Grade A steaks.

I had no family. I had left my native country, Germany, prior to my first marriage. My first husband's family was 'my' family. When I left him, I also had no family left. I desperately tried to make 'Hank's' family 'my' family. But I just could not, no matter how hard I tried. His family was the most dysfunctional family I have ever met. In fact, I think his family represents the personification of the term 'dysfunctional'. His dad passed on before I came into the picture and had been married five times. His mother had spent some time in an institution, declared mentally unfit by Hank's dad. Hank's twin brother was an alcoholic to the extent that he was drunk after about 10 a.m. every day. One sister was a crack addict and the other, well, let's just say her husband was caught transporting an entire vanload of pot across the States once.

Hank made them stick to the agreement about 'not in my house, not around me and not around my kids.' And I appreciated that. 'Oh, guys, come check out the remodelling we did to the bathroom!' was one of the signals for me to stay behind and shield my kids. But then, one year, as I was enduring yet another alcohol and drug laced Fourth of July picnic, always ending in a blast-off of a multitude of illegal fireworks on a crowded parking lot, I had my own blast-off.

I was not too happy about the recent increase of Tom's 'occasional' habit, now also coupled with frequent nightly bar visits. So instead of being the good wife and socialising during the pre-parking-lot-hullabaloo, I sat inside and read a book. When I made a dutiful appearance outside, I walked right into his family happily gathered behind the back of my van. Paraphernalia spread all over the back, joint doing its merry-go-round, while all the children were playing in plain sight. I knew his sister did not hesitate to light up in front of her kids (resulting in her eldest, at 19 now, being an alcoholic and pot-head, weighing 300+ pounds), but I guess, no one seemed to realise that Tommy was 'my' child, included in the 'not in front of my children' request.

So I did my own fireworks display, spewing flames of fury. Of course, that was extremely disrespectful of me, shame on me! A few days later I presented my husband with an ultimatum: counselling or divorce.

After his ugly response, I sat on our porch swing and cried for hours. I prayed my heart out, 'God, how am I supposed to support three children on my own?' A week of this and I repeated the ultimatum with the same reaction from him. Consequently I drove around town. I pulled into the first daycare centre and asked for a job. Two days later, I ran into someone who had just turned down a three-bedroom apartment at a decent price. A week later, I moved out of the marital home and started a new job. I guess God answered my prayers…

Two years later, I still work at the daycare and I still live in the duplex. I manage barely, but I do. I am one of those people who fall through the cracks. I went to apply for public assistance. What a joke! My income is low enough to place me into the 'below poverty' group. However, I make too much money to qualify for public assistance. Sounds oxymoronic, doesn't it?

I am 'in the crack' and I found out that there are too many of us. My children were put on Medicaid, thank goodness, but I did not qualify. I am enrolled in a 'spend-down' programme. If I accrue medical bills over US $300 in one month, then I get assistance. I am on medication myself, but am not taking it all of the time anymore, as I canot afford to pay for doctors' visits and prescriptions. Most of my creditors are leaving me alone, because I pay my bills. I do not always pay the entire amount, but enough to keep them satisfied.

My husband, on the other hand, decided to make a career move and quit his job at $25/hr and exchanged it for a $14/hr job. Being unable to budget money wisely even before the career change, he consequently lost the house to foreclosure, had a van repossessed, had power and water shut off, insurance cancelled, and filed for bankruptcy. All of these items are, of course, on my record as well, as I am still legally married to him (even if not by choice, I have begged my lawyer, at least weekly, to get me a court date…). It is clear: Hank needs a rescuer. I don't. And I am no longer a rescuer for anyone but my kids and myself.

I had to make a terrifying choice: stay in a marriage with a druggie and be extremely unhappy, but stay home and pursue my writing or leave him, return to the workforce and then what? As he was openly hostile against marriage counselling, I decided I had to leave. How I was going to manage with three children was beyond me. So when my husband returned from one of his drastically increasing bar trips, and I informed him that I was moving out the following week, he was stunned. He really did not think I would do it! My daughters were thrilled, to say the least, as they were completely fed up with their step dad's antics and treatment towards all of us. Our son was confused. Within one week of his life, mommy left his dad, moved into a new place, returned to the workforce and to top it all off, he started kindergarten. For the first two weeks at my new job, I faced getting let go every day as my son spent two hours or more in the office screaming his lungs out and throwing things. My new boss, however, really loved my work—she hired me as an art teacher for the Three's Room—and she was patient. My son is on medication for ADHD and his paediatrician and I decided to up his dosage temporarily. It did wonders. From one day to the next my child changed his attitude and we were able to return him to his regular dosage about a month later.

I get free childcare at work, a huge incentive. I also do not have to drive more than 1½ miles one way, to get to work. That, with today's gas prices, is yet another huge incentive. Nonetheless, I spend more than half of my income from my main job on rent and in the winter time, my gas bill is half as high as my rent. I still moonlight as a reporter and I still work as a Sunday school director on weekends. 'Me' time? My girls have moved out now and it's just me and my now 7 year-old-son. As he has ADHD, he is quite a challenge to raise, let alone by a single mom.

We live in a society where women are supposed to be equal. But in reality, we are not. We still have to work harder and more hours to get even close to the pay our male counterparts receive. And when we come home, we are still expected to be good and patient mothers and fun, sexy wives. The ideal of husband and wife sharing responsibilities is in about 50 per cent of marriages just that: an ideal—it sounds wonderful, but is seldom applicable in real life. Perhaps one could argue that my status as a single mother has made me disillusioned and bitter. In fact, I have been told so to my face. Recently, a married co-worker made a similar statement to me. Not much later, I overheard the same co-worker mention to someone else that no, she would not leave her husband, but given the choice, she would not marry him again. Why? Because despite the fact that her husband is not an equal partner—or more accurately, he does not treat *her* as an equal partner—her life is still just a tad bit more safe and secure than mine. Perhaps that goes to prove that those of us who do leave—reluctantly but openly accept the hardships that single motherhood brings with it—have a tad bit more courage and a heck of a lot more self-respect.

Take my story, for example. I left two years ago. For this entire time, I have slaved in a low-paying job (that allows me to closely monitor my son's well-being). I pay more than half of my monthly income to rent. Most of my bills are behind, but I pay enough to keep the creditors happy. Aside from that, I have saved $1,000 towards my son's college fund, and I add a little bit of money every week when my child support check arrives. In the same two years, my husband lost the house, had utilities shut off, had our van repossessed and ended up filing for bankruptcy.

This may sound like a made-up story, but I am telling the truth and I have met many sisters who can relate to such behaviour from their deserting males. As I live in a no-fault divorce state, the court system is letting my husband get away with all of this. As long as we are still legally married, his creditors have every right to go after me. Why am I not divorced, yet? I don't know. As of this writing, I am actually thrilled to report that I finally have a court date! It will be my Fourth of July and I plan on leaving the courthouse lit up like a sparkler! Every day when I ask God: 'Why me?' I try to remind myself: I survived. No, I WON!

I won, over my fear of losing comfort and security in exchange for being able to be proud of myself.

Addendum: At the court hearing to finalise my divorce, 'Hank' found a way to prolong my suffering: he contested the custody order. Not only did this result in delay of the divorce, but I was also forced to spend another $660 for a parental evaluation to prove that I am a fit parent and he is not....

3

Redefining the Meaning of Work

Millicent Daweti

INTRODUCTION

> The product of both early experience and later influence, this style is
> your own way of dealing with external circumstances and with the inner
> distress that they stir up. (Bridges 1980:15)

I grew up in a township[1] in the East Rand.[2] Township life was, and
still is, poor. Most of the working women and mothers in the neighbourhood were either factory workers or domestic workers in the
suburbs. Occasionally, our friends would share with us a treat of dry
lettuce-filled sandwiches or even better, spicy, oil-soaked crumbs that
their mothers had collected from some fish-and-chips restaurant. My
family was privileged in comparison. There was a geyser that supplied
hot water from our coal stove. We had a fertile vegetable garden in the
backyard—an innovation I found so simple I wished other families would
copy. We also kept live chickens in a run by day and in the bathroom by
night. One rooster gave me such a hard time that I had to watch the coast
each time I went out to play. The evening it died after my older sister
and a friend had 'taught that rooster a lesson' was painfully regrettable
for my sister but thoroughly exhilarating for me.

Overall, childhood was simple and predictable. We walked to school,
did gender differentiated chores, played many games in the street,
sometimes watched fights and defended ourselves from bullies at other
times. When our fathers could afford it, we joined school tours to the
Pretoria Zoo. Professions that we aspired to follow, based on the role
models in the community, were those of teacher, nurse, office clerk,
policeman or medical doctor.

MY MOTHER

Before I describe how my work life unfolded, I want to briefly state what I recall about my mother's education and vocation.

> An interesting sideline on your own course of life can often be found if you compare your chronology with that of the parent of your sex. Many of your life-experiences come from the model provided for you by that parent. (Bridges 1980: 54)

I remember my mother as a devoted wife and mother of five. She was brought up by her widowed mother and later by her maternal aunt. Both caregivers instilled in her the Bible based faith that she, in turn, passed on to us. Like most students of her generation she only went up to standard six.[3] High schools were very far and further education was generally considered a luxury, especially for girls. At 22, she got married and had her first child. Her role as housewife continued for another 15 years when the youngest child was about five. None of us went to preparatory school. Both my parents, but my mother in particular, gave us sufficient elementary education to sail through the first year of school.

To generate supplementary income, she made and sold hats, scarves and jerseys. At other times, she would sell a variety of household products or clothes which she had bought at wholesale cost. One day, I was probably in junior high school, she got an offer to work as an assistant at Dr Lipchitz's surgery. This was a convenient arrangement—the workplace was within walking distance from home and she worked either mornings or afternoons on a half-day basis. Moreover, she loved nursing and had received short training in first-aid. Some years later, just after I got married, she decided to register for a one-year programme that would qualify her as an enrolled nurse. My father had always attached high value to formal education, so he encouraged and supported her. Thus, at the age of 51, she started a full-time career at a nursing home and then at a public hospital. It is at that stage that she also assumed the role of breadwinner as my father had to leave full-time employment, and eventually stop working, owing to ill health. I will return to this story of my mother later.

TRIBULATIONS OF SCHOOL LIFE

> Every phase of life has ...a task, and failing to complete it satisfactorily means that the person makes the transition into the next phase with unfinished business. (Bridges 1980: 35)

That I started school when I was only four and a half was always a burden to me. All my school years, I had to pretend I was a year older—I appeared a little older and I was surrounded by peers who were at least two years older than me. Anyway, I did very well throughout the primary school years. However, my understanding of mathematics gradually deteriorated to a point that I accepted my mediocrity and simply shifted my energy and interest to other subjects. Just a few years ago, I read about the correlation between emotional maturity and mathematical excellence. I have since made peace with the circumstances that led my parents to convince Mrs Motlatle that I was ready to start school.

What I cannot shake off are the emotional flashbacks originating from an authoritarian school system. Added to the tough discipline at home was forced obedience through corporal punishment at school. Every teacher administered punishment, which ranged from caning on the hand or buttocks, to whipping the calves in a manner that left red and black stripes for days. Mr Kope—the mathematics teacher at grade seven—still stands out as the meanest, brutal and inflictor of pain.

'I want your hands to swell as though you were a potato digger', he would tell us as he hit our knuckles. In winter, he would bring long, moist willow twigs which he told us were 'carefully selected for special use'. I always wished I could repress tears like the big girls and boys who easily took the punishment with a straight face. Every time I thought I could muster the strength not to let myself cry, I would turn my face away in shame because tears just rolled down. Telling our parents would not change anything, so we never bothered to report every detail. I only know of one girl, Rose, whose parents had to come in because a teacher had mistakenly poked her eye with a piece of tyre-cum-sjambok.[4] An oral apology settled the matter.

I think I started enjoying school in the next grade. Punishment was not as severe and it was a pleasure to see Ms Moukangwe every day—a tall, delicately beautiful and hard working teacher whom I liked a lot. Sadly, in grade nine, there was a lousy teacher of English, Mr Mokono who hardly understood the plot of the prescribed reader, *Beau Geste*; we had to make sense of it ourselves. As was common among his kind, Mr Mokono taught little and punished a lot. One afternoon, he ordered us to keep quiet. After spotting three of us who had the unfortunate need to utter a word to a fellow student, he made us line up, eyes closed, in front of the class. There was silence; then I heard a loud slap. The next thing, I felt my glasses being removed from my face. I braced myself for an inevitable blow, which left an echoing sting after it landed on my left cheek. Ten years later, as my fiancé and I were taking one of our favourite walks in Johannesburg, I spotted the man, standing by a dingy corner and clumsily stuffing his fat face with some unappetising junk. I felt an uncomfortable mixture of vindication and pity.

High school life at a boarding school was no better. My father imagined it would do us good if we left the township environment for a while because the disruptive spirit of 1976[5] was still prevalent even during the early 1980s. The boarding school where my sister and I were sent to was a good choice in my father's eyes because it was the one that his brothers had attended. The problem, it turned out, was that many other parents were thinking like my dad. So, we had a mix of students bringing with them the ideas and attitudes that our parents thought we were being spared from. There were two riots against the boarding master and the food served at the dining hall. Teachers were corrupt in other ways than those I had known until then. Affairs between male teachers and female students were rampant, partly because age gaps were not very large. Even Mr Mahlong, an intelligent but sheepish mathematics teacher with a shaky voice wanted to date me. In grade eleven, our class teacher, known to all as 'Creature' made me keep and mark the daily class register. He was a drunkard who once came to school without shoes because the shebeen[6] owner had confiscated them in lieu of the money 'Creature' owed. In the final year of high school, another drunkard came to teach English. This one, who would always smell of spirits and never had a clean shirt on, also asked me to keep his scheme book. He got to be called 'Folks' because that's what he called us. One morning, a number of us were given, two whips in each hand for arriving late. This was carried out in the staffroom where there were at least two teachers at any given time. A few days later, 'Folks' came to me and said: 'When you were in the staffroom the other day, I saw ... [smiling, and then continuing softly and slowly] a pure white, tight fitting panty.'

I started believing that male teachers were a crazy breed struggling with underdeveloped self-esteem and aborted dreams. Except that there were brilliant teachers—male teachers. My favourite school year by far was grade ten, the year just before I went to boarding school. Mr Ncokazi made it all worthwhile. He taught English, but in his kind, firm and wise way he taught life skills. I had a feeling that he loved our class more than the rest. Maybe I was wrong, but I could not imagine him getting along with each of the four classes with the same enthusiasm and depth of personal engagement. He explicitly discussed sexual and teenage issues with such dignity that we had immense respect for him. He was a real father figure, a pastor by qualification, who made many of us wish we were part of his family. Not once did he beat us. Professor Mawasha, a seasoned lecturer of English as a Second Language at the university I went to, was another honourable person. He was a well-spoken and knowledgeable man whose teaching skill and professionalism made him a perfect role model. Missing his lecture was completely unthinkable.

PROFESSIONAL CHOICES AND MILESTONES

...there are times when you yourself turned out to be what you said and even believed that you were not. (Bridges 1980: 99)

Science and Mathematics were considered the right combination of subjects for a bright career future. Less prestigious high school options were History and Geography, and Biblical Studies with either Agriculture for boys or Home Economics for girls. My favourite subjects were English and Science. Whereas I could handle the application of mathematical concepts, equations and calculations in science, my brain did not like the gritty texture of theorems, logarithms and trigonometry. Because my matric[7] results were too poor to meet the admission requirements for

BSc in Pharmacy, I thought I should rewrite matric in order to get a better mark in Mathematics. My father and close family friends strongly dissuaded me. I had to proceed to university. During the first two weeks, I sat in at least one class of every Faculty—except Theology. Eventually, I had to make a choice to get the registration over and done with, and start studying.

'I'll settle for the Diploma in Pedagogy', I remember saying to myself after observing the crowd of people of all ages and capabilities that had filled the largest lecture hall of Education 101. 'Besides', my presumptuous teenage ego told me, 'schools need good teachers; and if this is the calibre of person that teachers are made of, I'm sure I will do better.'

Needless to say, I chose English and Science as my majors. In the third year, we presented a few practice lessons. Toward the end of my lesson, Professor Mawasha wrote something on paper and gave it to me before leaving the room. 'You are super!', it read. For the six-week formal programme of practice teaching, I decided to go to a newly established high school within walking distance from home. There was no doubt in my mind that I loved being a teacher. I got to teach in a real school and I had an opportunity to challenge my own views about what worked best and what did not. The learners responded well. Sis[8] Zola was a kind and supportive mentor. The principal and his deputy were pleased with her feedback about my teaching. One December afternoon, a teacher from the same school came to my house. He had been asked by the principal to recruit me to teach English and Science the following year. Thus, my career as a teacher was guaranteed to begin when schools reopened in January. I was 19 years old.

The five years I spent there as a teacher were very fulfilling. In the first year, I taught Mr Kope's daughter, who had missed the previous year of school to have a baby. I worked diligently, got along well with most colleagues and saw respect and appreciation in the faces of many of my students. I often told the learners that I took my work seriously and that I expected them to do the same with theirs. I think many of them did, and those who did not were successful at making me believe that they did. So there were very few occasions on which I had to give a strong reprimand. My tried and tested strategy to get the attention of the learners was to stand attentively and watch them without saying a word. What would follow was a quick settling down and an unspoken signal— 'you now have our full attention, major'.

Still, I had to face some unpleasant eventuality once in a while. I felt very small when I overhead senior female teachers lashing out disrespectfully at female students. Although the principal and other staff would address such matters in a staff meeting, by and large this pattern of abusive speech was silently condoned. A number of male teachers were known to use one of the smaller staffrooms as a drinking place on Friday afternoons. This issue was, however, sternly dealt with and the practice was discontinued.

After each day's work, I effortlessly switched over to my studies for a BA degree by distance education. At home, my sister and I contributed to whatever improvements our family could afford. When the town council made the supply of electricity more accessible to township residents, we joined the growing numbers who paid for the electrification of their homes. My father bought a refrigerator and a large television set. My sister bought a hi-fi set and I financed the erection of a new steel fence. For the first time in our lives we did not have to use candles or the gas lamp, we could play music albums instead of just listening to the radio, and we could catch up on the buzz about *Dallas* and what JR was up to. When my sister got married, I shouldered the bulk of the house renovation project. The house was extended and the boys moved from the kitchen to their own bedroom. Then I also got married; it was a good feeling, though, that I had made a significant difference in the lives of my parents and siblings. I had also completed all my BA papers but one.

NEW OPPORTUNITIES, ROLES AND CHALLENGES

> ...we achieve our breakthroughs not by setting out to break through, but by doing the work that is right in front of us. (Bridges 2001: 130)

The next school in Johannesburg was completely different. It was one of the first independent multiracial schools established in the premises of a former white school for girls. The principal and staff were all new, as were the students. The work ethic was very high, facilities were superior and parents from neighbouring townships were eager to give their children a better quality of education. I took more pride in being a teacher. However, after a total of eight years of being a school teacher and a couple of months before I was due to become a mother, I was feeling a pinch of burn-out and desperation to get out of the classroom.

A telegram arrived confirming my appointment as Subject Advisor for English as a Second Language in the West Rand. My prayers were finally answered; all I had to do was resign and move on. But I was very apprehensive. My baby was only nine months old and I felt that after taking up my new job I would not be able to come home as early as I used to. In order to be at work at eight in the morning, I would have to catch a 5:45 a.m. bus to the Johannesburg station and then travel by train for an hour and a bit. I had also put my studies on hold for that year to give myself some space to juggle the new demands of motherhood. It would now be doubly difficult to complete the rest of the honours papers. Mr Matabane was expecting my letter of acceptance by the end of that week. Pen and paper in my bag, I went to see him. After listening to me, he said, 'Do you have any idea how many teachers desperately want to have this job?' Then he pulled out a big volume from under his desk and continued, 'This is a dissertation that one staff member here has just completed. You too can do it.'

I wrote down a few lines and handed him the awaited letter. Although the first month was exhausting, I soon got used to the early morning routine. School visits were sometimes hectic but interacting with teachers was always a rewarding learning experience. While I was content with my professional progress, I was plagued by the guilt of leaving my daughter in the care of a stranger. I once came home to a heart-wrenching cry of my baby locked inside the house alone for hours. The door had shut locked after Sarah went out to dust a mat.

The following year I registered for the remaining honours papers. Within weeks I found out I was expectant again. I was not thrilled. As with the first pregnancy, I had to write my exams just a month before the baby is born. However, I found some comfort in the fact that my un-born babies seemed to love studying. I was mentally alert the first time and I got good marks for my papers. The second exams went so well I obtained the degree with distinction. I was rearing go on. Perhaps child bearing activated in me a subconscious instinct to accomplish more—to create better conditions for my offspring. When maternity leave expired, I took advantage of the study leave I had accumulated based on length of service in the Department of Education. It was a grand privilege to have 10 months altogether. I had an excellent supervisor, I used my previous school as locale of the research, and I could come home early to be with the children. I successfully completed my studies in one year and obtained a masters degree.

At this point, the Department of Education was restructured and I chose to be based in Johannesburg. At the end of the restructuring process several management posts had to be filled for various units. Being manager of a unit of 16 was not terribly difficult, but I was vulnerable. My counterparts in other units were older men. They thought they had an obligation to advise me how my unit should be supporting teachers, which resources we had to budget for and which individuals I ought to be tough on. At management meetings, there was a foregone conclusion that minute taking was my task. Within my unit, some individuals worked harder and cooperated better than others. Yet, acknowledging the same names all the time made me uncomfortable. Simultaneously, reminding the same people to submit their weekly itineraries and monthly reports was a pain. One morning when Olga became childishly difficult as usual, I retorted right away. That turned out to be a critical lesson in tact and conflict management. Never again should I allow anyone to make me feel provoked.

WORKPLACE NETWORKS AND SUPPORT SYSTEMS

> Who we think we are is partly defined by the roles and relationships that we have, both those we like and those we do not. (Bridges 1980: 13)

Fitting into a particular workplace culture can be a difficult process. At the school where I first taught, I became aware of the cliques with which I did not want to be associated. I was glad when a ladies club, based on the stokvel[9] system, was initiated. However, although the intention was sincere, I found their insistence on a particular method of using the income, unfairly prescriptive. My objection was lukewarmly received. Later that evening, Lindi called to thank me for the courage to speak out. That left me wondering if the club was a necessary support system or a vestige of a conformist education system. When I became head of the department, there was a competitive spirit that prevailed among my colleagues—even a dishonest attempt to downplay problems and challenges while overemphasising apparent successes. I was not sure if that was a 'typical male working style', but I knew I did not want to be absorbed in it.

Higher education is resourceful but isolating workplace. Work, particularly as far as research output is concerned, is territorialised and individualistic. Besides the orientation session that all new employees attend, there was no induction programme when three of us joined our department. Two individuals made a personal attempt to include us in their projects, which we found invaluable. Gradually our network of associates grew and we developed our own ways of surviving. I have observed interesting differences in the nature of the interactions I have with male associates on the one hand, and females on the other. My female friends are a small circle that provides essential encouragement on personal matters. We talk frankly about our personal frustrations and celebrations, our family lives, the papers we are writing and the struggles we have with our doctoral studies. We also pass on among ourselves self-help tips, reading material and websites of interest. With males, conversations are also useful, though less frequent. They tend to include the questions 'When are you completing your PhD?' or 'My paper or book has just come out; would you like to see it?' Occasionally, there is an attempt to test how far a collegial friendship can remain just that. Peppered into a discussion are repeated compliments, invitations to travel together to some exotic conference, and diagnoses such as 'you need somebody to spoil you'.

The notion of a Women's Forum as a transformational structure is a noble one. As it stands, however, I see it as an entity that promotes the visibility of a group who meet once in a while to declare their solidarity against gender discrimination. Outside the forum the sisters are as aloof as a monk. Could it be that we all, regardless of gender, have an untameable desire to rise above rather than with the other?

LOOKING BACK

> Rule number one: You find yourself coming back in new ways to old activities, when you're in transition. (Bridges 1980: 8)

Much as unfavourable circumstances can delay or prevent the realisation of our aspirations, I believe that significant people and events serve as catalysts for other meaningful trajectories. Professionally, I have grown into and out of roles that include teacher, teacher developer, instructional designer, manager, researcher, writer, facilitator and consultant. My interests have shifted from language teaching to adult learning and organisational development. Interestingly, when I took an online vocational assessment test recently, the results were as follows: 'Advisor... this is the role that is most in tune with who you are at your core. As an advisor, you are a quiet and reserved person who loves to help others achieve their potential through personal connections.' I then asked my children to describe the kind of person they see in me. After the praises they were in the mood to sing came what sounded like a more accurate assessment, 'You're a teacher; you are demanding', said one. 'Yes', confirmed the other, 'you read a lot and you like organising things, but you act crazy when you are happy.'

A great source of stability in my life has been the religious beliefs and values of my parents. Not only have I have grown to appreciate and espouse this value system but I have also instilled it in my own children. My mother stands out as an example of graceful resilience and knowing contentment. In one of my favourite conversations with her about work, she quoted Ecclesiastes 9:10, 'Whatever your hand finds to do, do it with your might; for there is no work or device or knowledge or wisdom in the grave where you are going.' Before cancer took her life two years ago, she joked that she would die a happy person because she had done a good job in raising us.

After obtaining my masters degree, I have been spending as much time with my children as possible. No greater joy do I derive than from reading with them, helping with homework and school projects, discussing money matters with them, hearing them describe their interests, dreams and fears, learning new dance moves and picking up brilliant ideas from them. At 41, I began to sense that I am at a similar state of transition that my mother experienced as 51. I am convinced that work should allow each of us to carry out assignments aligned with our natural strengths and talents. I want to earn a livelihood not out of resentful desperation or competition, but out of creative and expansive living. I want to make the most of myself in a manner that enriches the lives of those with whom I come into contact. I think I have begun to define in more specific terms what such living should look like for me.

I also think I am very close to the next step: 'stop getting ready to do it—and do it!' (Bridges 1980: 146).

NOTES

1. An urban residential area set aside under Apartheid policies for settlement by the Black population.
2. The East Rand and West Rand lie at extreme ends of the gold reef district of Johannesburg.
3. Equivalent to Grade 8.
4. Afrikaans word for a whip usually made from leather.
5. The year in which Black students protested against the Bantu Education system.
6. A drinking place that is usually unlicensed.
7. The last year of high school, now Grade 12.
8. Short for *sisi,* meaning sister in isiZulu. Also used, as in this case, in acknowledgement of seniority of the person being addressed.
9. A group saving system where members contribute a fixed amount on a monthly or weekly basis and then withdraw it in rotation.

REFERENCES

Bridges, W. 1980. *Transitions: Making Sense of Life's Changes.* Reading, Mass: Addison-Wesley.
———. 2001. *The Way of Transition: Embracing Life's Most Difficult Moments.* Cambridge, MA: Perseus.

4

Moving and Mixing: Stories of Migrant Women in New Zealand

Maureen Lewis

INTRODUCTION

Acculturation to a new country and workplace is for every migrant a time of navigating between a foreign present and a lost past. For every migrant the process of preparing to leave one's home country, of arriving in the new country and realigning one's values and approaches to become bicultural and bilingual is often complex, multifaceted and ongoing. The experiences of migrant staff who have made their new home in the host country are both similar and different to those of international students and hold significant implications for the sector.

The process of acculturation, or of people socialised in one culture moving to another has until recently been viewed in a linear sense as a movement starting from one cultural identification and ending with assimilation into the other. The notion of migrants being 'rooted' in a univocal, monolithic, English, Indian, Croatian or any culture is questioned and the reconstitution of identity in the host country has recently been framed as an interactive process which allows migrants to evolve without forsaking their cultural heritage. Acculturation is seen as a dynamic, interactive, 'mixing and moving' as the migrant adjusts to the discourses of the host country while holding on to their cultural values. At any one time the migrant may feel 'assimilated', 'separated' or 'marginalised' (Bhatia 2002). Letting go of the idea of cultural purity, the migrant assumes a hybrid identity or 'double vision', an ability to call on different perspectives and to integrate these in new ways according to different situations. Bhabha (1994) claims that the truest eye may now belong to the migrant's double vision.

The migrant seems to walk in two worlds, yet walk in none (Peeler 2002), feeling uprooted in their home culture, but not at home in any (Sarap 1996). This transnational experience of displacement is what Bhabha (1994) calls the 'third space', a productive space where 'new signs of identity, and innovative sites of collaboration and contestation' are created. Migrants enter this third space when engaged in inter-cultural dialogue.

Adapting to a new culture of education also involves intercultural exchange with similar 'mixing and moving' (Hermans and Kempens 1998), as new staff adapt to the interpersonal practices of learning and teaching, care and professionalism, and quality management in large organisations. Migrant staff undergo a complex process of orientation and learning as they construct new and different constellations of know-ledge and values in the new culture. The migrant teacher who reflects on 'the cultural' in relation to her own background, as well as to that which is new or different, has the 'migrant's double vision' (Bhabha 1994). People who are able to see relationships between different cultures based on critical understanding of their culture as well as other cultures, and can mediate for themselves or others, are said to be interculturally competent (Byram 2000).

As a process, intercultural dialogue 'encourages an identification of the boundaries that define individuals, then asks to relate across those boundaries and even to call them into question' (UNESCO 2003). Higher education institutions have an important role to play in providing structures and opportunities for intercultural dialogue to take place. Discipline objectives, teaching methods, student skills and knowledge itself can be deepened and strengthened through an intercultural dialogue approach. Intercultural competence should be a defining feature of organisational culture, in practice not merely in policies and charters.

APPROACH AND METHODOLOGY

I chose to use a narrative approach, collecting women's stories, primar-ily to allow for the individual richness that only individual accounts of personal experience can offer, and secondly to enable the type of creative expression and identity formation that the narrative process engenders in the story-teller (Giddens 1991). By telling a story, people engage in the conversation that explores and defines their sense of who they are (Taylor 1991; Benhabib 1992). The use of narrative identity theory or the telling of stories in which individuals construct a sense of their emerging identities opens the way to capture and theorise the experience of individuals who are marginalised from dominant social groups. It presents experience and subjectivity that would otherwise remain invisible and unheard.

My reasons for focusing on women were twofold. First, my understanding that identity is socially constructed (Giddens 1991; Taylor 1991; Benhabib 1992; Calhoun 1994; Somers and Gibson 1994) suggests that the intercultural experiences of women are likely to be different in a number of ways from those of men. Little has been written about the adaptation experiences of women migrants (Lyon 2001) and unless made visible, this useful knowledge is likely to 'remain in the closed space of individual experience' (Somers and Gibson 1994: 174). Second, it is my belief that women might feel more comfortable with other women when disclosing and sharing information that could hold emotional significance (Butler and Wintram 1993). Trust developed in conversation between women connects knowledge and knower in a meaningful way by honouring relationship and experience (Donawa 1998).

Both academic and administrative women who I had met in my capacity as staff developer while facilitating the induction of new staff were invited to participate. Despite a high level of enthusiasm expressed by the women for sharing their experiences, I had difficulty finding common meeting times for focus group sessions. I decided to hold one individual, unstructured interview with each woman, in which she was asked to tell the story of her migration to New Zealand and her experience as a staff member of the institute. A list of prompt questions was sent to each woman before the interview, relating to reasons for migration, experiences leading up to employment at the institute, differences they encountered there, the contributions they felt they had made and types of support that would have been useful. Transcripts of the taped interviews were examined for underlying themes and comments that most succinctly expressed particular thoughts or feelings. After a period of four years, I asked for their reflections on how their situations had changed in that time, and how their intercultural identities had developed.

Fifteen women participated in the original research: five were administrators and 10 came from the teaching staff. The women originally belonged to India, Pakistan, England, South Africa, Romania, Fiji, Malaysia, China and Croatia. One had been in New Zealand for 16 years and the others had been there for less than 10 years, only two women had migrated a year back.

Themes emerging from the women's stories are presented in four parts. Part 1 deals with their reasons for migration, the shock of arrival in a new country and the ways in which the women started to construct an intercultural or hybrid identity. Part 2 outlines their entry into the culture of a large New Zealand polytechnic, the challenges they faced aligning past and present values and the outcomes of these efforts. It also presents the reflections of women on what types of support might have helped their acculturation. Part 3 deals with a recent reflection of these women—four years after the original interviews—on how they have moved on in terms of their intercultural identities, their sense of belonging and their sense of what they contribute to the institute.

PART 1: MIGRATING TO NEW ZEALAND

Reasons for Migration

None of the women came to New Zealand to take up secured positions in the tertiary sector. In all cases, the desire for better social conditions and opportunities for development had been the women's motivation to migrate. Younger women who moved in their mid-twenties to mid-thirties sought to escape the constraints of communism and religious intolerance, and two women were happy to move to their husband's home country. Women who were already in their mid-thirties or older were motivated to migrate for the sake of their children's future. The effects of war, political unrest, compulsory military service, discrimination and corruption were major factors influencing their decision:

At that time, I wanted to get my family out [of the country]. My daughter was very sick. She had an anxiety disorder and wouldn't sleep. (Ana)

In such cases, both the women and their husbands left well established careers, willing to make financial, career and social adjustments in order to ensure greater personal and educational security for their children:

We decided [our son's] education was our priority, although it was a very difficult decision for us because my husband was in the academy. (Shireen)

Arriving in New Zealand: The Impact

Arrival was an anxious time for most of the women: a time of navigating between a foreign present and a lost past. Culture shock impacted on their identity as individuals, wives, mothers and employees, forcing them to rethink their status, usefulness, intrinsic values and goals.

Some women felt dependent and powerless. Others became the breadwinners while husbands struggled to find work. The women who admitted to the most profound sense of culture shock were those who, married to New Zealanders, least anticipated the overwhelming sense of difference:

I was hopelessly out of my depth on many occasions. (Vicki)

There were so many things that I as an Asian could not comprehend about how [Maori] define family and family support. (Daria)

The impact on family was for some of the migrants quite devastating, causing them to question the wisdom of their decision to migrate. A son who had shown enormous promise in his homeland, lost his motivation to succeed and gave up his studies; a daughter attempted suicide. The move resulted in at least one marriage break-up. The woman had found herself well suited to the less competitive environment in New Zealand, but her husband could not acculturate at all and returned to his home country. For many of the women, the intersection of expectation and experience resulted in a sense of failure, loss and guilt too painful to admit to family back home, to new acquaintances and especially to one-self: to keep on going was the only option.

> Initially it was very hard. We had a return ticket and I almost thought we needed to go back because the entire atmosphere was so dismal and I couldn't get a job easily, but we are Christians and so we had to hang in. (Sunita)

Engaging with the Host Culture

Finding work was the primary goal of the new migrants. Despite quali-fications and experience in other parts of the world, migrants were often rejected because they lacked New Zealand experience. Unable to find the equivalent of high-status, well-paid jobs they had left behind meant a complete restructuring:

> It's more or less like you're opening a whole new chapter. (Amelie)

Many started with casual, part-time or voluntary work often in fields unrelated to their original training, a factor that impacted on their financial means, as well as their sense of self. Through continuous 'mixing and moving' (see Hermans and Kempens 1998) the women were able to acquire sufficient intercultural competency to negotiate entry into the area of work where their skills and values could find some resonance. Others expressed humility, relief and joyfulness, as they were able to move away from the sense of displacement and failure to being able to share, once again, something of their knowledge and experience with others:

> And I crept back into the New Zealand workplace through voluntary work, which was a completely different way of entering a workplace. (Kim)
>
> I [had] been trying to get into teaching and all my applications [had] been rejected. It made us feel not good enough to be in this country... He was wonderful. He said he would be the first person to give me a chance and that's how I started. (Nishi)
>
> I loved it from then on! And that was at age 50, mind you! (Sunita)

For many of these women, migration had proved more challenging than they had anticipated. However, in most cases, finding employment in the tertiary sector was a significant step in re-defining a sense of self and purpose.

PART 2: ENTERING THE TERTIARY SECTOR: A DIFFERENT CULTURAL SPACE

Orientation

Finding work at a large urban polytechnic in New Zealand introduced the women to a culture of education in which they could construct themselves as education providers in their new country. Located in a region with the highest numbers of Maori, Pasifika and migrant peoples, the institute had developed strategies to attract and retain increasing numbers of students from these communities. It also recruited a high number of international students and as a result increasing numbers of migrant staff were being employed.

It is evident, both in the institutional charter as well as in practice, that the institute placed a high value on maintaining a welcoming and friendly work and study environment, where a culture of care was established and maintained (Manukau Institute Charter 2003). While bicultural strategies and support in language and study skills for Maori, Pasifika and international students were currently prioritised, the acculturation needs of the migrant staff into New Zealand's tertiary sector were still left largely to the discretion of individual heads of department and managers.

All the women acknowledged the friendliness of their managers, but while some managers went out of their way to help their new staff, others left the migrants to work out for themselves the new and unspoken approaches, and the procedures and policies.

The women's perceptions of the degree of empowerment they enjoyed in their new roles were formed in relation to their experiences in their home countries (Bhatia 2002). Two of the women who had experienced hierarchical employment structures were able to be less circumspect with their managers and peers:

[My boss] always encourages me when I've had a bad day, so that helps me emotionally. I think it's very important for a manager to do that. It was different because when you make a small mistake in China you were blamed in the meetings. You would be criticised. You would not be given the chance to make a mistake and learn from it. (Amy)

Here I became more assertive, that's it: I became more assertive. (Nishi)

Two others, however, felt that as migrants, their voices were not heard:

Having lived in a multicultural environment, I think I bring a multi-cultural perspective to the environment. I've come to this country pas-sionate about culture and its impact. I was hoping to make a change and it's really frustrating when you can't. I feel disempowered as a migrant. Ethnicity would be an issue; I feel that somehow I am not listened to. (Shireen)

I find that most of the colleagues who are immigrants are not part of any committee in which they can choose or change anything. And then you don't have a voice because you are left outside. (Ana)

From these accounts it would seem that the general culture of the in-stitution is less autocratic than that experienced in some countries. How-ever, the friendly welcome of managers in some cases appears to fall short of an actual openness to dealing with 'foreign' ideas and thoughts.

Different Cultures of Education: Some Observations

Administrative staff found more similarity between their previous work and their new positions than the teaching staff:

The systems are very, very similar to what I was used to. Whoever I've interacted with has been very, very nice. They culture has been so different from my home country because we are formal over there, but here everybody is pretty informal. (Larissa)

However, the contexts in which the teaching staff found themselves were, at times, very different to those they had known before. The women found differences in the educational focus in their new country that in turn shaped the roles and expectations of staff and students:

There are some major differences. I came from an environment where education was everything. But the way of learning was different. (Amelie)

Women who came from more teacher-centred, result orientated cultures of education had not anticipated the institute's more student-centred approach. They became aware that a focus on student-centred learning required a different set of responsibilities from teachers and made learning more relevant for students:

Everyone was working for an examination and you just had to [teach]. Whereas here the teacher plays a large part with the buffer skills and all that. We are responsible here and accountable too. (Sunita)

Some saw the easy access to education and the amount of choice as positive:

I think here you are given so many options. In China it was very strict, very narrow. Everyone is going [on] a bridge, a single bridge. You have to cross the bridge. You can't. Too many people cross the bridge and some of the people will not get a chance, maybe even fall into the water. (Amy)

However, other teachers pointed out that there was a lack of motivation among students. Whereas in their home countries students had to compete for getting an education that would give them a great start in life, their New Zealand students appeared to lack the same drive:

Students were motivated because work was the way to get somewhere. Here not like that, there are more choices. (Ana)

One of the women commented on the high degree of compliance in the educational sector which she evidently felt as a constraint:

Just follow the rules. I was never that sort of a lecturer, I was always trying to do more…that's what they taught me, to be very personal, to put your heart and soul and energy into it. (Marija)

Some women were conscious of a lack of rigorous foundational learning that could support further, higher level learning:

I thought they should know the basics. The reality is they don't. At one point, I wanted to quit, because the pressure was on me to make it simpler and simpler…so I found I was not challenged. [But] I was challenged in another way because I was relearning how to deliver it in a language and a manner they can understand. (Katrina)

Developing Intercultural Competence

Through trial and error and much reflection the migrants began to navigate their way through the issues and practices of teaching in New Zealand:

When I got my first feedback, that's when I realised I wasn't delivering the way they wanted it, I was delivering the way I thought was right. (Jill)

By comparing their past and present experiences the women started to negotiate new values and practices. Their shared experience of having been 'on the other side' (Kim) gave them a double vision—an ability to work with different perspectives and approaches and to integrate different ways of being and knowing. For some, communicating cooperatively with several cultures was already a well-honed skill that gave them confidence and satisfaction:

I used to have to deal with a lot of different cultures. I came from a nation whereby we have four different cultures. (Daria)

Lillian was excited by the differential needs and challenges posed by her students. She continuously constructed new teaching strategies based on their own experience of different cultures of education:

It's just amazing how [international students] have been taught. I think that's what some of the students appreciate again, that they're allowed to use their own logic. With my students I try and use a little bit of every-thing. I usually ask how many people had learnt in this way…and how many people have done it this way. So every time I put something on the board, I've got to do it both ways, so I use different coloured markers and stuff like that to show them different ways of dong the same problem, and then people just choose the one they like. (Lillian)

The motivation of migrant staff to adopt responsive strategies is large-ly altruistic, often based on a sense of mutual loss and displacement.

Ana created an immediate bond with her classes, acknowledging their struggle and making a commitment to working together to succeed:

> The first thing in my class, and my class is 80% immigrants, I tell them I am an immigrant and I tell them [what] is important, helping them to make something out of their education. And [they] need to fight. Yes, I do reach them. And I am very proud of them. (Ana)

> The fact that I'm a woman helps a lot. I think women, generally, very often are not afraid to talk. (Ana)

Other migrant staff were conscious of modelling their successful negotiation of the educational and employment situation to both students and staff, thereby assuring them that intercultural survival was possible. Knowing that her students appreciated her advice on how to succeed, Vicki was happy to guide them, where necessary.

> They find it easier to talk to me and if I think they are not doing the right thing I tell them about it. (Vicki)

With their ability to deconstruct and compare different aspects of different cultures of education, the women were able to mediate the learning processes of their students and support their development of required learning skills.

Looking Back: Supporting the Process

When asked what could have been done to support the women's acculturation into the institution, participants said they valued the adult education courses which many of them had taken, but orientation and mentoring could have addressed issues of a more particular nature. Very few of the women had had an opportunity to join the twice-yearly orientation sessions conducted by the institute.

Some women felt the need of a mentor to provide guidance and to support progress at work:

> You need to have a mechanism in which you check up on somebody, you allocate a mentor. (Katrina)

Some felt that membership to an informal group would have helped them to talk about their issues and sometimes speak to someone in their own language.

Four of the women indicated that support with English usage in the educational environment would have been welcome. Discussion groups with a focus on educational issues and procedures would have helped them to tackle difficulties that they could not take to their managers and provide a space in which they could, through dialogue, establish communication skills and networks and construct themselves more powerfully as teachers and administrators:

> In an interview a person asked me what I'm going to do, because I said I think I need to improve my language, honestly. They didn't say what they are going to do to help me. (Ana)

> We must be more encouraged, not told your English is OK, it's OK. I see the difference from three years ago. I can now have better relationship with the students. And they think differently now about me as a lecturer. (Marija)

An introduction to Maori culture would have empowered new staff to interact more meaningfully with Maori students and staff:

> An introduction to Maori culture, like don't sit on the desk and don't pass things over people's heads. This is how you pronounce names. (Jill)

Many of the women were still on casual contracts that contributed to a sense of marginalisation:

> I'd like to see more security for casual employees. Because when you are casual, I think you miss many of the advantages of working here and one of them is continuity of tenure, your job. We're wanting to grow and to offer a lot and contribute a lot… 'cos I don't think, from a personal point of view I could be any more committed. I said before, what I do is my self-image. (Kim)

PART 3: FOUR YEARS LATER: ONGOING DEVELOPMENTS

Women still working at the institute four years later, said they continued to derive much satisfaction from their work with culturally diverse students with whom they could share their experience of difference. Most felt more confident in their engagement with staff and systems, though their sense of belonging varied according to context. Marija had made significant input to her department in designing a new system, and had embarked on the doctoral studies that had been interrupted on her arrival. For Katrina however, professional survival was still an effort:

> I can't see myself ever integrating. The two value systems can never merge, but you do mellow and become more flexible. You know now, an awareness is there. As a migrant you are always the first target. You are in survival mode from here on. (Katrina)

On a personal level, most of the women's initial anxiety had been replaced by an easier relationship with their social environment. Kim realised after a crisis that she actually had built up a working network of women in her life again, something she thought she'd never replace. Amy felt that her independent spirit had in fact been nurtured in the New Zealand context in a way it would never have been in China.

CONCLUSION

The acculturation stories told here speak of difficulty, resilience and transformation. They speak of their love for children that motivated so many women to migrate, the sacrifices in terms of personal ties, job status and incomes, the tireless pursuit of meaningful work, the stress of confronting contradictory value systems and the ways in which they reconstructed their lives. But mostly they speak of an energetic and powerful commitment to supporting and inspiring others, be they staff or students, who find themselves at a cultural boundary.

As their experience of acculturation into New Zealand differed in the degree of ease of matching or integrating values past and present, so did their adaptation to the culture of learning they found at the institute. It is evident that allied staff, working collaboratively in teams, found a better match with the new culture of learning than did academic staff working in a more individual capacity, and left to learn through trial and error. Having children in the educational system added to the women's intense interest in the nature and quality of learning and teaching in New Zealand. By 'mixing and matching' (Herman and Kempens 1998), they were able to be more discerning and appreciative of both the new culture and their former roots (Kim and Gudykunst 1988). Their own hybridised approaches were a working together of what they considered the strengths of the different systems and were based on the responsiveness to the needs of their students and the approaches promoted through the institute.

The most significant theme running through the stories, however was their empathic bonding with staff and students from diverse cultures, evidence of Freud's notion of loss and mourning being that which binds society together (Rose 1996).

Implications for Polytechnics

In Bhabha's view we need to support cultural exchange in our institutions because it is exactly in this way that cultural hybrid and intercultural identities arise (Bhabha 1994), and response to the needs of a diverse student body can be initiated and developed. Institutions that are fully responsive to the learning experiences of increasingly diverse staff and student bodies are committed to functioning as learning communities. Current research on how professional learning communities are created and sustained suggests that clear leadership, management and coordination of professional activities, as well as teamwork, networking, critical friendships and mentoring are key factors in the process (Scherer 1999; Stoll et al. 2003). This indicates shared values and vision directed towards student learning and a greater reliance on collaboration will be more effective than reliance on individual problem-solving. Communal professional learning is recommended over individual professional development which has been the lot of classroom teachers. Reflective professional inquiry, through frequent interaction amongst staff, is acknowledged as an essential in converting individual unspoken or tacit knowledge into shared knowledge, and applying new ideas and information by problem-solving to meet students' needs. Such interaction and learning fostered and managed by leadership processes supports an ethos of intercultural engagement, which is otherwise difficult to sustain on an ad hoc basis.

REFERENCES

Benhabib, S. 1992. *Situating the Self: Gender, Community and Postmodernism in Contemporary Ethics*. Cambridge: Polity Press.

Bhabha, H. 1994. *The Location of Culture*. London: Routledge.

Bhatia, S. 2002. 'Acculturation, Dialogical Voices and the Construction of the Diasporic Self', *Theory and Psychology*, 12(1): 55–77.

Bhatia, S. and A. Ram. 2001. 'Rethinking "Acculturation" in Relation to Diasporic Cultures and Postcolonial Identities', *Human Development*, 44: 1–18.

Byram, M. 2000. 'Assessing Intercultural Competence in Language and Teaching', *Sprogforum*, 18(6): 8–13.

Butler, S. and C. Wintram. 1993. *Feminist Groupwork*. London: Sage.

Calhoun, C. 1994. *Social Theory and the Politics of Difference*. Oxford: Blackwell.

Cortazzi, M. and L. Jin. 1997. 'Communication for Learning across Cultures', in D. MacNamara and R. Harris (eds), *Overseas Students in Higher Education*, pp. 79–90. London: Routlegde.

Donawa, W. 1998. 'Friendship: An Epistemological Frame for Narrative Inquiry', *Connections 98*. Available online at http://www.educ.uvic.ca/connections/Con98donawa.htm (downloaded on 14 May 2000).

Giddens, A. 1991. *Modernity and Self-identity*. Cambridge: Polity Press.

Hermans, H.J.M. and H.J.G. Kempens. 1998. 'Moving Cultures: The Perilous Problems of Cultural Dichotomies in a Globalizing Society', *American Psychologist*, 53, 1111–1120.

Kim, Y.Y. and W.B. Gudykunst (eds). 1988. *Theories in Intercultural Communication*, Vol. 12. Newbury Park, CA: Sage.

Lyon, C. 2001. *Cultural Mentors: Exploring the Role of Relationships in the Adaption and Transformation of Women Educators who Go Overseas to Work*. Paper presented at the AERC Conference. Available online at http://www.edst.educ.ubc.ca/aerc/2001/2001lyon.htm (downloaded on 15 July 2003).

Mills, C. 1997. 'The Lived-in Realities of Internationalism', in H.R.M.H. Silins (ed.), *Learning and Teaching in Higher Education: Advancing International Perspectives*, pp. 91–114. Special refereed preconference edition of Proceedings of HERDSA Conference, Adelaide, Australia.

Manukau Institute of Technology Charter. 2003. Available online at http://mitnet.manukau.ac.nz/ydrive/executive.asp (downloaded on 20 July 2004).

Peeler, E.J.B. 2002. *Changing Culture, Changing Practice: Overseas-born Teachers in Victorian Educational Contexts*. Paper presented at the AARE Conference 2002. Available online at http://www.aare.edu.au/02/pap/pee02345.htm (downloaded on 15 July 2003).

Rose, J. 1996. *States of Fantasy*. Oxford: Clarendon Press.

Sarap, M. 1996. *Identity, Culture and the Postmodern World*. Atlanta, GA: University of Georgia Press.

Scherer, M. (ed.). 1999. *A Better Beginning: Supporting and Mentoring New Teachers*. Alexandria, VA: Association for Supervision and Curriculum Development.

Somers, M.R. and G.D. Gibson. 1994. 'Reclaiming the Epistemological "other": Narrative and the Social Construction of Identity', in C. Calhoun (ed.), *Social Theory and the Politics of Identity*, pp. 37–99. Oxford: Blackwell.

Stoll. L., D. Fink and L. Earl. 2003. *It's about Learning and it's about Time: What's in it for Schools?* London: Routledge Falmer.

Taylor, T. 1991. *The Ethics of Authenticity.* London: Harvard University Press.

UNESCO. 2003. Conference on Intercultural Education, 2003. Available online at http://www.jyu.fi/kyl/unesco2003 (downloaded on 23 January 2004).

Yew, S.L.T.T. and L. Farrell. 2000. *The Root of Confusion: Identity.* Paper presented at ERCCS Conference 2000. Available online at http://www.latrobe.edu.au/lasu/conference/tanyew.doc (downloaded on 28 June 2002).

Yourn, B.R. and A. Kirkness. 2003. *Adapting to a New Culture of Education: Not Just an Issue for Students.* Paper presented at the HERDSA Conference, Christchurch, New Zealand, July 2003.

PART TWO
Exploitation in the Workplace

The global workplace continues to exploit workers in this century and women remain the primary victims. Forms of exploitation are diverse and often covert. Occasionally, women are aware of the exploitation but they succumb because they are between 'the devil and the deep sea'. In other words, they are cursed if they do continue under oppressive circumstances and they are damned if they don't—they have to feed children and take care of the household. Sometimes the form of exploitation is very harsh, but it is so difficult to get justice that women have to resort to desperate measures—some of that may be criminal, unjust or even immoral—to avenge those who are responsible for committing the injustices.

In Part Two of the book, Shelda Debowski and Lynne Hunt raise important questions about women who bully women in the workplace. Why do women take on 'male-like tendencies' and keep or put other women down? Both authors bring out the positive aspects from their experiences and demonstrate that it is possible to come out stronger in spite of the challenges or obstacles faced. Shirley Mthethwa–Sommers focuses on the issue of empowerment of democratic South Africa and raises pertinent questions. Does the visible representation of women in the South African government and market place, for example, mean that women are empowered? Multiple struggles across barriers of poverty, class, family roles and morality form the basis of Kay Sexton's story. As Mandy, the main character in Sexton's story finds out, sometimes the only form of justice lies in enacting an immoral act.

5

Homeless Women and the Choices They Make

Kay Sexton

When Mandy walked through the Mecca Brighton doors, she was made small by the beauty around her. Mandy's mother used to come here, before she died, 'in tragic circumstances'. The circumstances have been tragic only for Mandy. When the end came, mum must have thought she had struck lucky for the first time and only time.

Once, when Mandy was working for Mrs Phillips, she was required to relocate the ironing board and a hamper of Mr Phillips shirts to the living room to watch a documentary about Faberge eggs. Mrs Phillips was full of such insistencies. 'Mandy, listen to the Afternoon Play today while you clean the oven, you'll enjoy it', or 'The Afternoon Concert on Radio 3 is Shostakovich, you'll find it a perfect accompaniment to cleaning the dining room windows.' Then Mrs Phillips would leave to do whatever she did in her 'workroom'. From the chinking of the 'oh so witty' bucket handbag that accompanied her, Mandy assumed she stared at the wall and poured vodka miniatures down her throat.

If you were half an inch tall and you walked into a Faberge egg it would be like entering the Brighton Mecca Bingo Hall. It was round and scarlet and blue, bedecked with gilt lion heads and stern faced women—who could just as easily be poker faced men, gender seemed less important when it came to beauty—who were straight-browed, lovely and unsmiling. They stare resolutely out from the balconies, judging, and finding wanting the scenes below. Mandy assumed Bingo was a bit of a come-down for them. The Mecca had been a theatre originally, although where the stage had been was a puzzle, unless it was in the middle with seats all round.

She had seen a nightclub like that in London, before they moved
down here. She had tried for a job there in the desperate days when she
thought that if she paid off her mum's debts she could also teach her
not to gamble and they could live like normal people. She had got up on
the round stage and danced a sort of striptease down to the red G string
she had bought at Camden Market. The manager had said, 'Very nice
love, but we need something with a bit more oomph. The audience
can see all round you, so you have to give them a bit more—how about
acrobatics? Can you do a handstand? Dancing upside down would be
a pull!' She could not, so it was back to charring and moonlight flits
whenever they could not pay the rent.

Mandy came to the Mecca egg twice a week usually, but only once
through the front doors. That was tonight, Thursday evening, when
she got her tickets free, ate her chicken and chips supper, and went home
again. Most Sundays she visited the Mecca again, but then it was through
the back doors at 8 a.m., and only if Anya called her. Anya got let down
pretty frequently by her cleaning team. Sunday morning charring was
hard work, and the Mecca Sunday clean was a biggie. It started at 7: 30
a.m. and by 7: 40 a.m. her phone would ring, 'Mandy, we're one short
at the Mecca. Can you come down?'

'Cash in hand?'

'If you insist.'

And that was that. Thirty quid for three hours work. Hard work! but
so what? Mandy needed five thousand pounds to escape. Thirty quid
cash was a tiny step towards freedom.

That was why she carried a mobile phone. Alongside her cash-in-hand
chippie shop job, there were a dozen opportunities that arose urgently
enough for her to demand real money as payment. Nobody quarrelled.
She was a good worker—the choice between handing off a few notes to
Mandy and finding somebody else to do dirty work at half an hour's notice
was a no-brainer. Mandy got the money every time. As well as being
a stand-in for Anya's cleaning gang on the Sunday morning Mecca
contract, she was a short notice chalet cleaner, a cash-in-hand racecourse
char and she worked 'black' for two catering companies as a washer-up.
Dirt earned money.

The Mecca was cold in summer, hot in winter. It had the biggest,
cleanest toilets, the brightest gilding, the cheapest chips, the fastest

callers and the finest interior in the South of England. The architecture was accidental but everything else was deliberate. Mecca ran the best bingo halls in Britain. Mandy knew about the toilets; she poured bleach into them on Sunday and let them stand while she used dry ice and *'gum-go'* on the carpets. She had just bought a coffee from Joe at the food counter and while he was chatting and she was stirring two sugars into it, she had slipped another three milk cartons and four sugars into her hand—from her hand to her bag, without a blink. Thank you, Mrs Phillips, for the introduction to capacious handbags, it made life so much easier. That was two cups of coffee at home that she would not have to buy milk and sugar for.

When her mum died, Mandy was expecting debts. Gamblers have debts like Irish have freckles. But 7,000 pounds of debt was a bit of a bracer. It would be a lifetime of work to pay back that kind of money and Mandy wasn't up for it. Worse than the debt was the name attached to most of it. Not Deidre Chambers, but Amanda Chambers. Three store cards, two credit cards and a hire purchase agreement on a car that had never been found as far as Mandy knew. But that was not the worst of it. It was pretty bad that Mandy was now wanted by more debt collectors and bailiffs than she could shake a payslip at. For three months they had kept appearing at the door. She told them her mother was dead, that she had been a known gambler and a high credit risk and they showed her the agreements, signed with her own name—agreeing to pay and pay and pay. It even looked like her signature.

Worse than the debts and the signature, was wondering whether mum knew what she was doing? Did she know she was going to die and plan this last mad fling at Mandy's expense? Or did she believe she would talk her way out of it when the duns turned up with menaces and court judgements? Did she carry on, unknowing, until the moment when the massive stroke stopped her forever, or did she feel the slow creep of death and decide to damn Mandy to a life of poverty and fear by spending until she dropped?

Three months after Deidre died, Mandy ran. She ran away from the flat in Hastings where they had lived, from being 'educated' whilst charring for Mrs Phillips, and from the debts. She gave no notice, she just flitted.

Now she rented a room for cash: no laundry, no cooking (toaster and kettle grudgingly permitted), no visitors and communal bathroom with a 50 pence meter for the bath. She worked for cash. No union, no health and safety, no tips, no time off, no bonus. No questions asked. She had saved 2,000 pounds, not just by working, but by selling everything they had owned. She had flogged all the jewellery, the good clothes, the CDs, everything. The TV, mum's sewing machine and three piece suite had been left behind when she ran.

Five thousand would buy her a new passport and National Insurance number. Mandy Chambers had already disappeared, and one day a new person would appear, with a clean credit record. A person who could work, rent property and pay taxes without expecting a stream of hard-faced men to knock at the door and demand money. And until then…

Take today for example. All day in the fish shop, frying food and clearing tables. She finished work at seven. Then straight to bingo, buying her dinner there although she was so sick of fried food she could hardly force it down. She had to eat, to stay fit. When the big game started, she had already drifted to the door of the toilets, and for the next 10 minutes she could bet she would have them to herself. They were the least used ones, far from the main bingo area. They were never as messy as the ones right alongside the chip stall, or those nearest the counter where they sold books of bingo tickets. In 10 minutes, working with precision, she could wash and half-dry six pairs of knickers, one bra and six pairs of knee-highs. The Mecca had the biggest basins, hottest water, and the most blasting hand-dryers in the south of England. Half-dry was enough—she could finish them on the radiator in her room overnight without her landlady noticing. That meant one load of laundry less to pay for.

Then it was a good strip-wash with a hot flannel and a Tupperware bowl of water carried to a cubicle and set on the closed toilet seat. She had locked the cubicle door in case some incontinent oldie could not hold out till the big game is over. Wring out the flannel, put it in a plastic bag, dry the Tupperware with loo roll, put the barely damp washing inside and pop the lid on. Fifteen minutes in total and she had saved valuable pennies. In any case, she knew the Mecca toilets were clean—she cleaned them often enough—but the shared bathroom at the bed-sit was disgusting. She would rather wash in the toilet cubicle here than use the bath there.

Clean undies for a week and a good wash, plus dinner and free bingo tickets—total cost, two pounds ten including two cups of tea. The electricity meter in her room would cost 50 pence for the same amount of time, and she had won 16 pounds in five weeks on the free tickets. When she was here she felt closer to mum, and that was important. There were women here who chatted to her because they remembered Deidre, and that stopped her feeling as though she had already vanished.

When she stepped out of the toilet cubicle she walked into the arms of Pat Monaghan, literally. His big soft arms were spread across the doorway and his big soft Hush Puppy shoes had carried him right up to her in silence. She shrieked. She didn't mean to, because she saw it was Pat straight away, but the sound was out before her brain could stop it. He liked the shriek. It made him smile. Pat's big soft smile was not nice. Assistant Manager Monaghan was known for that smile—like finding a razor blade in suet.

'Well, well,' he said like a Hammer Horror villain. 'What have we here then?' Mandy recognised that something had moved awry in the world and that Pat was going to do something bad. She looked round the shiny toilet block, trying to encompass the nastiness that she could feel building up in him. How could anything unpleasant happen here, in the lovely Mecca?

His big hand pawed through her bag, pausing at the Tupperware, fingering the sugar sachets, then rubbing the chilly flannel suggestively between blunt fingertips. 'What can I say, Mandy? I don't want to have to ban you, but this isn't exactly the proper way to use the facilities, is it?' Mandy recognised that the questions were a kind of bullying, but she was too upset to be defiant. She hung her head like a shamed child. Propriety, like cleanliness, was vital. Poverty was acceptable if you were honest, honesty could be negotiated if you were rich, but poverty and dishonesty together were insupportable. That was Mandy's view, her bottom line, her creed. That is what had pulled her along in mum's wake all these years. That, and the fact that Deidre created fun and happiness. And she had adored Mandy.

'Mandy love', that is what mum called her. Never Amanda—even though it was her birth certificate name. Never just Mandy either; always Mandy love, or Mandy pet, Mandy sweetie, Mandy baby...a name full of love. Mum could make a party out of a bus queue. She never raised her voice or her hand. There was just one problem—she could not deal with money. It flew from her like confetti and melted like candyfloss. Whether she spent it or gambled it did not matter, because it was just gone. It had always been that way. And from as early as she could remember, Mandy had been the one to find ways to hang onto it.

'Don't ban me Pat,' she said, trying to look appealing, 'You know I come here because of mum, she loved it here.' 'We loved her too Mandy, she was a star player, your mum,' Pat's voice was empty, the words routine. He was thinking about something else, turning it over in his mind. 'Tell you what, stay here a sec. I've got an idea that could make both of us happy.' And he was gone, out of the toilet, with his big key chain jingling merrily in his hand.

She thought about running, for a second, but she knew if she did Pat would ban her. He was a mean bastard. He might appear big and jolly but it was all show. Looking at him from the side, she saw all the bulk was in the front, like an Easter egg. He was a hollow shell of a happy man and the mean side was the back—flat and stealthily muscled. Look at how he had crept up on her.

He had returned already. In his hand was the little yellow sign they put up when there were spillages to clear away or a toilet got blocked. He turned nimbly, showing her his back again, and put the sign outside the door to the toilets, which he locked. He came across the shiny floor towards her like the front half of Father Christmas, all smiles. 'Well then, Mandy, you do something for me and I'll forget about the pilfering and the misuse of Mecca facilities. I won't ban you forever from your mum's favourite place. How's that?' As he spoke, he was unzipping the big soft trousers that draped around his lower body and pulling from them a small hard penis.

It was not as bad as she thought it might be. He was a very clean man—she had to give him that. His clothes smelled of fabric conditioner and talcum powder and even with her nose buried in his paunch all she could smell was the sweet scent of a freshly washed body. But he was very slow. He was watching in the mirror as she knelt in front of him, trying to preserve her tights, a ladder now would be the final straw. His hands roamed and clutched at his own flabby torso, as though he'd lost something in his acres and could find it only by touch. Eventually, long after her lips went numb and her neck began to ache from holding herself still as he blundered back and forth inside her mouth, he made a whinnying sound, and came.

'Next week then, same time, same place, Mandy love,' he smirked, as he twitched his organ back inside the generous underpants and whisked to the door on his light, sly feet.

It was not the sex that upset her as much as the way he said 'Mandy love', as though he had a right to call her pet names. Her own cowardice made her feel sick. She washed out her mouth with the foamy soap from the dispenser, scrubbing at her gums and teeth with the flannel in a frenzy of disgust. As she walked out of the toilets onto the bright carpet of the bingo hall she heard mum sigh, 'Mandy pet, you should have walloped him', and she knew mum was right. But Mandy could not do the things Deidre could.

Anya did not call on Sunday, so Mandy did not char at the Mecca that weekend. On Thursday night Mandy won 10 pounds with her free book of tickets, and sucked Pat off during the big game. This time she brought her toothbrush and when he was done, she brushed her teeth with vindictive force. But first, she watched to see where he put the yellow sign. This time, mum said, 'Well ...?' and Mandy looked at her own blotched face in the mirror and said, 'Give me time mum, give me time.'

Anya called and Mandy spent most of Sunday morning hanging over the Mecca balcony with a big feather duster, scooting dust from the gilded statues. She cleaned the toilets too, and peeked into the staff room, a poky little hole with a kettle so disgustingly furred up that she could not see how they got enough water in it to make a drink. Anya had keys to the main doors and she knew the alarm code too. A security officer was supposed to be on hand to let the cleaners in and out, but on Sunday the Mecca did not open for business until noon, and as the security and cleaning contracts were run from the same company, Anya counted as both cleaning supervisor and security officer. She did not gamble. She had never been in the Mecca in its open hours. Pat had never been in the Mecca outside them. Mandy thought she might be the only person who knew the Mecca in both its guises: full and noisy with dozens of avid bingo players, empty and noisy with vacuum cleaners and floor polishers. Mandy knew the alarm code too, they all did, they punched it every time they carried out a ticket-stuffed rubbish bag.

Thursday night and Pat was ready when they announced the big game, as soon as the lights started to dim until the tables were spot-lit and the voice of the National Caller began to echo through the public address system, he was there, with his little yellow 'closed for cleaning' sign, his voluminous clean underwear and his tiny hard cock. He locked the door and put his hands on her shoulders, pushing her down to her knees so that she could open her mouth for him to enter. This time he came quicker; he thought she was getting to like it, so he patted her on the bottom as she moved past him to spit into the basin afterwards. But he had misunderstood the situation. The urgency of her movements and the action of her mouth was not for his benefit. It was for mum's. What she was doing was saying, 'Not long now, mum, not long now' under her breath.

On Sunday she was at the Mecca again, and this time she spent more time in the staff room, blocking open the little window with a skinny slip of cardboard. The cleaning crew finished at 10.30 a.m. and Anya handed over Mandy's cash. Then, while the others headed for home or the pub, Mandy sauntered round the back of the Mecca and eased the cardboard gently to and fro until the window swung inwards slightly. She propped it open with a tiny pen from the betting shop while she pulled on her cleaning gloves.

Wriggling through the window was a total bastard. Twice she thought she would not make it and would wedge there until the Mecca staff found her. Desperation pushed her on until suddenly her hips went through and she smashed head-first into the old easy chair under the window, knocking over the kettle and the card table it sat on. She had emptied the kettle earlier, expecting that she might snag the cable on the way in or out, and while she rubbed ferociously at her forehead to ease the stinging that made her eyes water, she felt smug at her foresight.

The next steps were easy. After whacking the code into the alarm keypad, she found the yellow 'closed for cleaning' sign tucked behind the flap door to the ticket sales section. She rifled the jacket Pat left hanging over a chair in the staff room and found a red chisel-tip marker pen, the kind he used to double-check winning tickets. She pulled the little betting shop pen from the window and a book of last week's bingo tickets from her bag. The pen was useless, thin and scratchy, the ink gave way at several points so she was etching the paper rather than writing on it. That was fine—she considered that part of the plan.

While Pat was engrossed in her mouth on Thursday, she had been sliding her hands into his pockets. She had snagged a matchbook with her nails and prised it out gently while he was doing his impression of a distressed horse. The matches, the pen and the note she had written were her master plan. The chisel end marker just added a bit of style. She tore the first sheet, the one she had written on, from the tickets and placed the rest of the book in Pat's jacket pocket, well tucked down.

She lit the fire with the ticket and some shiny paper rescued from the bin under the ticket sales counter. She had had to pretend to empty that bin and then—when Anya was not looking—she had filled it up again with corrugated cardboard, the kind that doesn't burn well, but that was deliberate too. The fire-retardant carpet didn't even smoulder and the yellow sign kept most of the smoke down, developing a rich black layer of soot on one side where it rested above the burning paper, the bubbling marker pen and the matchbook.

She had less trouble getting back out through the window. She had had to move the chair a foot or so to allow her to get back up to the right height, but she did not think anyone would notice.

As soon as she thought the staff room was suitably on fire she trotted down the street as fast as she could without looking suspicious. Then she made a quick call to the fire brigade from the nearest call box and carried on down the hill to work. Within half an hour she would smell of fish and chips so strongly that nobody would notice a bit of bonfire odour too.

On Thursday she walked through the doors of the Mecca, shrinking once more under the weight of its elegance. Pat was not on duty. 'Where's Pat then?' she asked Joe at the tea counter.

'Where have you been? Did you not know? Pat's been arrested for arson! He tried to set fire to the place over the weekend apparently. It seems…' but then they announced the big game and Mandy had to wait until the lights dimmed and the National Caller was intoning the lucky numbers before she could get Joe to continue his story in hushed tones.

'Well…there was a note, written to Pat by one of the customers, you know? It said that she'd had enough, she didn't care if he did tell the management that she'd stolen a book of tickets or two over the years, she wasn't going to let him get away with the kind of sexual abuse he was doing to her.' Mandy looked sceptical and Joe continued, 'No really, he'd set fire to the note, do you see, but she'd written it on the back of a book of tickets and he'd just torn the front one off and put the rest in his jacket. They could make out what she'd written from the way the pen had pressed through—it's very thin paper you know.'

'And there was one of his pens in the fire, all burnt, as if he'd dropped it in there by mistake. It looks like he'd tried to burn the whole place down but one of those cleaning signs fell down and put the fire out. Amazing really, it couldn't have gone worse for him.'

Mandy stirred her tea and listened to the National Caller for a few seconds before asking, 'So how did he get found out then?'

'Now that is a mystery. Somebody called the fire brigade, saying they could smell smoke in the alley outside. And guess what? He'd tried to start the fire with an old catalogue! You would have thought he was smart enough to realise that shiny paper just smokes and never really burns. Still, he was always a strange one…,' and Joe rambled on, telling tales of the many strange people the Mecca had incubated over the years.

Mandy nodded to the golden people holding up the balconies. She was certain they would understand. After all, she was their servant too.

6

Pencilled in at the Margins: Dealing with Bullies at Work

Shelda Debowski

PENCILLED AT THE MARGINS: A CRITICAL REFLECTION ON BULLYING AND ORGANISATIONAL CULTURE

Higher education needs more women in leadership roles. As various institutional barriers diminish it is pleasing to see more women progressing to senior positions, although they may generate new hurdles to be overcome. Unfortunately, some of the challenges may relate to the resentment from other women who have also achieved higher status and recognition. The 'sisterhood' is not necessarily a positive or supportive phenomenon.

It is important for senior women to share their stories and to reflect on their experiences to enable learning by others (Cotterill and Letherby 2005). Unfortunately, there is a paucity of stories about hard times and the strategies that assisted in navigating through those difficult stages of one's career. This critical reflexive account explores two major issues: the impact of bullying on an individual's career and personal well-being, and on the wider organisational culture.

A BRIEF SYNOPSIS

After 23 years of working in the field of higher education as an academic, I accepted a position as a senior leader in a research–intensive university. For the first time in my career I was responsible for a group of people, budgets and strategic support for the university. I was attracted to the position for a number of reasons. First and foremost, it offered the opportunity to apply my leadership and organisational knowledge and skills into a university setting. I was attracted to the fact that the role incorporated an academic and leadership/management emphasis. With five qualifications in education, I was also able to provide the leadership and guidance in teaching and learning which the role encompassed. A passionate idealist, I was keen to apply best practices in the university and help to take the institution forward.

In my first year of appointment, I was provided with enormous support. I reported to the Deputy Vice Chancellor who was very generous in his guidance and advice. He accepted a number of major innovative proposals and sponsored them positively. They became ongoing initiatives in the University. In the following year, the lines of authority evolved and I moved to a new reporting relationship.

There began the worst two years of my career. I experienced significant bullying over most of that period. My contribution regressed from being a creative, active participant to a marginalised bit player who was regularly denigrated in public settings. My credibility was greatly undermined by my detractor, who was very senior and very powerful. I was pushed to the edges of many activities, and excluded from working groups, discussions and projects in which I had previously taken part. My unit was restructured and I lost over half of my team following a very difficult and unpleasant review. I was firmly pencilled at the margins. I no longer had direct access to knowledge and was increasingly invisible. My peers advised me to keep a low profile and avoid being noticed. This was a most unnatural strategy for me to follow and caused high emotional dissonance. After two years, I was carefully reviewing my options and future, reluctantly recognising that I would need to move, to gain any further opportunities or work satisfaction. I knew I would remain a target until one of us moved on. Fortunately, the bully resigned before I did. I had survived… but at a great cost.

BULLYING IN THE WORKPLACE

McMahon describes bullying as 'an abuse of power… It may involve verbal intimidation, the undermining of the victim's professional work and the bully taking credit for other people's work.' (McMahon 2000: 384.) Simpson and Cohen (2004) describe a number of bullying tendencies, including that it is normally located in those with organisational power and primarily work-oriented. In most cases, the bullying targets an individual's personal characteristics and is psychologically focused rather than physical abuse. They note that many instances of bullying are linked to restructuring in the workplace. They note that 'the occurrence of such behaviour [is] related to power relationships and conflict, uncertainty and change as well as organizational norms and culture.' Many workplace bullies demonstrate characteristics that are also reflected in organisational psychopaths. These include manipulation of people, unethical practice, intolerance, erratic behaviour, failure to take responsibility for actions, a desire to create conflict and dissension and a strong desire for increased power and status (Clark 2005). In many cases, these people are very charming to those who can further their goals. It is only those they wish to marginalise become targets of aggressive behaviour. The variant faces of the bully makes identification of poor behaviour even more challenging. Those who support the bully are unlikely to experience the unpleasant behaviours that are levelled at the target. This creates high cognitive dissonance if a victim does manage to register his or her concerns.

Studies of bullying suggest that between 25 and 50 per cent of workers experience bullying sometime in their career (McCarthy et al. 2001). And yet, in literature there is only limited advice on how to cope with continued harassment of this nature and very limited consideration of how the bullying of one individual can impact on many others.

The Impact of Bullying

For the most part, writers explore the impact on the individual. Certainly, my personal experience correlates with typical documented responses, namely:

- Initial assumption of personal guilt for the negative experiences which were occurring.
- Inability to sleep.

- High anxiety and emotional stress.
- Increased blood pressure.
- Loss of self-confidence.
- An inability to think beyond the bullying and its impact.
- Diminished trust in those around me (particularly as my activities were being documented and reported by an adversarial colleague).
- Tendency to burst into tears at very inconvenient moments.

However, the impact of bullying can affect many other individuals—particularly if they are working closely with the target. In our situation, 20 people were directly affected by the changing context. Some of our members experienced physical and emotional deterioration as a consequence. Most of those who were shifted to a new organisational setting have since left the unit. And those remaining in my unit had to work very hard to maintain morale as they experienced the destabilising effects of a change that they had not supported or felt was justified.

The visibility of the bullying also made concealment difficult. In the early period of the harassment many colleagues intimated that I must have antagonised the bully in some way. This initially accorded with my nightly recriminations. As time progressed it became more evident to many that this was a concerted campaign. Others started to experience some of the same difficulties, and this helped greatly—although it was not a desirable outcome. However, I remained the most singled out target throughout and had to manage as I was pushed aside completely.

COPING AT THE MARGINS

When one is bullied the goal is to both survive and maintain one's own self-esteem. These are major achievements if they are accomplished. However, they do not come easily. It is very difficult to keep these goals in mind when self-doubt and a constant barrage of negative messages are delivered by the bully and whoever else is enlisted. Over time a range of strategies were employed.

Name It as It is

My first response to the evidence of bullying was disbelief. I have always managed to build good relationships with people—particularly senior people, and this was a very new experience. Initially I found it hard to name and label the responses and behaviours that were evident. I withdrew from the workplace dynamics as I tried to identify why my work setting was imploding. (Lewis 2005 notes that this is a very common response and can further isolate the bully's target.) I internalised the blame and assumed I was at fault. Perhaps it was some form of miscommunication? I lay awake at night worrying about what errors I might have committed to generate the ill-will I could perceive. I spent considerable emotion trying to amend, correct and adapt. All to no avail. It was only when I could finally recognise and name the aberrant patterns as bullying that I could start to limit my own perceptions of culpability: this was not my fault; I could not have prevented it. It was going to happen because this person wanted it to. And I also accepted that it was not going to change regardless of what I did or did not do. The position was immutable. This made acceptance and coping much easier.

Know Your Enemies

It is not possible to combat bullying if you do not understand the person/s involved. Over time it became evident that three people were the prime instigators of my difficulties. Clark notes that sociopaths tend to bring in reinforcements, and this was certainly my experience. I monitored and then started to predict the likely issues that would act as conflict triggers. For example, whenever I was highly profiled, I anticipated flak in some form or other. Being aware of the factors that most rile those who hate you, makes it easier to be forewarned and forearmed. It was clear that I, and others with high level expertise, were progressively marginalised. It also became apparent that a desire for resources and additional power were elements of the agenda. The recognition of these motives greatly assisted in working through the issues and externalising the causes. Reading on the causes and effects of bullying was also very helpful as it assisted in affirming that this is a very common phenomenon in workplaces.

Know Yourself

A time of great pressure forces an individual to become more reflective about what is important in life and what qualities one possesses. I had never really taken stock of who I was and what I contributed to others. These events necessitated a more active focus on self-management and self-review. Richards and Freeman (2002) describe a number of reasons a person may be targeted for bullying. They may, for example, be more competent, popular, respected, conscientious and dependable or too independent for the bully. It can be hard to pinpoint what factor/s became triggers. But it is certainly most important to reaffirm the personal qualities that should be retained as valued and desirable attributes—regardless of the negativity that is emanating from other sources.

I could see quite early on that anything I held to be important to me would be challenged by the bullies. Fortunately, I decided to take advantage of an opportunity to undertake a 360 degree appraisal. When my skills as a manager were called into question, I was able to present a very detailed and very supportive review of my leadership skills which totally refuted that claim. I became more focused on seeking opportunities for external validation.

Clark (2005) notes the importance of documenting everything and correcting untrue rumours as rapidly as possible. I found it necessary to keep attuned to what was being said and spent considerable time trying to resolve unfair statements about my performance and actions. My dossier was maintained as evidence of abuse if I finally decided I needed it. I also kept a journal where I poured my angst each night. The recording of my feelings removed them from my soul and provided a cathartic daily cleansing. Poetry became another avenue of release for me. It had been nearly forty years since I had last penned a poem! It proved an important emotional distillation.

I also began to develop a leadership portfolio to document what we had achieved as an organisational unit. This turned out to be most important, as it was used for a number of purposes to show that despite our various travails we had maintained our exemplary performance. When I was accused of poor management, I was able to demonstrate this was not the case. Notably, the accusation that I was a poor leader was never provided in writing to enable my refutation of the charge. Following the restructure, I was subject to an investigation of every item of expenditure made while I had been the Director. While this appeared quite malignant in its intent, it again served to demonstrate my good management, not otherwise.

It is also important to recognise that sometimes the accusations are right. I was, for example, informed that I needed to learn how to write. I found this very hurtful—especially, as I was informed by email while overseas and there was no constructive feedback. I subsequently realised that my academic writing skills were not being called into question; it was my report writing skills. I sought guidance on writing executive reports and also identified several useful models that I could emulate.

I can honestly say that I have a much stronger sense of self as a result of these two years. However, it has had some interesting impacts on who I am and how I respond to situations. I am much more assertive and frank. I aim to be authentic in my leadership and in my response to the world. Interestingly, it has enriched my life hugely and I have gained a stronger sense of self-worth as a consequence.

Recognise the Issues

Once I realised I was being harassed I grew more proficient at reading the political landscape. For example, it was clear that we were at great risk in terms of our credibility and access to sponsorship. When the official sponsor is unsympathetic to the cases one puts forward, the situation becomes very dire indeed. I talked to my staff about the situation and we ensured that everything we did was absolutely professional and exemplary. We worked closely as a team to negotiate our new organisational context.

I sought new sponsors to support our initiatives. They became new channels for support, although it was much tougher to gain resources for these initiatives as the new sponsors were often less influential.

Recognising that the main issue was an intense dislike of me as an individual, I worked through people rather than trying to manage the situation head on. One of my staff became the negotiator and presented our ideas. I would feed ideas to other colleagues and they would then present those concepts for successful consideration. We all knew that if my name was on it, it was not a strong proposition for support. This required quite a bit of fortitude. I am by nature a high achiever who seeks recognition! To be forced to send my ideas on their way through other voices was very hard, but a most essential strategy if I was to keep supporting the institution.

As a manager it was also important to talk about and recognise the issues that were surfacing. My career was not the only one to be affected, 20 people were ultimately changed by the actions that were taken. While my staff relied on my management of the dynamics, there was also a need to keep everyone supported and positive as the various issues arose. We spoke honestly and openly of our concerns and I maintained very open communication channels about changes to our organisational context. On the other hand, my own emotional responses had to be contained as much as I could. I found this hard as I am a gregarious person.

Clark (2005) recommends team building programmes to reduce the vulnerability of the target. While we had not consciously sought to do this, our community retained its solidity through most of the journey. It was only following the decision to split the unit that fragmentation began to occur. Those with new reporting lines realised they could no longer be protected and began to seek new positions. As their sponsor and previous manager it was very difficult to see their distress and have no capacity to provide tangible support.

Seek Help

Namie and Namie (2000) suggest that most targets will be unsupported through their workplaces. Their support networks will generally be drawn from external sources. More senior bullies, on the other hand, will generally be supported by human resource services, senior management and the target's peers. These principles were reflected in my experience. My supervisor initially instructed that I speak with no one about the situation. From an institutional perspective, this contained the damage. From a personal perspective it was very poor advice as I felt I had no support or assistance to guide or sustain me. He too must have felt anxious as his unit was also vulnerable. My colleagues were similarly dismissive of my concerns and anxieties, exhibiting either 'denial' of the problem or 'personalising the problem' as being caused by my own behaviours (Lewis 2005). Over time I realised that my silence indicated complicit acceptance and that I could not continue to simply accommodate the bullying. I needed help to cope and to explore my anxiety, fear and frustration.

Lyn, my coach, entered my life at the lowest ebb just as a review of my alleged (mis)management was announced. She was a breath of fresh air. 'Well of course you're a threat', she said airily. 'Just look at you, my dear. You look good, you speak well, you know the territory. How could she not regard you as a threat?' That simple affirmation annealed some of the hurt and pain that had been festering. Lyn met with me regularly to review the newest events, discuss strategy and to bolster my sense of self-worth. Through her support, I managed to navigate through the whole period without one day's sick leave. Lyn counselled me to be strong and to maintain my *sangfroid*. This I did. It was hard at times. I would go into meetings quaking inside, but with an outwardly calm demeanour. I would smile, joke, look confident and at ease, despite the fact that I had not slept the night before. A goal would be to shake the hands in greeting of each of my detractors—something they were most reluctant to do. Each opportunity to look in control was another important campaign to win and to maintain my professionalism and credibility.

I did try other sources of help too. I visited employee assistance programme specialists, but they just threw their hands up in horror and said it was an unacceptable organisational practice. Well, I already knew that! I visited a psychiatrist and was placed on anti-anxiety/sleeping medication for a while. I also consulted a lawyer several times on matters of work-related security and he advised me on my letters of response. Two of the executive became mentors, which I valued greatly. They provided covert protection through their sponsorship. I also investigated the possibility of mediation, but realised that this would only work if both parties were keen to resolve the issue. In this case, where the prize was power and resources, there was little chance of a successful resolution (Hare 1993).

Perhaps, my biggest source of support were my loved ones. I remember going to a family gathering one Sunday and walking in, and then bursting into sobs which continued for hours. My family passed me around like a parcel, with someone or other holding me for that entire time.

Of most support was my nuclear family, listening to my trials and tribulations and remaining by my side each step of the way. My experience has shaped my children's perceptions of how they wish to work. My daughter, an undergraduate law student, is now interested in workplace relations as she has a strong desire to protect others from the same experience. My son now has a passionate desire to prevent people being bullied or unfairly treated and has assisted his school in addressing cultural issues in that setting.

Find New Avenues for Fulfilment

As I was placed more firmly in the margins of the university, I realised that to survive, I would need to seek new and different outlets where I could operate free of the restrictions and animosity that clouded my internal relations. I was aware that it would not be possible to sustain working in a toxic setting of this nature for many years, and so, I was also aiming to build my profile to open some new career opportunities.

I nominated and became president of the Higher Education Research and Development Society of Australasia (HERDSA). The society enabled me to continue supporting higher education's enhancement and the profiling of the university. HERDSA has been one of the most important avenues for my ongoing growth and healing. It has been a strong professional community that has grown, expanded and offered many exciting avenues to build enduring and respectful associations.

It was important to keep occupied and to develop new paths towards my unknown future. My book on knowledge management was written and published over those two years. I also studied for my Company Director certificate to increase my knowledge of corporate affairs. I continued to set new goals that would assist my career, albeit in a new direction to that I had intended. During that time I worked with colleagues in other universities to build a collaborative project, and we made some significant contributions to higher education development as a consequence. Again, this also provided the intellectual engagement not possible through my work context.

My diminished leadership role within the university was counterbalanced by high level leadership roles and consultancies across the nation. However, I still sought to contribute in a more substantial way within my own institution. I applied, for example, for a Dean's position. I saw it as an opportunity to again affirm my qualities and their relevance to the institution. While interviewed but not appointed, this proved still a very important mechanism to promote my capabilities and re-engage with the senior university members. Several new projects have come my way as a consequence.

SOME OBSERVATIONS

Till date there has been little research on how senior women support other senior women as they move towards higher roles. There is much anecdotal evidence that many female appointees are threatened by other women. Those who should be sponsoring others may, in fact, do everything possible to destroy others. On the other hand, there will be many who also provide support, mentorship and emotional sustenance to other colleagues. The need to build a supportive network is an important strategy for those moving towards more senior roles. If the networks and mentors are established early, they can act as a protective barrier between potential bullies and the individual.

It should also be recognised that despite the best policies and systems in the world, an institution is vulnerable if the bully is very senior. Grievance processes only operate effectively if they cover all staff within the institution. The introduction of an ombudsman is a possible option that could protect the integrity of the system. However, Simpson and Cohen (2004) note that many bullies can subvert the organisational processes for their own ends, particularly with respect to performance reviews and similar processes. While I attempted to express concern and raise various issues along the way, my powerlessness greatly reduced my voice. And, of course, the bully was able to counteract most of my efforts by being so well placed in terms of influence and power. An associated issue relates to the goals the organisation sets. If the desired outcome is to effect organisational change, no matter what the cost, the setting becomes a natural breeding ground for bullies. If the focus is on cultural enhancement, people will become more confident that speaking up about poor behaviour will be supported.

Institutions need to recognise the potential damage to organisational reputation, productivity and talent management from bullying (Clark 2005; Field 2006). The potential costs of litigation must also be recognised: in some cases, the target may decide legal action is the only course of action to redress the wrong done to them. Clearly this is highly undesirable for all parties and action needs to be taken long before the difficulties reach this point. Clark (2005) recommends that dysfunctional bullies should be recognised early to minimise the impact on those around them. Organisations need to become more receptive to the cues of victims and more careful about their recruitment and selection processes. In many cases, there is a history of abuse which can be traced to previous work settings.

Another issue also arises when aggressive behaviour is permitted to thrive. Bullies breed new bullies, who can receive significant sponsorship from their senior colleague as they gain promotion and high profile. The ascendance and rewarding of poor behaviour sends a significant message to the wider community which needs to be counteracted strongly. The impact of bullying extends beyond the individual. It has been estimated, for example, that 20 per cent of those who witness bullying will leave a workplace, along with 25 per cent of the bullied targets (Field 2006).

The development of a cohesive corporate culture is a very challenging task in higher education. Many universities comprise a number of fiefdoms which are led by unique individuals. Kouzes and Posner (1999) note the importance of building communities with heart. In particular they indicate the need for leaders to pay attention to the cues that surround them. This is critical in heeding the soft pleas for assistance that may percolate through the institution. It takes courage to stand up and say one is being bullied. It is not done lightly and needs to be recognised as a desperate plea for leadership and response. Namie and

Namie (2000) indicate that most targets feel little was done to prevent or address the bad behaviour. While this may not be the reality, the lack of follow through and feedback reduces the perception of a responsive organisation. Targets need to know that someone cares. In particular, when they open up to share their distress, colleagues need to be guided in how to respond (Lewis 2005).

CONCLUSION

At the end of the process I breathed a heartfelt sigh. I had survived—albeit, a very different person. I view people differently and my political radar is far more acute. These days I feel confident and at ease in times of stress—after all, I have managed to navigate around some very tricky shoals. I am still re-building my reputation and recognise that this could take considerable time. And my career is moving into a very different focus, given loss of the more influential half of my portfolio. However, in a twisted way, I am very pleased that I had the experience of being so marginalised. It has exposed strengths I did not know I possessed, and encouraged me to move into new frontiers and creative spaces. I feel enriched, empowered and confident that I can meet the challenges life throws. I am far more resilient.

And as I look back at that margin, I can see that the blank space has been filled with many notes of import. The margin, after all, became a small and fertile space for growth and knowledge. And now it's time to move back onto the page.

Make way. I am ready.

REFERENCES

Cotterill, P. and G. Letherby. 2005. 'Women in Higher Education: Issues and Challenges', *Women's Studies International Forum*, 28(2–3): 109–113.

Clark, J. 2005. *Working with Monsters: How to Identify and Protect Yourself from the Workplace Psychopath*. Sydney: Random House.

Field, E.M. 2006. 'Workplace Bullying'. Available online at http://www.bullying.com.
au/workbullying.html (downloaded on 10 August 2006.)

Hare, R.D. 1993. *Without Conscience: The Disturbing World of the Psychopaths among
Us.* New York: Pocket Books.

Kouzes, J.M. and B.Z. Posner. 1999. *Encouraging the Heart: a Leader's Guide to Rewarding
and Recognizing Others.* San Francisco: Jossey-Bass.

Lewis, S.E. 2005. 'Women's Experience of Workplace Bullying: Changes in Social
Relationships', *Journal of Community and Applied Social Psychology*, 15(1): 29.

McCarthy, P., J. Rylance, R. Bennett and H. Zimmerman. 2001. *Bullying: From Backyard
to Boardroom.* 2nd edition. Sydney: Federation Press.

McMahon, L. 2000. 'Bullying and Harassment in the Workplace', *International Journal of
Contemporary Hospitality Management*, 12(60): 32–51.

Namie, G. and R. Namie. 2000. *The Bully at Work.* Naperville, Illinois: Sourcebooks.

Richards, H. and S. Freeman. 2002. *Bullying in the Workplace: An Occupational Hazard.*
Pymble: HarperCollins Publishers.

Simpson, R. and C. Cohen. 2004. 'Dangerous Work: The Gendered Nature of Bullying in
the Context of Higher Education', *Gender, Work and Organization*, 11(2): 163–86.

7

Gender Equity in a Post-Apartheid South Africa

Shirley Mthethwa-Sommers

INTRODUCTION

Post-Apartheid South Africa has made remarkable achievements in terms of gender representation in the government sector and considerable advancement in the private sector. More than 40 per cent women are members of the national parliament, which is one the highest women representation in government worldwide. According to the Nedbank Index (2006), women in the private sector constitute almost 20 per cent of executive managers and 6.2 per cent of chief executive officers and board members. Such an achievement within 12 years of democracy must be undoubtedly applauded; however, it is also important to focus the lens on how South Africa could go beyond representation to women empowerment in its quest for gender equity.

Women empowerment is not merely about having women in jobs that were historically occupied by men; or having female bodies without a female empowerment agenda. It is the provision of space, policies, structures, resources and means for a woman to make decisions that are suitable for her development and general well-being. If one is then to take the latter as the definition for women empowerment, one would then argue that the grand achievements that have been made in South Africa during the last 12 years are not ostentatious at all as the majority of women still do not have space, structures, resources and means to make decisions that are suitable for them.

This chapter, through feminist theoretical lenses, examines the working lives of 10 young African women who are at entry-level positions and have been working for a total of three years or less each.

Some of these young women are in nebulous social class as they cannot be classified as belonging to a specific socio-economic class. Their educational qualifications distinguish them from the definition of confinement of lower socio-economic class and yet they do not earn enough money or possess capital to be classified within the confinement of middle or higher socio-economic class definition. Some are in positions that do not promise upward mobility, which in turn stagnate their socio-economic level. All participants come from lower socio-economic class backgrounds; they all had an initial upbringing in the rural areas and came to the urban areas in search of better educational and work opportunities.

PARTICIPANTS

This study comprised of 10 young African women between the ages of 22 and 30. In-depth interviews were used as research method in order to get a deeper understanding of workplace issues or concerns for young entry-level African women in a politically democratic South Africa. Two of the young women have a university degree and hold occupations that can be termed professional (Casale 2004) as they involve skills and some intellectual engagement.

Six of these women completed high school and received some form of post-high school training. They hold jobs that can be termed semi-professional, because their work involves neither physical labour nor intense intellectual engagement. Two women are involved in non-professional work. They both work as physical labourers within an office environment.

All participants, with the exception of one, are single parents and none of them is in a committed relationship with the paternal parent. This is typical of young urban and rural African women's lives today. The percentage of young women rearing children outside any formal or informal partnership is estimated to be considerably higher than any other racial groups in the country (LoveLife 2006).

These participants were selected because their backgrounds are typical of young African women. Furthermore, most studies focus on professional women who have made it in the workplace, overlooking the majority of the women (other than domestic workers) who remain at the lower levels of the workplace ladder.

THEORETICAL BACKGROUND

In examining the women's workplace experiences, the author used the lens of feminist theory, in general and womanist feminist theory, in particular. What is feminist theory? Feminist theory is an umbrella of feminist theories. It is mainly concerned with experiences of women vis á vis power structures as it 'recognizes the genderedness of all social relations and consequently of all societal institutions and structures' (Shrewsbury 1987: 7). In other words, feminist theory is about disruption of patriarchy and promulgation of alternative configurations of gender relations. Feminist theories range from *inter alia*, liberal, radical, post-structuralist, socialist to womanism.

Liberal feminism is attentive to three main areas: (*a*) individual rights; (*b*) eradication of traditional and stereotypical beliefs about what constitutes femininity and corresponding masculinity; (*c*) attainment of equal opportunities for both men and women. The main criticism for liberal feminist theory is that it does not seek to disturb or transform institutions but seeks to acknowledge women's right to make choices on how they interact with those institutions (Weedon 1987).

While liberal feminist theory calls for eradication of stereotypes which serve as a hindrance for women's advancement in society and in the workplace, radical feminist theorists posit that women's liberation can be achieved in two fundamental ways, namely, reclaiming women's bodies and lives from the perennial control of men, and separatism of women from men in order to free them from the strong grip of patriarchy. Hawthorne (1991) postulates that separatism advocated by radical feminism is a 'politically motivated strategy for empowering women and undermining patriarchy' (Hawthorne 1991: 312). Separatism has been a reason for criticism of radical feminist theory as many argue that such societal re-organisation is unrealistic and thus unattainable.

Similar to both liberal and radical feminisms, socialist theory also critiques patriarchy. Socialist feminists argue that a patriarchal and capitalist system engenders social class, gender and race subjugation. Socialist feminism calls for a complete overhaul of structures, institutions and practices for all men and women. This theory has been largely criticised for its emphasis on capitalism as the foundation of sexism. Critics of this theory argue that while capitalism contributes greatly to the oppression of women, women can be oppressed outside the economic system as well.

Feminist post-structural theorists principally focus on language as socially, culturally and historically constructed, deconstructed, interpreted and reinterpreted to place people in power—full/less positionalities. Emanating from post-structural theorists' work such as Derrida and Foucault, feminist post-structuralists call for analysis of power issues and transformation of institutions to sites of empowerment as opposed to disempowerment for women.

Womanism is feminist theory that is promulgated by 'women of colour' and specifically black women. As Walker (1993) puts it, womanism is to feminism 'what purple is to lavender' (Walker 1993: xi). In other words, womanism has similar traits to feminism except for that it highlights what Hill Collins (1990) calls intersectionality of race, gender and class. Womanist theorists posit gender oppression alone is not what is faced by 'women of colour'. Instead they face multiple forms of oppression and therefore have to call for eradication of all those forms of oppression not merely gender oppression.

All of these feminist theories have a common thread: abolition of gender oppression albeit the strategies they employ differ. The author utilises womanist theoretical lenses to explicate the working life experiences of the young women.

FINDINGS AND ANALYSIS

This is Not Where I Want to Be

All the women interviewed in the study revealed great discontent about the jobs they currently hold. Many of them pointed out that they were not happy about their current positions because they had not planned to be in those positions. Two of six semi-professional participants in their early 20s who are receptionists, indicated that they took their positions because they were no other alternatives, one said, 'it was either this or nothing else and I had been at home doing nothing for nine months.' These young women also revealed that being unemployed, with newborn babies, compelled them to take the very first opportunities that came their way because 'such opportunities are rare'.

Similarly, the young woman who is a physical labourer and renders cleaning services for offices, pointed out that she did not wish to be in a position that 'everyone looks down upon'. She stated that 'being a cleaner, people treat you as the rubbish that you have to pick-up from their offices.'

It was not only the labourer and receptionists who were doing work in which they were not interested. The study revealed that even the women who are in what can be termed professional positions—a Human Resource (HR) officer, training manager and IT support specialist—were also highly unhappy about their positions. The HR officer reported that she would like to be working in another field not in HR, but she took the position because she needed the money not because it is harmonious with her educational background and interests. The IT support specialist reported that she had a 'different idea of what IT specialists do, not what I am doing. I am interested in that not this.' She finds, even with her qualifications, people in the office 'think they can get better assistance from my male colleagues than me. So what I do is just sit around 80 per cent of the time'.

Such dissatisfaction with employment may be taken at face value as entry-level positions which are almost always paved with dissatisfaction. After all, how often do people love and stay in their first jobs. However, it is important to note that some of the participants feel 'trapped' in these positions as they have no alternatives for upward movement. In case of the IT specialist, it is sexism, the placement of male colleagues above her that makes her unhappy with her position. Had she been in an environment which values her knowledge and capability as woman she would not be unhappy with her position.

These young women complicate and problematise the orthodox understanding of entry-level positions as a passage or stepping stone to a better job as they view their entry-level jobs as an impasse. All participants pointed out that they feel like they are in a *cul-de-sac*. One receptionist said, 'I have been here for three years; I am not challenged. I just function like a zombie.' The HR officer pointed out that she has been in the job for two years, 'which is too long. Doing a job you don't like is like dating a man you don't like but can't dump; imagine that.' They did not perceive their entry-level work as a stepping stone but viewed it as only a means to survival, albeit undesirable.

While the findings undoubtedly reveal the participants' unhappiness with their work, could they be also revealing what Heilbrun (1988) calls the state of fantasy in which women in general engage, for example, if I get into college, if I get this work accepted, if I get that job—there always seems to loom the possibility of something being over, settled, sweeping clear the way for contentment. This is delusion of a passive life. When the hope for closure is abandoned, when there is an end to fantasy, adventure for women will begin (Heilbrun 1988: 130).

The state of fantasy that Heilbrun speaks of is paralysing to young women in the study who feel a sense of helplessness and hopelessness. They seem to have internalised patriarchal norms which dictate that they are not active players in the moulding and shaping of their lives but passive spectators. They feel that there is nothing that they can do to alter the situation.

Comparison of an undesirable job to a boyfriend one can not 'dump', is symbolic of an unhealthy relationship that women are willing to endure at the workplace as long as they get monetary gain at the end of it all.

Notwithstanding the state of fantasy, these young women are aware of the corrosive realities of the economic system in South Africa, which make women willingly subject themselves to 'dehumanising' work ('treated like rubbish', 'zombies'). It is the dehumanising aspect they believe men would not have been able to handle for too long. 'Men could have done this job but perhaps they would not have stayed as long as I have. They would have moved on to something better' one receptionist reported.

Notably, all the young women believed that there were equal opportunities for women and men in the workplace, however, they all believed that men would not have been 'stuck' in the same positions. In other words, while they believe that there are equal opportunities, they also believe that men are in better positions to tap into those opportunities.

How Did I Get Here?

It is crucial to understand that these women did not mysteriously find themselves in undesirable positions. One of the participants pointed out that she did not have any aspirations when growing up:

> I am from a rural area where I went to school because everyone went to school but there was no certain goal that I was trying to have. I got pregnant in my matric, had a baby and just stayed at home as did everyone else around me. It was only when I visited my sister in the city that I started thinking that I need to make something of myself; especially because women of my age were doing it.

Such directionless existence was echoed by other participants, who reported that they were no expectations for them as young women, which is congruent with what is generally experienced by girl children. When Sadker and Sadker (1994) conducted their landmark study on how girls are treated in schools, they found that girls were not expected to amount to anything in schools, whereas boys were expected to be 'breadwinners' later on in life and therefore encouraged to work harder in school and aim higher in life. The young women in the study were socially moulded and institutionalised to believe less of themselves as women, and therefore had no particular goals, which is one of the reasons they found themselves in undesirable positions or doing work that they did not want.

I Am Not a Mother I Want to Be

All of the young women between the ages of 22 and 30 are single parents, with the exception of one; each raising a toddler or a young child. They all had their children while in high school, immediately after completing high school or during their college years. All of the pregnancies were unplanned and only one of the participants is still in relations with the biological father of the child. This is typical of many young African women in South Africa today. According to LoveLife, a youth awareness organisation, close to 60 per cent of children born to African young women are born out of any kind of parental partnership.

While this statistic is informative about the high rates of unprotected sexual relations, it is also telling that the responsibility of child rearing and financial support for the child is largely left in the hands of the young mothers and their families. It seemed unquestionable to the young women that they would be the ones who keep the children. When asked why *they*, not their partners, had decided to have sole custody of the child, they unanimously answered that it was the 'natural' decision. As mothers they are 'supposed to take care of their babies, not their fathers', as the training manager pointed out.

As women attempting to find equilibrium between their work and parental demands, the participants find themselves unable to cope with their parental responsibilities. Most of the participants have some sense of guilt about leaving their children in the rural areas to be taken care of by their mothers: 'I think I need to be more responsible in raising my child. But I had her at such a young age that I really did not feel that I could be a good parent to her,' one participant pointed out.

Another participant has brought her child to the city in order to 'experience motherhood'. She has since learned that motherhood is not as easy as she had thought. 'I would like to spend more time with my son but I can not. I feel badly about it but there is nothing I can do.'

Guilt seemed to be pervasive in all discussions vis á vis the paritcipants' children. They were torn between having to work in order to provide materially for their children and physically being with their children as their sole parent. Socialist feminists would argue that the capitalist system compels them to choose between working in order to survive and staying at home to provide nurture, that they believe their children deserve, especially in the absence of their paternal parents. Socialist feminism thus insists that South Africa's democracy is lacking in its affirmation of women as it does not provide 'conditions necessary for the realisation of the right of women to make choices' suitable for them.

While working outside the home has been one of the feminists' achievements (especially western white elite feminists, as 'women of colour' and Africans in particular have always worked outside their homes), it is noteworthy that young African women would also prefer to have the option of *not* working outside the home.

It is rather ironic that African women under the system of apartheid had no choice but to leave their children unattended to attend to their fellow white, Indian and coloured people's children, young women today still have to be brimful of guilt for leaving their children behind in a politically democratic country. This highlights the interrelationship between political and economic democracy. While South Africa has political democracy, such democracy can only be truly experienced by many women when it is coupled with economic democracy. Macedo (1994) argues that to speak of a democracy and capitalism simultaneously is contradictory as capitalism hinders democracy. That is, the young women have political democracy—they can vote and have access to institutions from which they were barred as Africans under the system of apartheid. However, socio-economic democracy eludes them as they have no choices but to work outside the home even when they want to work inside the home. The lives of these young women as workers elucidate that political democracy independent of socio-economic democracy cannot generally have an effectual impact on the lives of young African women in the workplace.

Surrogate mothers

All the participants had their children stay at home with older neighbourhood women, their own mothers or aunties assuming the role of surrogate mothers. The system of surrogate mothers in the African community is completely different from having a childminder or a person who is paid to take care of the child with minimal emotional connection. The participants pointed out that surrogate mothers treat the children under their care as if they were their own children. One participant said, 'sometimes it hurts to hear someone else talk to you about your child as if she was hers. But I have to understand that she takes that child as hers and I would not want it any other way.' Women who act as surrogate mothers in African communities are what Hill Collins calls community mothers who do self-sacrifice for the upliftment of the Black community. Hill Collins asserts that 'community mothers model a very different value system, one whereby Afrocentric feminist ethics of caring and personal accountability move communities forward (Hill Collins 1990: 132).' The 'Afrocentric feminist ethics of caring' emanates, from oppression of African women under colonialism and apartheid as it did for African Americans under slavery. In other words, in a democratic

South Africa, African women continue to employ feminist tactics used for survival under the most inhumane systems. Usage of such tactics in the post-apartheid South Africa unveils that political democracy has ushered economic emancipation for a few women but not for the women in entry-level positions.

CONCLUDING REMARKS

The working lives of the young women unveil the intersectionality of class, gender and race oppression. Young African women in entry-level positions are highly dissatisfied with their current occupations. This dissatisfaction stems from, among others, class disadvantage. When the young women were growing up they had no role models of working 'successful' women. Young affluent women of their age are likely to have had role models and mentors. Dissatisfaction is also due to the fact that many young women do work that they do not particularly like because there are no alternatives. In other words, high unemployment levels compel young women to take whatever work is available for survival. Contributing to dissatisfaction is also that young women feel guilty for leaving behind their children in order to work. However, it is equally significant that they remain optimistic about the future and opportunities available to them. In summary, the women's working lives demonstrate that women lack empowerment in the workplace as they do not have space, resources and means to make decisions that are suitable for them. Undeniably South Africa has made great strides towards women representation in all work sectors, but the chapter shows that women empowerment remains elusive.

REFERENCES

Casale, D. 2004. 'What has the Feminization of the Labour Market "Bought" Women in South Africa? Trends in Labour Force Participation, Employment and Earnings, 1995–2001', *Journal of Interdisciplinary Economics*, 15(3): 251–276.

Hawthorne, S. 1991. 'In Defence of Separatism', in Sneja Gunew (ed.), *Reader in Feminist Knowledge*, pp. 312–318. New York: Routledge.

Heilbrun, C. 1988. *Writing a Woman's Life*. New York: Ballantine Books.

Hill Collins, P. 1990. *Black Feminist Thought: Knowledge, Consciousness and the Politics of Empowerment*. London: Harper Collins Academic.

LoveLife. 2006. 'New National Survey Examines HIV, Sexual Behaviour among South African Young People'. Available online at kff.org/southafrica/sa04070nr.zacfm (downloaded on 04 July 2004).

Macedo, D. 1994. *Literacies of Power*. Boulder,CA: Westview Press.

Nedbank Index. 2006. 'Women Still Lag Behind Men in BEE Playing Field', cited in *City Press*, Johannesburg, August 13.

Sadker, M. and D. Sadker. 1994. *Failing at Fairness: How American Schools Cheat Girls*. New York: Maxwell Macmillan International.

Shrewsbury, C.M. 1987. 'What is Feminist Pedagogy?', *Women's Studies Quarterly*, 25: 6–14.

Walker, A. 1993. *Warrior Marks: Female Genital Mutilation and the Sexual Bondage of Women*. Orlando: Harcourt.

Weedon, C. 1987. *Feminist Practice and Poststructural Theory*. Oxford: Basil Blackwell.

8

In Search of a Title

Lynne Hunt

INTRODUCTION

'What's the title?' the editor asked, when I agreed to write this chapter. This became a challenge, which I posed to colleagues, 'If you had to choose a title to characterise your career, what would it be?'

The book focuses on women's careers, alluding to glass ceilings and discrimination, but I did not want to describe my career in this way. I started work as an academic in the 1970s and I have been helped by the feminist revolution, and the expansion of the university system. Yet, there have been barriers, so I cannot pretend all is well—when it is not. I am a migrant, so maybe the title *upside-down* would signal changes in my career arising from my move down under. My greatest success has been in teaching. So perhaps the simple title *Teacher* would paint the best picture of my work; but it ignores the role of family in my life. I will just have to road-test a number of titles.

Resilience appeals, but Anne Deveson (2003) beat me to it. It is a title that acknowledges difficulties without victim status, and it leaves room for success. It also characterises the early years of any British baby boomer, a time when parental resilience facing post-war stringencies created a hidden agenda for offspring to 'just get on with the job'. Travel was unheard of in the British working classes. Neighbourhood was the limited horizon. Kids played in the streets. Life was grey, beige and tweed. Men smelt of Woodbine cigarettes and beer—in particular my dad, who spent every evening at the pub before coming home to make life miserable for my mother, my three sisters and me. I do not feel scarred by this. What is normal to a child is normal—even domestic violence. Personal resilience was developed through this.

SURVIVING AS A YOUNG WOMAN

The daily absence of a father meant that I grew up in an all female household. I also went to a single sex high school. I had attended nine primary schools before I passed the high school admission examination known as the 11+. I did not realise, until I was in my mid-40s, that a girl had to pass at a higher level than a boy for selection to an academically elite grammar school. Given my chequered primary school years it is not surprising that I did not pass the 11+ outright. I was one of four 'borderline' girls in my village primary school to be invited for interview. It is difficult to believe that it was considered normal for a headmistress to interview 11-year-olds: that the future career of these girls would hang by such a fine thread. The interview was a comprehension test. I had to read a passage and then answer questions on it. I also had to say what I wanted to do when I grew up. By chance, *Cherry Ames* (Wells and Tatham 1943–1968) came to the rescue and landed me a place. These career education books had introduced me to the work of almoners, which was seen as a ladylike profession that appealed to the headmistress. So, maybe *Chance* should be the title of this chapter; but for indicating this career I may not have attended an elite academic school, or university, nor become an academic.

Traditional though it was, the school did many things right, including creating a context that supported the development of relationships. These school mates have provided a strong base of female friendships throughout my life. 'It's relationships that count', a colleague said recently when discussing our work team. What was true of school and work is also true of teaching: One student wrote to me some 25 years after I taught her: 'I've been wondering what it is that made you such a good teacher for me. I remember you as very supportive and affirming of me as an individual and as a young student teacher. That relationship you fostered affirmed me and supported my learning and my growth.'

She had remembered this for a long time, so it must have been important. *Relationships Matter* is a title that might well characterise my career.

Mentoring is a structured manifestation of friendships at work. In the late 1990s, I decided I had had enough of watching less qualified men getting promotion. I entered a mentoring programme for women who wanted to enter senior management at my university. I chose my mentor strategically. 'I don't know why you chose me,' she remarked, 'You are better qualified than me and you are older.' I replied, 'But you've had more promotion than me, so you must be doing something that I'm not.' It was a wise choice and friendship has grown from it. She advised me to apply for a newly created senior position. 'You won't get it,' she said, acknowledging that there was a front-runner, 'But you will show your wares to a new faculty hierarchy. It's not who you know but who knows you that counts.' As predicted, I did not get the job, but the front-runner had withdrawn his application, leaving the field wide-open. I surprised everyone by coming a close second. My mentor offered to come with me to my de-briefing. She seemed prepared for what might be said. 'You didn't get the job because they said you are difficult to work with', affirmed the chair of the selection panel. My mentor launched a challenge, noting that nobody on the interview panel had ever worked with me. 'That was gossip and hearsay, and you should have dismissed it.' The boy's club had been alive and well!

THE WORLD OF WORK

Exclusion could be a possible descriptor of women's careers, including mine. All cultures have exclusive practices that maintain boundaries. For example, dress codes and dietary patterns in religious groups distinguish the believers and provide a framework for living. The world of work is no different. However, the creation of in-groups, through exclusive practices, by definition, means that there will be out-groups. Indeed, much of the feminist discourse of the 1970s explored the exclusive, male strategies that marginalised women. Exclusion comes in different packages. I was once a senior member of staff in a department that had no regular staff meetings for two years. I had no clue what was going on.

When I asked for meetings I was labelled unsupportive of management by the two female managers in the department. Their reaction was to call me to endless disciplinary meetings. It was time-wasting, career sabotage. 'What you need is reputation management,' advised the young woman who was interviewing me about life as an academic. 'Reputation management!' This was a new one on me. I was still naïve enough to think that doing a good job was all that was needed. Some time later, a loyal and caring colleague burst into my room saying, 'You need to go and see the dean and tell him your side of the story.' 'I haven't got a side to tell', I replied, 'I'm not sure what my sin is.' The situation had escalated; I had taken the line that the dean and I were too busy to deal with baseless innuendo. My strategy was to rise above it. This just allowed the attack to gain momentum. Eventually the harassment was stopped and the managers were moved on. It would have made for easier, feminist analysis had my career been shaped by male discrimination, but this harassment was at the hands of women. 'You'll leave,' said the steadfast union woman who had supported me throughout this stressful period, 'People who are bullied, nearly always do.' She was right. I resigned some time later.

ADVOCATING INCLUSION

'I've never had anyone come to me and say they want more meetings,' said a senior man at my new university. We were discussing low staff morale. The solution I had been advocating was inclusion. It was an evidence based observation: the literature notes that change management works most effectively when the hearts and minds of workers are engaged in the process. 'Well, if you want people to be involved they've got to actually meet,' I replied. I had encountered, for a second time, difficulties associated with exclusion. As a professor at my new university I sat on only one decision-making committee and it met only once in my first year there. I had no leverage to provide the leadership for which I had been employed. Apart from any feminist, ideological commitment I had to implement participative decision-making, it just made good sense to en-gage staff because it provided the university the best value for money.

University staffs are knowledge workers. They are employed for their brain power. What was the value in excluding them from the decision-making table?

My new job involved management. I took with me the lessons I had learned from being harassed and was determined to be inclusive in my approach. I developed structures for the staff to participate collegially in decision-making. We experimented with communities of practice. As I see it, managing is much like teaching: set ground rules, scaffold processes for development and provide opportunities for autonomy so that people can create their own learning journey. Support, reward, extend horizons and sketch visions! It had worked for me in teaching so why not in management. Just recently, a student I taught five years ago wrote to let me know that he had graduated successfully and won a major scholarship. He referred to his first year experience when life was a mess and he was failing. He then noted:

> One simple comment from you on my assignment put me onto the path to great things. I believe it went something like, 'this assignment is well researched with an excellent writing style and you have all the makings of a postgraduate student.' That comment gave me such confidence in my own ability that I got my life in order and went from being a student who was failing badly to one who was disappointed with any mark under 70.

Little things mean a lot would be a title that shows how a few positive words can extend people's horizons. A positive, inclusive approach had also worked in my new job. When I left, to return to my home town, the department was buzzing.

When I got home, I found that a recent string of horrific murders of young girls had alerted the community to the fact that violence against women is endemic in the Australian society. Does this mean that feminism has failed? At least my generation of feminists can be proud of their work to provide services for women who suffer violence. Many of those early feminists now occupy senior positions in their place of employment and they work in ways that sustain a feminist vision about the quality of human life in an increasingly corporate world that measures success only in terms of cost-effectiveness. One group of diehard feminists I know actually refer to themselves as the 'Alternative Public Service'. *Subversion* is the name of their game, and a possible title for a chapter on women's careers.

The problem with subversion is that it has resonance with stereotypical 'women's' behaviour, often typecast as manipulative. *Resistance* might be a better title. French theorist, Michel Foucault (1982: 216), observed that personal resistance is available to us all: 'Maybe the target nowadays is to refuse what we are ... We have to promote new forms of subjectivity.' My mother raised me on proverbs and she said much the same as Foucault: 'You can take a horse to water but you can't make it drink.' In brief, women might have to run their working lives in the context of overt and covert sexism, but we do not have to play the game. The problem is that those playing the sexist games are often unaware of what they are doing. One of my favourite cartoons shows a group of workers sitting in a meeting. There is only one woman present. The chairperson is saying, 'That's a very good idea Miss Smith. Would one of the men like to have it?' Sad, but true. I was dismayed at an incident at the first senior staff meeting I attended. I deferred to a female administrator for an opinion. She was an old-hand and had been sitting on that committee for years. Later, she told me that it was the first time any academic had asked for her point of view. What explains this exclusion? Is it gender or the academic–administrative divide that exists in many universities? What a difference when, recently, I sat on a committee chaired by a high-powered, committed, woman. When the boys interrupted she stayed quietly focused on the woman who had been talking. When a bloke said something hopelessly gauche, which one did with monotonous regularity, she refocused on the discussion at hand. This was professional resistance at its best.

Dale Spender's work had an enormous influence on my perceptions of the world of work. She advised direct action, 'When a bloke does something stupid in committee meetings women rush in to rescue him,' she announced. 'Don't do that! Ask him to repeat it—twice if necessary! Take notes!' She has turned resistance into an art form. Her research (Spender: 1980) demonstrated how men jostle for position at committee meetings. It is all talk and no listening. She also showed that teachers (including me: my male students clocked me one day) give boys two-thirds of their attention. In example after example she exposes the layers of sexism in language and communication. 'Take the word legitimacy,' she said at a public lecture, 'Women would have to learn that off by heart. What woman is going to give birth and ask: "Is it mine?" Wonderful stuff!'

LIFE EXPERIENCES AND CAREER CHOICES

Transitions may prove a fitting title. Attending nine different primary schools certainly attuned me to change. Yet I was sick the first day of high school—wound up with anxiety about the fact that I was borderline: not a great transition! In the first year of high school we studied all subjects together. Subsequently, we were streamed by some subjects but returned to our home classroom for many lessons and routine tasks. I can still recite the entire class register because roll-call was taken twice a day for five years before the early school-leavers departed for the world of work whilst the rest of us entered the Sixth Form to study for university entrance exams. This was a significant transition because sixth form was run on university lines with independent study time and small tutorials. By this time, I had grown in academic confidence. In fact, I can date a transition point. The school had 'form captains'—two each term per class. We were voted in by classmates, so it established something of a pecking order of popularity. I was voted 'form captain' at the beginning of second year. Thereafter, my marks improved so that two years later I was an 'A' average student and on track for university, even though I did not know what it was. Maybe *The accidental academic* would make a better title for this chapter.

I was the first in my entire extended family to go to university. I studied sociology, which was necessary to be—yes, an almoner! That ambition had stayed with me but never came to fruition. My headmistress had to research what sociology was. Such a trendy subject had not, so far, reached her ken. She suggested Liverpool University because it had one of the longest established sociology courses. I reacted favourably: It was also in a city known for its pop groups—a great place to be, at the end of the 1960s. The transition was easy. Why wouldn't it be when I was living in a hall of residence with some 500 other students of the same age? I loved it. The city boasted poets who were clever wordsmiths.

One poem by Roger McGough, entitled *Come Close and Sleep Now,* stays in my mind (Henry et al. 1967). It expressed the reality of the so-called sexual liberation of that era: In the morning, 'you will put on a dress of guilt and shoes with broken high ideals.' Truth to tell, the 1960s were pretty tame and monogamous. That may be the best kept secret of the baby boomer generation.

'I only lived there for the first twelve years of my life,' remarked Australian novelist and playwright, Dorothy Hewett, 'but it's like a microbe in my blood'. In this way she identified her sense of place and bonding with the rural western Australian environment of her childhood. She was giving a public lecture on her life's work, and I interviewed her the next day. 'That's how Liverpool is for me,' I commented. My transition from a rural village to the big, port city of Liverpool was liberating. Of course, it coincided with leaving home—liberating in itself. I liked the anonymity of city life and I liked studying sociology: so much so that when postmodernism became the hot theory in Australia, many years later, I did not 'get it'. It took me some time to realise that I already had it. Perspective-taking, critical-thinking and phenomenology were the essence of my undergraduate learning. Much of my intellectual development can be credited to my lecturer, Dr Nikos Kokosalakis, in voluntary exile from his country that Sir David Frost satirised in the joke: 'There is going to be a general election in Greece and we all know which generals are going to be elected.' At least academics in those days stood for something politically.

Academic transition to university study had not been a problem for me because of the sixth form experience at school. However, I was aware of the social limitations of my home life. I had rarely been to theatre; we had no car; and, what's opera anyway? Food at home was good, country cooking. Exotic fruits like grapefruit were unknown, causing me great embarrassment when, in front of more sophisticated university friends, I cut one in half the wrong way. Fortunately, I had spent three summers with a French family to improve my French. They were well-to-do and had shown me a different way of life, both intellectually and socially. The issue was class: working class girl makes good through education. In fact, the title of this chapter might well be taken from the play by Liverpool writer, Willy Russell, *Educating Rita*, which depicts the cultural gulf that prevails when working class kids attend middle class universities. So, gender does not explain all aspects of my career trajectory; class influenced as well. Despite the fact that I was an avid reader, I lacked middle-class fluency. 'What's the lingua franca of Israel?' asked a senior member of staff, when I returned to college teaching after a summer working on a kibbutz. 'Buggered if I know—what's lingua franca?'

Such experiences have influenced my teaching career, which started with my appointment to a lecturing position when I was 22—a lucky break at that age. As a university lecturer I have concentrated on working with students to introduce them to the culture of university life and to extend their horizons. 'The social atmosphere of this class has improved enormously since you started teaching us,' observed a young, male student in the first class I taught, 'But, you'll have to work hard to gain our respect.' At least he was honest! When I quizzed him, he said that middle-aged blokes in suits had a natural authority, mostly because they were middle-aged blokes in suits. My long hair and miniskirt, it seems, did not quite crack it in the academic credibility stakes. It is not uncharitable to observe that my teaching career had a head start because I had followed the world's worst lecturer. Bad though I probably was as a rooky, I could only be better than her. She described everything in terms of complex models, leaving the students, and me, bewildered. So, my first two lessons about teaching were learned: develop a positive and supportive environment in class, and keep things simple. Apparently, I learned well, because 20 years later an American colleague drawled, 'Gee, you're such a good lecturer, because you're so simple-minded.' Apparently this was a compliment!

My first two heads of department taught me a lot and demonstrated, once again, that relationships have been important in my working life. The first is a lifelong friend and I married the second. The first could extemporise. He was an inspirational lecturer. A member of staff was absent one day and he had to takeover at short notice. He gave a memorable, off the cuff lecture on the sociology of hot pants, which were in vogue at the time. I was impressed but it was several years before I developed the skill and confidence to do the same. Storytelling is the basis of this approach, but it is still lecturing. When I arrived in Australia I had the good fortune to work in a new college that was experimenting with pedagogies that involved learning-by-doing and continuous assessment. My second head of department encouraged this move away from lectures and exams, and engaged staff and students in creative, social science projects that used a particular community as a social science laboratory. These were great beginnings and I went on to win university and national prizes for teaching.

Clearly, my first two male heads of department opened doors for me. However, as the feminist mantra of the 1970s indicated, 'It's not the doors that open that concern me. It's the ones that close.' When I started work in Australia, it became apparent that my salary level started a rung below where it should have been. Actually, after backpacking across eastern Europe (crossing the Berlin Wall at dawn), the Soviet Union and a number of countries in Asia, I was glad to earn any amount. However, there was a pattern. Another young, 'Pommie' colleague was also short-changed. Was this because we were women, young or migrants? Who knows? In fact, I did not even know I was feminist. Having been raised in an all female household and school, I did not know that I was supposed to be a second-class citizen. My first inkling came as I was graduating from university. I had applied for a management position in Marks and Spencer, a major retail store. This was considered a prestigious job and only two from my university, a male student and I, were offered positions there. He was put on management track and I was put on personnel track at significantly less salary. I did not take the job. Later, when I started work at the new college in Australia my feminist consciousness grew. The first draft of the conditions of service indicated that a lecturer could take his wife and children overseas with him on study leave. The blokes thought it was a bit of a laugh that I took seriously such exclusive language, but they did change the wording. I became active in the academic union and was labelled because of it. However, I started to take a back seat in union affairs after I had children. There was room for only one activist in the family, and in those days, unions did not pay baby-sitting costs.

'Do you enjoy your work?' This opening question of my annual performance review took me by surprise, but it is an interesting question. It became even more so when I listened to a radio talk on happiness, which suggested that academics are unlikely to be completely happy because they are trained to levels of scepticism incompatible with karma. The context in which academics work has also undergone rapid change, and staff careers and employment conditions have been affected. My own career was influenced as the teacher training colleges, in which I first worked, became colleges of advanced education and, ultimately, universities. Teaching workloads increased with higher student numbers and the imperative for research and publication mushroomed. The pressures are enormous. However, I have reached professorial status and this would not have happened without these changes. Titles associated with *adaptability* may need to be considered.

'How many of you planned to be career advisors?' I had been asked to talk to career teachers from nearby schools. Unsurprisingly, nobody raised their hands. I doubt that many school kids aspire to being an academic or a professor either. As Dorothy Smith (1987) noted, life can be more messy than planned and many simply fall into careers. So really, as one of my friends is given to observing, *Life's a mess and then you die.* This might be the best title yet. However, my career has been reasonably ordered and stable. At least it felt like it when it took me 20 years to get my first promotion! These days, longevity in a workplace is not rewarded. 'But you're not an old-timer,' said my vice-chancellor. 'I've been here more than 30 years,' I replied, 'How long do you have to be here?' Clearly she had an image of old-timers that was unrelated to longevity. Rather, they were stick-in-the-muds. Yet, those who had worked at the university for years had to adapt to change: the context had been so fluid that they experienced change just by standing still.

GENDER-BASED BATTLES

'The writing's on the wall,' mused my husband (a fellow academic) at the end of the 1980s. 'You'll have to get a PhD. Take a couple of years off work and I'll keep you in the manner to which you have become accustomed. I'll take early retirement when you return to work.' Thoughtful and supportive though he was, it did not escape my attention that he had achieved promotion without a doctorate. So, resigning myself to the fact that I needed either a willy or a PhD for promotion, I took two years off work and wrote my thesis quick time. My husband is older than me, so the deal worked well for him. I had two years off work and he is now into his twelfth year of retirement! The drop to one salary cost us, but it improved our quality of life. He retired just as our eldest child entered high school and he did a great job endlessly chauffeuring our sporty kids from one training session to the next. He also did household chores. That is when my 70-hour-working-weeks started.

I was a second year student in the 1968 year of student revolutions. I was not a great participant, but I inherited from that era the notion that it is possible to make the world a better place. Yet the opposite has happened in Australian universities: 'I no longer encourage my postgraduate students to apply for jobs in a university,' observed a colleague. She is feminist and, like me, has fought, won and lost gender-based battles, but as she and I see it, today's problems arise not from sexism but from resource-poor universities, staff doing more with less, and increasing time spent on accountability processes. The most laughable of these is activity-based costing in which academics must 'guesstimate' the time they spend teaching, marking, researching, and engaging with the community. The numbers have to add up to 100 per cent. Given that most academics work at least 50 hour weeks, the 100 per cent baseline of a 37 1/2 hour week is shot before the guessing begins. 'Just tell them you do 100% teaching', goes the corridor advice, 'then they can't get you to do more'. We had to 'guesstimate' on-line. The programme provided the opportunity to indicate that things were the same as last year. One busy colleague thought he would kill the job with a quick tick in this box. But these computer programmes are wily. It popped back the observation that he had not filled it in last year either! *Well, you've got to laugh or you'd cry*: is this a possible title?

CONCLUSION

Crying is easy because good staff are leaving. I recently joined with a colleague to research why good university teachers quit. One respondent summarised the pressures of academic life thus: 'We've got to give... [students] just as much education in the smaller...time frame...I can be creative but I can't be that creative...I can't fit a city into a house.' *'Fitting a city into a house'*: not a bad title! It irritates people when I say that

I work long hours. They think that I am either inefficient or showing-off. But the work is there to do and I am no orphan. It is the same across Australia, now reputed to be the hardest working country in the world. So much so that the Tourism Commission pleads with employers to make workers take leave to boost domestic tourism. Maybe *Working 9 to 9*, could be the chapter title—or *Open all Hours*.

So why continue if the hours are so long? Is it for the money? Yes! I had good, if sexist, career advice from my mother who wanted her daughters to have 'a job to fall back on'. Despite everything she experienced she still thought marriage was the main game in women's lives'. She clapped her hands at my wedding, thankful that I was finally 'off her hands'. 'Mother', I replied, 'I'm now 31 and I left home at 19.' But work is about more than money. I like the creative side of teaching, research and development work. Yet time marches on and the American–Indian expression, *Like rain without thunder* describes how something, such as retirement, creeps-up unawares. There's a story about an old-timer in the Australian outback. When asked if he had lived all his life in remote areas, he replied. 'Not yet.' Nor is this the end of my career—not yet! So which title describes my career so far? All of them.

REFERENCES

Deveson, A. 2003. *Resilience*. Sydney: Allen & Unwin.
Foucault, M. 1982. 'The Subject and Power', in H. Dreyfus and P. Rabinow (eds), *Michel Foucault: Beyond Structuralism and Hermeneutics*, pp. 208–226. Brighton: Harvester.
Henry, A., R. McGough and B. Patten. 1967. *The Mersey Sound*. Harmondsworth: Penguin.
Smith, Dorothy E. 1987. *The Everyday World as Problematic. A Feminist Sociology*. Boston: Northeastern University Press.
Spender, D. 1980. *Man Made Language*. London: Routledge & Kegan Paul.
Wells, H. and J. Tatham, 1943–1968. *Cherry Ames Series*. New York: Gosset and Dunlop.

PART THREE
Health and Wellness

Women often avoid expressing their concerns publicly when it comes to matters of health and wellness. Of course, this varies across diverse cultural communities, but in many communities it is generally taboo to talk about personal health and wellness in a public forum. However, today when global communities interact more frequently, it becomes necessary to focus on some of the illnesses and diseases such as cancer and HIV/AIDS that can no longer be restricted to private domains.

In Part Three, Arlene Fester brings to the fore the human capacity for understanding and accepting pain and suffering caused by disease, and the interrelationship between acceptance of that experience with one's cultural and religious worldview. Again, Arlene takes us on her journey and we discover that family loyalty and honour along with an infused spirituality become the primary factors in dealing with adversity. Nokujabula Myeza and Dennis Francis in their chapter bring to us the reality of those living with HIV/AIDS in South Africa. They work with AIDS sufferers and their families, in the education and training of society that is plagued by a medical condition, which is not well understood by those suffering from it and others (friends and family) who are also affected personally. Their paper celebrates the dedication and courage of women who are HIV/AIDS positive and who choose to use their unwelcome illness to educate others. Nirmala Gopal and Reshma Sookrajh provide another perspective to the stigma of being HIV/AIDS positive and share the experiences of women who choose not to declare their truth for fear of consequences to themselves and their children. This perspective is one that addresses current homophobic reactions and the impact on orphans who will remain the real victims of the disease.

9

Our Lives with Mother and Alzheimer's Illness

Arlene Fester

This story is about a 78-year-old woman who was once very strong. She fought, struggled and survived during the apartheid years, raising three kids and now has become a child herself, because of Alzheimer's. Many a night my mum sat at my bedside as I was a sickly child. Doctors did not think I would live to be 12 years and my mum did not think I would see my 21st birthday. In 2006 I turned 42. Although Prudence, my sister, did not have a good relationship with my mum she decided to look after her anyway. Prudence one day said to one of my colleagues that she always thought Arlene would be the one to take care of mum. But God had to get me out of the way, so He could work on Prudy's relationship with our mother. When God changes your heart, He changes your attitude. It was beautiful to witness the relationship which developed, irrespective whether she was now the adult and my mum, the child.

Five years ago (June 2003), my mum was diagnosed with vascular dementia. It is when the blood in the body is not circulating properly and thus, insufficient oxygen gets to the brain (family of Alzheimer's). I remember the day Karin (my eldest sister) called to tell me. I cried for a whole week. Every moment thinking about mum just made me cry because I could not believe that this woman who was once so strong, would now become a baby. One morning I said to the Lord:

> When You're ready to fetch her, make us ready to release her; but this one thing I ask: would You keep Your hand over me and stay so close to me as I go through, on this journey; so that when I get to the other side, I'm still able to say that You're faithful and that You're a good God.

On Monday, 22 May 2006, around 11:45 a.m., Karin called to say she was on her way home. Margaret (the lady we appointed permanently to look after mum) phoned Karin to say that my mum did not look well. We had a terrible incident the day before. Sunday morning Melanie (my cousin) called Karin to say that my mum is not eating and she does not look good. They then took my mum to hospital. They were there from the morning until after 8:00 p.m. and still no one had attended to my mum. We did not have medical aid, but Karin took my mum instead to Gatesville Medical Centre, where they put her on a drip.

I told her, if possible, to rather keep my mum at home and find out whether they can come and put her on drip at home. I was sitting in my car crying not sure whether to go home or not, feeling so helpless. Irene, the tea lady, saw me and called Yvonne (one of my colleagues). She came and asked me if it was my mum and I shook my head. She asked whether I wanted to go home and I said I do not know because with Alzheimer's one can not really tell. About a month ago my mum had a severe stroke that left her paralysed on the right side. Doctors were amazed at her recovery. Yvonne phoned Karin and came back to tell me that Karin said I should come home and that Koos (the director) said it is OK.

The earliest flight back to Cape Town was 6:30 p.m. The plane landed at 8:30 p.m. and Mark (Karin's husband) fetched me. When I got home, Karin was standing at the entrance of my mum's bedroom and opened her arms to greet me, but then held onto me and said that mum is no longer with us. I broke down and cried and as she still held me said: 'She went so peacefully, Arlene...'

Karin asked whether I wanted to see the body (the duvet was thrown over mum's head). She uncovered her and I lay across her body and stroked her hair and cried and said to her that I am so sorry I was late mummy. She was so cold and yet it seemed as if she was only sleeping. My cousin, Cheryl stood behind me and stroked my back and said you were not late, you were on time. Then she asked me what do you want to say to your mummy and I said: 'I just wanted to say Goodbye,' and Cheryl said, 'Now say Goodbye, talk to your mummy....'

Karin had phoned the undertakers and asked them to come and fetch the body. The undertaker came around 10:30, his name was Stan. I watched in amazement as this gentleman handled my mum's body with so much dignity and respect. He threw what looked like a baby's receiving blanket (just much bigger) over the duvet and then shifted the duvet out from under the receiving blanket and wrapped her body in it. Melanie was helping him; which was quite amazing since she is afraid of touching dead bodies. They moved the body onto a sheet of plastic and tied a knot at the head and foot end, and lifted it by the knot to place on the stretcher bed. He pulled a cover over the body and then a royal blue blanket halfway which had a big gold cross on it. I said bye-bye mummy as they wheeled the body out of the bedroom and Cheryl standing next to me said, 'No walk with your mummy. Go all the way'. It was raining terribly hard outside and they threw my coat over me. Stan had reversed the Toyota Hilux Van to the back gate because the bed was too long and the angle from the front door through the lounge into the passage was too awkward, so they brought it through the kitchen.

As they lifted the bed into the back of the van and he closed the shutters, I said again, 'Goodbye mummy,' as the tears rolled down my cheeks and the rain was pouring down, at that very moment it felt as if all the angels in heaven were crying with me. Stan slowly pulled out of the grounds and slowly he drove down the street with his hazards on as I stood and waved goodbye and I had the sense of the Queen herself, being driven away (she was driven away like royalty). It's a memory I will treasure for as long as I live….

Thursday evening was the prayer meeting. Uncle Joseph led the prayer meeting and Aunty Esmé played the piano. It was such a memorable prayer meeting. My cousin Cheryl shared the word. She said that she went to the Book of Acts because she was looking for a woman of 'ACTS' (Deeds) and she came across Lydia. She compared Lydia to my mum saying that this was not just a woman, but she had a name and whenever anyone mentioned Aunty Ellen or Uncle Attie (my dad); everyone knew who they were speaking about. Lydia was hard working and my mum could work hard. Cheryl said that each one of us had actually inherited something of my mum. My mum was a good gardener and Karin is good in gardening. My mum was a good cook and Arlene can cook well. My mum was straightforward and said a thing just as she saw it, and Prudence is like that.

My Aunt wrote a message that she read to us and this is what it said:

Dear Karin, Arlene & Prudence

I admired you the way you handled your mother. You spoke so nicely to her; not a shout. You cared for her so tenderly. You showed your love to her. You always took her with you wherever you went. One could see that she appreciated it. You have done your best. If I look at you three sisters, I see your mother in you. She had a strong and firm personality. She loved to cook and sing. She was hardworking. She loved gardening. She was always prepared to help others. She had a strong faith in God. Your mother left you a good and solid legacy. I salute you! Be assured that the Lord will bless you richly. He is able to strengthen you. Keep the faith. Psalms 91: Safety of Abiding in the Presence of God.

Love, Aunty Esmé

My mum had a beautiful service on Saturday, 27 May 2006. Uncle Langdon shared such an awesome word out of the book of James:
    'What is Life, but a vapour...here today...gone tomorrow...'
As they wheeled the Coffin out of the church the song of David Phelps played:

No more night, no more pain, no more tears, never crying again, and praises to the great I am, we will live in the light of the risen lamb. See all around, now the nations bow down to sing. The only sound is the praises to Christ our King, slowly the names from the books are read, I know the King so there's no need—no need to dread...

I am extremely grateful to Alzheimer's Related Dementia Association (ARDA). Though I was not in contact with my mum everyday, I felt I needed to be 'informed' so that I could support Prudence better (she cared for mum). There were times I went down to Cape Town only for a weekend, and I felt I did not want to waste time becoming angry with my mum because I did not understand the disease. The most important thing I have learnt through this illness is that the sooner one changes and accepts what is happening, the easier it becomes; handling the person as well as the situation. The illness deteriorates with time. If you remain ignorant, you will fight the person and fight the illness and you will feel more frustrated and drained after that because the person cannot change; you will have to make a decision to change yourself. The choice is yours...

Alzheimer's is a very humiliating and degrading illness. It was very sad to see my mum becoming like a baby. They start to wear nappies again because the message to the brain does not get there fast enough and so they wet or dirty themselves. Their walking also becomes affected. It is as if their brain gets stuck and then they do not know to put the one foot before the other and thus do not move forward. Towards the end, she even started crying like a baby (when, for example, her tablets did not taste good. I think it left a bitter taste in her mouth).

I promise you that if you change within yourself you will even be able to see the humour in the illness. Many people thought we were laughing at my mum and making fun of her, but it is a kind of coping mechanism. We could choose to laugh or cry, so we chose to laugh and that in itself brought so much joy to our lives that I miss that humour. At times my mum was so sharp with her remarks that she totally caught you unawares. I remember one day Prudy made her tea and later she and my cousin joined my mum in the lounge with their cups. She noticed my mum's cup was empty and said to Melanie it is impossible, my mum could not have drank her tea so quickly because it was quite hot. So she leaned over the table where my mum sat and noticed that the windowsill was wet. She asked mum, 'Why is the windowsill wet?' to which my mum replied, 'ask the windowsill!' At times my mum was very difficult and would not cooperate with Prudy. At times, they do not want to undress, do not want to bath or get dressed (part of the illness) and Prudy would say to her, 'Who is in charge here?' and she would say, 'You are!'

Many times my mum went missing (that was before we realised my mum was ill). She went for a walk; got disorientated and confused and could not find her way home, then she just kept walking. One day she walked from our home in Greenhaven to Tygerberg Hospital (about 30 km). One evening as I was praying and saying thank you to the Lord for always protecting my mum and that nothing bad ever happened to her when she went missing (one always hears these stories about elderly people getting mugged or raped), the Lord said to me, 'His Eye is on the sparrow and He's watching over her...'

My sister Prudence did not have a very good relationship with my mum, so it was a very difficult decision for her to take care of her. But I want to tell you that I stand amazed to see the miracle of change in my sister's heart and approach toward my mum. When I look at my sister I am reminded of, 'The God of the second chance…'

My favourite Scripture:

Isaiah 40:31: 'But they that wait upon the Lord shall renew their strength. They shall mount up with wings like Eagles, they shall run and not grow weary, they shall walk and not faint.'

10

'Openly Positive': Living and Working with HIV/AIDS

Nokujabula Myeza and *Dennis Francis*

INTRODUCTION

Nearly 15 per cent of all people living with HIV/AIDS around the world live in South Africa. Of this group in South Africa, 5.6 million are in the economically active group (Shisana et al. 2005). These statistics reveal the serious impact that the virus has on our workforce. Within the education sector itself, at least 12 per cent of the South African educators and administration staff are thought to be living with HIV (Theron 2005; World Bank 2002). This is not surprising when one considers that the disease is affecting both the demand and supply of education as argued by Shisana et al. (2005: 2), 'Not only do children drop out of school because of HIV/AIDS, thus reducing the demand for educators, but educators, school managers and policy makers are themselves dying of HIV/AIDS, thus reducing supply.'

Despite this knowledge most educators are silent and unlikely to disclose their serostatus. Disclosure, for many, is like a 'double-edged sword' (Mthembu 1998: 27). On one hand, it may be constructive and enable people living with HIV/AIDS to get support and services that they need whilst on the other, it can be destructive. This view is further articulated by Maile (2003: 79) who argues that disclosure is important as it would promote 'trust and proper human resource management,' however, the prevailing climate of discrimination against people living with HIV/AIDS would result in the targeting of educators who have disclosed their HIV status by school managers and others. Upon examination of these insights, it is not difficult to understand why seropositive people often keep their serostatus silent in the workplace and elsewhere. This occurs despite legislation that prohibits discrimination. The South African Constitution explicitly states that everyone has a right to fair labour practices and includes more general provisions that promote the right to equality and non-discrimination (Section 9) and privacy (Section 14). The Labour Relations Act 66 of 1995 and the Code of Good Practice also serve as a guide to employers and employees and protects any employee living with HIV/AIDS from unfair dismissal. The legislation referred to is relevant to the education sector as it provides recourse for educators living with HIV/AIDS to challenge unfair discrimination and to participate in a free and fair democracy.

The purpose of our article is to describe the experiences of educators who are living 'openly' with HIV in their workplace, in the Ethekwini region in KwaZulu-Natal. We use the phrase living 'openly' to describe these women as they have chosen to disclose their seropositive status to people in their families, schools and communities, despite the prevalent stigma and silence around HIV/AIDS. While much has been written about the experiences of people living with HIV/AIDS, there is a dearth of literature available pertaining to people who have disclosed their HIV status in the KwaZulu-Natal region. Hence, this study represents an attempt to fill this gap.

We highlight the conditions under which disclosure happens; describe the experiences of these four women in their work contexts and draw attention to how the four women participants have come to define their role as educators in the struggle against HIV/AIDS which they view as their personal and professional responsibility. We conclude by arguing that educators living 'openly' with HIV have a critical role to play within the context of HIV/AIDS in South Africa and more particularly in KwaZulu-Natal as well as the potential to move beyond mere delivery of the curriculum in their teaching practice. The narratives demonstrate the possibility of bringing the voices and experiences of such educators into the centre of the learning process related to HIV/AIDS.

WOMEN AND HIV

Women are over represented in the prevalence of the pandemic. In the UNICEF study (2001), gender was a significant factor in response to seropositivity within the context of the family. Daughters, wives and daughters-in-law experienced higher levels of stigma and discrimination than sons, husbands and sons-in-law. In instances where both partners were seropositive, men enjoyed greater familial care. The women, however, were labelled as being of 'loose character' and the potential source of their husband's serostatus. The women's burden of care increased as they assumed the caretaking responsibility of their seropositive partners. This can be attributed to gender norms which dictate unequal caretaking responsibilities for women and girls, where this is viewed as a natural part of being a woman. Women were often ousted from the houses of parents-in-law when their partners died (UNAIDS 2002: 41). Extending this argument, O'Sullivan (2000) contends that women in many parts of the world are denied access to basic treatment, isolated without proper information or support and many live in fear of discovery because of continuing stigma and discrimination still attached to a diagnosis of HIV. In fact, the literature is full of stories of the differential treatment to men and women living with HIV/AIDS (Francis and Francis 2006; Aggleton 2001; Francis 2003; O' Sullivan 2000; Bujra 2000; Mtembu 1998).

In South Africa, the story of Promise Mthembu (1998) highlights some of the challenges that seropositive women face in this country. Mthembu represents the trauma of disclosure and the stigma attached to HIV/AIDS which can result in many seropositive people being evicted from their homes, losing their jobs and being denied medical care. The story of Gugu Dlamini, a KwaZulu–Natal woman living with HIV/AIDS who was murdered by members of her community, illustrates the fatal consequences for individuals who disclose their serostatus in contexts where stigma is rampant. Newspaper reports stated that Gugu Dlamini was stoned and beaten to death after she had spoken out about her HIV status. Neighbours went on to accuse her of shaming the community (Selsky 1999).

While HIV is not readily transmitted in the majority of workplace environments, numerous employers have used the supposed risk of transmission as an excuse to terminate or refuse employment to those who are HIV positive (Aggleton 2001). Some employers have opted to get around the demands of providing medical and pension benefits to people who are living with HIV/AIDS by denying employment (Whiteside 1993). In Ukraine, people living with HIV/AIDS reported that when their serostatus was known they experienced rejection by colleagues and excuses were found to dismiss them. Some Ukrainian employers enforced pre-employment testing as part of their recruitment process, refusing work to those who were HIV positive. (UNICEF 2001: 19–21). In South Africa, two flight attendants were denied employment based on their seropositive status. In one case, the airways company admitted unconditionally that the exclusion of the applicant for the post of cabin attendant was on the grounds of his HIV status (Whiteside and Sunter 2000).

Participants in the Francis (2004) study reported that when they first disclosed their serostatus in the workplace, colleagues verbalised that they will not discriminate against them. However, as time lapsed the participants expressed feeling exclusion and discrimination which sometimes led to the termination of their working contracts. Some of their responses were: 'They would talk very softly with one another but when I joined they would keep quite. I knew they were talking about me' and 'I noticed that none of the other colleagues were using the toilet that I was using and that my teacup was placed far from the other cups.'

In view of this, it is not difficult to appreciate why people living with HIV/AIDS choose to keep their serostatus secret. The manifestation of HIV/AIDS related stigma creates a climate of harassment and discrimination that forces many living with HIV/AIDS to conceal their HIV status thereby making the virus invisible and allowing it to spread.

RESEARCH STRATEGY

All four participants in the study are African women educators employed by the KwaZulu-Natal Department of Education (See Table 10.1

Table 10.1 Biographical Data of Participants

Name of participant[1]	Age	Marital status	No. of children	Geographical district	School	Level
Zama	35	Married	2	Urban	Primary	PL1
Zethu	35	Widowed	1	Township	Secondary	PL1
Nonsizi	43	Widowed	3	Urban informal	Primary	PL1
Zemvelo	54	Married	2	Deep rural	Secondary	PL1

for biographical data). They are also members of the South African Democratic Teachers Union (SADTU). Gaining access to the participants was made easy by the fact that the first author is also an educator and chairperson of the Gender Desk responsible for HIV related support at SADTU.

There were specific criteria considered in the selection of participants. First, they had to be educators teaching in the Ethekwini region and second, had to be living 'openly' with HIV. Initially, 16 women belonging to the SADTU support group for women living with HIV/AIDS were approached. Seven women agreed to participate in the study. However, only four were living 'openly' with HIV and could be included in the study as they met the sampling criteria. The women educators were asked to sign a document outlining informed consent, the issue of confidentiality, and the right to withdraw at any stage. They were quick to point out that there they were living 'openly' with HIV and that there was no need for anonymity or confidentiality. Despite this, we emphasized the need and importance for confidentiality and anonymity throughout the study.[2]

At the root of our study is an interest in understanding the experiences of four women educators living 'openly' with HIV and the meaning they make of their experiences. For this study, in-depth interviewing, as suggested by Seidman (1991), was used as it allows for the stimulation of conversation through open ended questions. It proved especially useful in troubling the silence and secrecy around HIV. Two interviewing sessions of 90 minutes were scheduled per participant. The interview questions were structured to assist the participants in telling their stories. All interviews were taped and the data was transcribed. Notes were also taken during the interviews to assist us in reconciling the audio and written data. The recorded and written data was coded and pseudonyms were used as codes for each participant. During the analysis phase the interview transcripts were transformed into a logical and manageable structure that attempts to address the research question and communicate a thick description of what the four participants' experiences were and why their experiences were constructed in particular ways. Following, is a discussion of the themes that emerged from our study.

DISCUSSION

All four participants in our study chose to disclose their seropositive status in their workplace as they believed that the relational and environmental contexts were sufficiently supportive:

> My good principal is very supportive. She goes all out to make me feel I am still important. She shares with me all the useful information concerning AIDS. [I] Knew I could count on her support. (Nonsizi)

> The people I work with are wonderful and I knew that nothing would change if I told them [about] my HIV status. (Zama)

In some ways, Zama and Nonsizi continued to receive support from their colleagues, school managers and learners after they disclosed their seropositive status:

> I [received] supportive response from the staff and my senior management (mostly women). I [receive] counseling and help when needed. (Zama)

> They are very supportive of me and when I have to stay away from work they visit me and take care of my duty load. I am aware though, that behind my back some of them are saying, 'Why doesn't she go for medical boarding?' (Nonsizi)

For Zemvelo and Zethu, a different scenario emerged. Both disclosed their HIV status believing that the relational and environmental conditions were safe to do so. Regardless of policies referred above which offers protection to people living with HIV against discrimination,

both participants experienced discrimination and even expulsion as
Zemvelo recounts:

> My principal (male) could not put up with my condition and the school
> governing body (comprising of men only) could not deal with my illness.
> They made headlines with my HIV [status]. I was suspended from work
> without pay when the Department of Education discovered, through print
> media, that I had AIDS. My salary was blocked and I had to live without
> any income. (Zemvelo)

Nonsizi, Zethu and Zemvelo recall that when they first disclosed their
seropositive status they were promised support and friendship. However,
as they became ill, the friendship and support dwindled:

> They are very supportive of me and when I have to stay away from
> work, they visit me and take care of my duty load. I am aware though,
> that behind my back some of them are saying 'Why doesn't she go for
> medical boarding? (Nonsizi)

> To them (colleagues) HIV is a disease of the prostitutes. (Zethu)

> AIDS to them (educators) is a disease of lower class, not educators.
> (Zemvelo)

Our findings reveal that conditions for disclosure change and do
not necessarily remain fixed as suggested by Maile (2003). This is seen
in the experiences of the four participants in our study who initially
believed that the contexts were favourable for disclosure. However, as
time passed these conditions became less constructive. Maile (2003: 80)
states that disclosing one's HIV status is a difficult process. He mentions
three 'disclosure conditions'—individual, relational and environmental
conditions—under which educators reach a breakthrough before they
disclose their seropositive status. Individual conditions are when an individual is forced to undergo testing by the employer. For example, when
an individual applies for employment or as a condition for employment.
Relational conditions refer to the 'need for an enabling environment for
disclosure to take place'. Maile mentions that when teachers develop
relationships of trust they are more likely to divulge their HIV status.

Environmental conditions refer to the prevailing climate around HIV/AIDS. For example in South Africa, with the prevailing climate of HIV related stigma and its associated prejudice and discrimination in the workplace, the environment is not favourable for disclosure.

Our findings are also at variance with the findings of Vollenhoven's (2003) study with members from five school governing bodies and Theron's study (2005) on educators perceptions of educators HIV status. In the Vollenhoven (2003: 245) study, members of five school governing bodies were asked what they would do, if anything, to support teachers who are HIV positive. Participants responded that educators living with HIV should be supported, allowed to continue teaching and have a right to confidentiality and privacy. Similarly, the responses in Theron's survey study (Theron 2005: 57) revealed that educators perceive their co-workers living with HIV as 'people who may not be discriminated against' and 'to be treated with dignity'. This illustrates such a contrast between the espoused attitudes of the school governing body members (Vollenhoven 2003) and those of the educators (Theron 2005) to the experiences of the four educators living 'openly' with HIV.

The response from the community in which the educators worked was no better. The stereotypes, misinformation about people living with HIV/AIDS and discriminatory attitudes were abundant.

> The community that I work for thought only prostitutes could get HIV. Prostitutes are perceived as dirty people and this makes HIV a dirty disease that can never affect educators. (Zethu)

> They have different views and ideas about HIV and I feel they need a lot of teachings about HIV/AIDS. Nasty jokes are told about people living with HIV. (Nonsizi)

> Most people in my community are educated and they responded in a positive and supportive way. Other community members, more especially the illiterate people, are very rude to people living with HIV. They use ugly words like 'simnandi' (we are nice); we are suffering from 'iqhoksi' (high-heeled shoes). (Zama)

> When you approach a group of people on the street, you can see that they are gossiping about you, but when you get closer, they stop talking until you have walked past, then the conversation resumes. You try to ignore that but it is hurting. (Nonsizi)

In addition to experiencing discriminatory attitudes, Zemvelo also had to live with the knowledge that she must fear systematic harassment and violence. She reports:

> I was attacked and assaulted by local community members who had read the Zulu newspaper that reported, 'Lixoshiwe ithishelakazi elinengculazi' (a female teacher with AIDS has been expelled). They (the community) felt I had brought shame to their place of residence. I was living in fear of being attacked at home when we received threats of damaging our property.

Physical violence and systematic harassment has been a common experience for many people living with HIV/AIDS (Francis and Francis 2006; Francis 2004; Webb 1997) and is indicative of very high levels of prevalent stigma and prejudice. HIV/AIDS related stigma, with its subjective notions of shame, disgrace and cultural misinterpretations has resulted in the educators being given a spoiled identity by their colleagues, school managers and most of the community.

The learners in the educators' context responded differently. Learners were less judgmental and more supportive.

> I received letters of support from different schools in KwaZulu-Natal. Learners at my school were initially confused (by my ill-treatment at school and in the community), but gradually they understood. (Zethu)

> I enjoy teaching learners about this reality called AIDS. They give me their undivided attention, ask clarity-seeking questions and applaud my bravery. I receive cell-phone messages from them and letters and cards with personal messages. I identify with a number of them who look very healthy but are living with HIV. (Zemvelo)

One of the questions that emerged from our study was why the learners in the four participants contexts reacted differently to the participants than the others did. Two possible reasons can account for this. First, we can only speculate that our findings support the arguments put forth by Zisser and Francis (2006) that classroom interventions have had some success in increasing knowledge of HIV/AIDS among young people and therefore have been successful in lessening levels of stigma and its associated prejudice and discrimination. And second, in the absence of other prominent South African figures disclosing their seropositive status, it is possible that the learners recognise the educator's activism and view their disclosure as courageous.

Finally, we draw attention to how the four women participants have come to understand their role as educators in the struggle against HIV/AIDS, as their personal and professional responsibility. The high HIV/AIDS prevalence and infection rate, particularly among the youth, has lead to a need that all educators should integrate HIV/AIDS content into their subject areas with understanding. For this reason, the Department of Education has tasked educators with facilitating the Life Skills programme aimed at targeting behaviour change amongst youth.

The four participants in our study spoke candidly about how living with HIV challenged them to move beyond mere delivery of the Life Skills component of the curriculum to a more meaningful interpretation of the content. Unlike Ngcobo's concerns, noted above, the four participants highlighted issues of HIV/AIDS and sexuality and contributed significantly to the struggle against HIV in their teaching.

> I do justice when it comes to teaching sex education...I always use HIV/AIDS as a cross-cutting issue in my teaching. We also talk about dealing with grief and what death is, with my young learners. They have a lot to share about death, irrespective of their ages. (Zama)

> Being a walking and a living testimony has encouraged me to teach the truth. I tell it all as it is and feel good thereafter. Whenever I do my reflection for the day, I always check if I did justice in terms of empowering learners about AIDS. (Zemvelo)

> I was able to reach out to other AIDS sufferers from various workplaces, being an AIDS focal person for the Education Department. What made me influential was the fact that I identified with the people. (Nonsizi)

In particular, both their presence and their teaching challenge discriminating attitudes amongst learners.

> I teach them tolerance and the importance of caring for others, irrespective of what their condition is. (Zethu)

The four educators living 'openly' with HIV demonstrate their ability to draw on their personal challenges and experiences to educate learners and in the process benefit their community in terms of transforming mindsets about HIV and stigmatised groups. In this way, all four educators bring their own voices and experiences into the centre of the learning process related to HIV/AIDS. As one participant shared, 'It happened to me and I do not want it to happen to somebody else.'

NOTES

1. Names have been changed.
2. The study was approved by the Ethics Committee in the College of Humanities, UKZN and permission was obtained from the KZN Department of Education and Culture.

REFERENCES

Aggleton, P. 2001. Comparative Analysis: Research Studies from India and Uganda: HIV and AIDS related Discrimination, Stigmatisation and Denial, Geneva: UNAIDS.

Bujra, J. 2000. 'Targeting Men for Change: AIDS Discourse and Activism in Africa', *Agenda*, 44: 6–24.

Francis D.A. 2004. 'HIVism: A Pervasive System of Oppression', *Journal of Social Work*, 40(1): 61–71.

———. 2003. 'Conversations around Amagama Amathathu', *Perspectives in Education*, 21(3): 121–127.

Francis, D.A. and E. Francis. 2006. 'Raising Awareness of HIV-related Stigma and its Associated Prejudice and Discrimination', *South African Journal of Higher Education*, 20(1): 48–59.

Maile, S. 2003. 'Legal Aspects of the Disclosure of HIV Serostatus by Educators', *South African Journal of Education*, 23(1): 78–83.

Marshal, C. and G.B. Rossman. 1989. *Designing Qualitative Research*. Newbury Park: Sage Publications.

Mthembu, P. 1998. 'A Positive View', *Agenda*, 39: 26–30.

O'Sullivan, S. 2000. 'Uniting across Boundaries: HIV Positive Women in Global Perspective, *Agenda*, 44: 25–31.

Seidman, I.E. 1991. *Interviewing as Qualitative Research*. New York: Teachers College Press.

Selsky Andrew, 1999. *Charges Dropped in HIV Killing*. Johannesburg: The Associated Press, August 16.

Shisana, O., K. Peltzer, N. Zungu-Dirwayi and J. Louw. 2005. *The Health of our Educators: A Focus on HIV/AIDS in South African Public Schools*. Cape Town: HSRC Press.

Theron, L.C. 2005. 'Educator Perceptions of Educators' and Learners' HIV Status with a View to Wellness Promotion', *South African Journal of Education*, 25(1): 56–60.

UNAIDS. 2002. *A Conceptual Framework and Basis for Action: HIV/AIDS Stigma and Discrimination*. Geneva: UNAIDS.

UNICEF. 2001. *Stigma, HIV/AIDS and Prevention of Mother–to-Child Transmission: A Pilot Study in Zambia, India, Ukraine and Burkina Faso*. London: UNICEF.

Vollenhoven, W. 2003. 'How School Governing Bodies in South Africa Understand and Respond to HIV/AIDS', *South African Journal of Higher Education*, 23(3): 242–247.

Webb, D. 1997. *HIV and AIDS in Africa*. London: Pluto Press.

Whiteside, A. 1993. 'The Impact of AIDS on Industry in Zimbabwe', in S. Cross and A. Whiteside (eds), *Facing Up to AIDS: The Socio Economic Impact in Southern Africa*. New York: St Martins Press.

Whiteside, A. and C. Sunter. 2000. *AIDS: The Challenge for South Africa*. Cape Town: Tafelberg Publishers.

World Bank. 2002. *Education and HIV/AIDS: A Window of Hope*. Washington: The International Bank for Reconstruction and Development, The World Bank.

Zisser A. and Francis, D. 2006. 'Youth Have a New Attitude but are They Talking About It?', *African Journal of AIDS Research*, 5(2): 2–20.

11

Children Left Behind: Voices (Ukhuhebeza)[1] of HIV+ Mothers

Nirmala Gopal and *Reshma Sookrajh*

INTRODUCTION

While developing countries account for approximately 90 per cent of new infections, sub-Saharan Africa bears the largest burden of the HIV/AIDS epidemic (Taylor 1998). Taylor further asserts that over two-thirds of all the people in the world, nearly 21 million men, women and children, are in sub-Saharan Africa, and 83 per cent of the world's AIDS deaths have occurred in this region. An estimated 87 per cent of the world's children living with HIV are in Africa. Taylor describes the HIV epidemic in Southern Africa as explosive. According to the UNAIDS Report on the global HIV/AIDS epidemic (UNAIDS 2000), the number of new infections in most sub-Saharan countries during 1999 was 4 million, AIDS is now the leading cause of death in sub-Saharan Africa. In 2000, 25.3 million Africans were estimated to be living with the disease, 3.8 million of whom were infected with HIV during that year. The 19 countries with the highest HIV prevalence in the world are in Africa (UNAIDS 2000).

Studies have revealed frighteningly high prevalence rates of infection among teenagers and women in their early 20s in various urban and rural areas in Africa (UNAIDS 2000). The Report further informs that in 7 of the 11 studies conducted more than one woman in five in her early 20s was infected with the virus. A large proportion of them will not live to see their 30th birthday.

Although ignorance, fear of ostracisation and inaccessibility to health care are some of the contributing factors that are responsible for posing practical challenges in ascertaining an accurate extent of the HIV/AIDS infection rate, the use of projection models has allowed South African researchers to estimate the level of HIV infection in the general population. Statistics generated indicate that approximately 5 million of the 43 million people in South Africa are currently HIV positive. The prevalence rate of HIV infection was 24.8 per cent at the end of 2001, while the national incidence rate in antenatal clinic attendees has hovered at 6.5 per cent for the past five years. In young women aged 20–30 years, the mortality rate has risen almost four-fold in the last five years Karim and Karim (2003).

The inevitable consequence of these infections is thousands of children orphaned by AIDS (UNAIDS 2000). According to the 1999 Progress of Nations Report (UNICEF 1999), South Africa is one of the seven countries where the number of children orphaned by AIDS between 1994 and 1997 increased by more than 400 per cent. In 2002, there was an estimation of 300,000 AIDS orphans in South Africa and it is predicted that by 2015 there will be almost 2 million AIDS orphans, an increase of over 600 per cent (Whiteside in Gow and Desmond 2002: xi). In the same year, Mtshali[2] indicated that KwaZulu-Natal[3] had an estimated 80,000 HIV/AIDS related deaths in 2001. In 2001, about 40,000 of our children were infected with HIV/AIDS by their mothers. It is estimated that possibly 36 per cent but as much as 40 per cent of our women giving birth are HIV+. In 2005, figures based on a sample of 16,510 women attending 399 antenatal clinics across all nine provinces by the South African Department of Health Study (Noble 2007), estimated that 30.2 per cent of the pregnant women were living with HIV with KwaZulu-Natal recording the highest figure of 39.1 per cent.

This chapter examines within a context of small scale research, the perceptions of eight HIV+ women, hospitalised in various areas in KwaZulu-Natal, on the impact of their HIV+ status on their lives generally and particularly on their children. An initial definition of AIDS orphans is examined, and then the focus moves to the voices of the selected women with special reference to concerns around declaring/denial of their HIV status, fear of ostracisation, cultural beliefs, poverty, knowledge of the HIV/AIDS epidemic, the lives of their children.

RESEARCH METHODOLOGY

This study was dictated and grounded in the manner in which women made sense of their medical and social circumstances and presents their experiences and understanding of their own lives as was communicated to the researchers. The focus presents the opinions of these women with minimal interpretation by the researchers.

An opportunistic sample of eight HIV+ women from hospitals in KwaZulu-Natal was used to respond to the key question asked, that is, what are the perceptions of HIV+ mothers of their lives, and especially that of their children? It also attempted to understand the day-to-day realities of these women and gain insights into their concerns around the educational, financial, social and psychological needs of their children. Each respondent was interviewed twice for approximately two hours at each interviewing session. The interviews were conducted in isiZulu[4] with the assistance of an interpreter. All interviews were tape recorded and subsequently transcribed and translated into English. Interviews were held intermittently and were interrupted because of respondents' need to attend to their babies. The ad hoc interviewing rooms were utilitarian in nature, that is, a 'dispensary' and therefore the interview process was constantly interrupted. The interviews had to be conducted only when the mental and physical constitution of the women was suitable. Such disturbances may have influenced respondents' comments.

This study examined the perceptions of eight HIV+ women from hospitals around KwaZulu-Natal, namely, King Edward VIII, Clairwood Provincial, McCord's Mission and Prince Mysheni. The women ranged in age from 19 to 31 years of age. The levels of education ranged from grade 5 to grade 12. With respect to the number of children each mother has, the data revealed the following: one mother had five children; two had one child each, three had two children each; and two had three children each. Seven of the mothers were single, and one was married. Two were employed and six were unemployed.

All respondents were assured confidentiality because of the highly sensitive nature of the issue.

VULNERABILITY OF AIDS ORPHANS

Perusal of literature has identified an inconsistency in the definitions of AIDS orphans:

- Maternal orphans: children who have lost their mothers.
- Paternal orphans: children who have lost their fathers.
- Double orphans: children who have lost both their parents.

The age range of orphans, according to the US Bureau of Census, 2002, is children under age 15 which is the traditional demographic cut-off point for childhood. However, in most countries, children do not reach the age of majority until 18 or later. UNAIDS defines AIDS orphans as children from 0–14 who lost their mother due to AIDS (Taylor 1998).

Francois Xavier Foundation an orphan institution in Switzerland, however, claims that after research conducted in nine rural villages in Uganda's Luweero District, it was decided that the definition of 'AIDS orphan' used by UNAIDS and other agencies excludes many children whose lives are severely affected by the HIV/AIDS pandemic while the parent is still alive. By excluding children who have lost their father and young people between the ages of 15 and 18, the UNAIDS definition fails to recognise many of the children rendered vulnerable by the pandemic. Hence, the need for the term 'virtual orphans', which, according to the Francois Xavier Foundation, includes children who, al-though not orphans according to the strict definition of the term, are subject to similar hardships as that experienced by orphans. This includes children whose both parents are sick with HIV/AIDS. This implies that for many AIDS orphans the true point of orphanhood may occur before either parent has died. Whiteside and Sunter (2000) argue that a child may experience stresses and have needs that the family cannot respond to when the parent falls ill and the family income decreases. Therefore, children may be orphaned prior to the death of the parent. In addition, these authors demonstrate that a child may be orphaned more than once: first, when the parents die, and second, when the subsequent caregiver, often the grandparents, die. The researchers suggest that this would effectively make these children *multiple orphans.*

In the context of this article, an AIDS orphan is defined as a child from 0–15 years who has either lost one or both parents, is heading or living in a household in which one or both parents are infected with HIV/AIDS. Although according to the South African law a child is described as being between 0 and 18 years, unless by law, majority is attained at an earlier age (Smart 2000).

Halkett (1999) and Harber (2000) have pointed out in many countries there will be adolescent and child-headed families where dying adults of AIDS would have to be attended to by children. This suggests that children have to now bear the economic, social and emotional burden of the family. Children who themselves need nurturing are now providing this to parents.

Households headed by orphans are becoming common in high-prevalence countries. UNICEF (1999) explains that children whose have been orphaned when their parents die, assume roles as the head of the household when the guardian, caregiver or grandparent dies. In such roles, these children are even more vulnerable to sexual abuse and may be forced into exploitative situations such as prostitution as a means of survival (Smart 2000).

UNICEF (1999) explains that deep-rooted kinship systems that exist in Africa and extended families have proved to be social safety nets for children who are vulnerable, that is, children who have been orphaned and have been resilient even in the face of major social changes. These networks are now being slowly eroded by the strain of AIDS. The UNAIDS Report on the Global HIV/AIDS epidemic reports that (UNAIDS 2000) as the number of orphans grow and the number of care-givers shrinks, traditional coping mechanisms, capacity and resources are stretched to breaking point. In most cases, those providing the care are already impoverished. It is likely that they themselves were dependent financially on the very son or daughter who has died of AIDS. Orphans, therefore, in these households run the risk of being malnourished.

AIDS DISCLOSURE

Eight women indicated that they would not disclose their HIV status to anyone. The reasons given for not disclosing to family, friends or the community are several. Many of the respondents feared that their lives were in danger, since the murder of Gugu Dlamini,[5] a young KwaZulu-Natal woman who disclosed her HIV status. A conspiracy of silence amongst women infected with HIV/AIDS does exist. According to Giese (2002: 62), the fear of disclosure makes it difficult for women to make informed decisions on choices such as breastfeeding, family planning and planning for the future of her existing children without raising suspicion about her HIV status. She is therefore forced into continued childbearing and breastfeeding which might significantly compromise the health of her children.

At least three of the eight women feared ostracisation and rejection by the community:

> I was living at my home. Another woman mentioned that she is HIV positive. I saw the people... they don't go near her, they say she is 'ungcobile'.[6] They will do the same to me and my children. I will be sad.

Smart (2000) explains that the stigma associated with disclosing an HIV diagnosis remains prevalent in many communities, and results in many ill and dying parents choosing not to disclose to their caregivers, families or children.

Similarly, Schreedhar (2000) claims that stigma and discrimination against people living with HIV/AIDS is widespread in India to the extent that a wife was thrown out of her house. The belief was that her HIV/AIDS status might jeopardise the chances of her brother-in-law procuring a decent bride.

For the South African scenario, Noble (2005) notes that the authorities are largely to blame:

> Social stigma associated with HIV/AIDS, tacitly perpetuated by the Government's reluctance to bring the crisis into the open and face it head

on, prevents many from speaking out about the causes of illness and deaths of loved ones and leads doctors to record uncontroversial diagnoses on death certificates... The South African Government needs to stop being defensive and show backbone and courage to acknowledge and seriously tackle the HIV/AIDS crisis of its people.

Fears that their children may suffer shame, rejection and social isolation was common in the responses: 'My first born will not be treated well if the people know. I have seen this happen in the community before' (R1).[7] 'If the community gets to know they will alienate my older child. At school she will have no friends' (R2).

People affected by HIV/AIDS suffer rejection and shame, because of the stigma attached to AIDS. According to UNICEF (1999) children may be denied access to schooling and health care, and may be denied their inheritance to property. Lovelife (2001) argues that the stigma and secrecy around HIV/AIDS exposes children to discrimination in their community and even their extended family.

At another level, the women fear that they may be derided or even harmed by their partners who may believe that they have been infected: 'I will never tell him because he is rude. I don't know what he will do to me. He comes to see the baby but I will never tell him' (R4). 'I am scared to tell him (her boyfriend). He will say I infected him' (R2).

According to Baylies (2000), the AIDS discourse moves from being viewed as hidden to blameworthy, and then as marginalised. Through the discourses of blame—'whether as prostitutes infecting their clients or mothers infecting their children, along lines characterised by Patton (1990) of women being treated variously as vaginas or uteruses, by Carovano (1991) as whores or mothers and, more gently by Sherr (1993) as vectors or vessels,' (cited in Baylies 2000: 1), these women are viewed as responsible for transmitting the virus.

Dorrington and Johnson (2002:17) maintain that South Africa remains a patriarchal society in spite of the new political dispensation in 1994, in which women are vulnerable to sexual abuse. In many cases, women have limited control over their sexual activity, and thus continue to be more vulnerable to HIV infection.

DEALING WITH CULTURAL AND SPIRITUAL BELIEFS

The mothers revealed the difficulties they experienced with having to deal with the conflict between modern medicine and cultural beliefs. Two of the women explained:

> The father of my baby says the nurses are lying to me. He went to a witchdoctor or Umthakathi, and that witchdoctor said I must leave the hospital and go home. There is something I must do at my boyfriend's house. He didn't tell me what. He just said the baby needs something from the ancestors. He only got this information while the baby and I were in hospital. (R5)

> My boyfriend says this is not AIDS. You see the isangoma, told my boyfriend that my ancestors, want me to be a sangoma that is why I am losing weight. The sangoma, says I must come and visit him, and then I will be okay. Even now I am not sick. (R6)

'I think my boyfriend has another girlfriend. She sent this thing to me. Now she thinks she can have him but I will never leave him.' (R7)

> The people where I live are jealous because I have a nice boyfriend. Now they don't want to see me happy and dressing well. They went to the witchdoctor and put the muti. I will get better and the witchdoctor will return the muti to them. They will suffer. (R8)

Four of the respondents believed that they were not infected with HIV/AIDS but instead believed they were bewitched as illustrated above. Van Dijk (2005) argues that the belief in witchcraft helps people give meaning to the things that happen to them. She further clarifies that such beliefs provide answers that science cannot provide such as explanation of the personal or the ultimate cause of illness. Attributing HIV infections to witchcraft may also help the bereaved family to avoid feeling stigmatised by their community (Campbell and Kelly 1995). In a survey by the Kaiser Family Foundation (2001) it was found that 13 per cent of the teenagers between the ages of 12 and 17 believed that traditional African medicine had a cure for AIDS. It is evident that illiteracy, geographical isolation or misinformation could be cited as reasons for ignorance of the basic facts of AIDS.

DENIAL OF HIV/AIDS STATUS

Five of the respondents deny of their HIV status. There was evidence that their cultural beliefs influenced their view. All the eight women appear to have a lack of knowledge, and misconceptions or myths about the disease. This is captured in the following responses:

> I still don't believe the nurse because when I was pregnant for my last born five years ago, the nurses at the clinic told me that I was HIV positive. The baby was born HIV negative, and I have never been sick since. How is it that there has been no suffering for five years. (R6)

A study of pregnant women in KwaZulu-Natal found that although more than 50 per cent had at least one infection of the reproductive tract, none volunteered symptoms of STD[8] (Sturm et al. 1998). A second problem is that even when symptoms occur, individuals will often not seek treatment, either because treatment is inaccessible or because the infection is not regarded as being serious.

KNOWLEDGE OF THE HIV/AIDS EPIDEMIC

All eight women obtained knowledge on HIV/AIDS from people and institutions outside of the school environment. There was no indication that they had any kind of formal exposure. None of them was educated about the epidemic at school. Five of the eight women had acquired knowledge from informal discussions in the community, workplace, clinics and hospitals, and the media in particular, the radio. 'I learnt about HIV at the clinic and on the radio' (R4). 'I learnt at the clinic and hospital and from the doctor' (R8). 'I heard the women in my community talk about it' (R2).

CONCERNS FOR THEIR CHILDREN

The mothers expressed concerns about whether their extended family members would be able to provide for their children. The financial circumstances of their extended families were poor. Although the women were of the view that the children could be cared for by grandmothers, uncles and aunts, they were very aware that this help might not be sustainable as resources are depleted. Two of the women felt that it was inevitable that the older children would have to drop out of school in order to work and care for the younger siblings. The women's responses provided a bleak picture of the future of the children which include poor schooling experiences, having to take on adult responsibilities at an early age and a lack of basic needs.

> The grandmother of the children will take care of them. She will get money from the children's father. But if he doesn't provide, the grandmother will have a problem. The children can't go to school if there is no money. This troubles me. My children won't get good jobs. I am afraid they will end like me. (R1)

> The uncles and granny can look after them. I know they are many but they can look after them. The granny may ask the first born to leave school and support the other ones. I am not sure how they will cope financially because they are seven altogether, and only two uncles are working. They are not paid well. The children may not have food to eat. I pray to God everyday about this. (R5)

> My mother is the only one who will care for them. She is getting a pension. My children will go to school if she has the money. The year she doesn't have money the children will stay at home. My mother did not have money to send me to school so I finished school in standard five. I am not sure that she will have money for clothes and food and school fees. (R7)

In investigating how the energy, expertise and traditions of mutual support among women can contribute to the struggle against AIDS, we have drawn on Ulin's (1992: 64) observation that: 'The solidarity of women in rural African communities may be their greatest source of strength for coping with the AIDS epidemic.'

Educational Concerns

Orphans are often the first to be denied an education when extended families do not have the financial resources to educate all the children in the household: 'My first born is in grade 6. She must leave school and find a job. If she doesn't do this then all the others will go through a difficult time' (R2). 'The first born girl who is fourteen years old takes care of the other children, and on days when I am very sick she stays away from school and cares for me. She also cleans the house and takes care of the younger children' (R1).

Studies in Uganda and Zambia (UNICEF 1999) have shown that following the death of one or both parents, the chance of orphans going to school is halved and those who do go to school spend less time there than they did formerly. Webb (1997) suggests that these child-headed households have their own unique problems such as poverty, lack of supervision and care, poor nutrition, disruptive educational experiences, lack of adequate medical care, psychological problems, disruption of normal childhood and adolescence, exploitation, early marriage, stigmatisation and discrimination, poor housing and child labour. Webb also suggests that AIDS orphans drop out of school, particularly in cases where caregivers cannot afford to provide uniforms, food, school shoes, school fees and other basic needs. AIDS orphans also drop out of school as a result of stigmatisation, rejection and isolation by other students, and occasionally by teachers. Coombe (2000) argues that in the South African context, many AIDS orphans after the death of their parents are increasingly absent from school. They are also distracted owing to the fact that they will have to move long distances to find new homes, and because of illness, poverty, lack of motivation and trauma. The dearth of studies on AIDS orphans in South Africa suggests a gap in empirical evidence on the correlation between the absence of the parent and school attendance as estimated by US Bureau of Census, 2002 (Eun Jung Cahill Che 2000).

Another social discourse that appears to be emerging is that AIDS orphans are not repeatedly absent from school as not a consequence of the absence of the parent but as a consequence of the financial demands made by the school in terms of school fees although legislation has it that no learner may be denied access to learning on the basis of non-payment of fees. It would appear that disempowerment of disadvantaged communities creates a situation whereby caregivers accept rather than question administrative injustices.

According to Giese (2002), children living in child-headed households thus typically live in conditions of poverty, without adequate adult supervision and suffer from hunger and stunting—these children have reduced opportunities for education, limited access to health and welfare services and no access to social security:

> My children have become responsible around the house. They complete adult chores. I am very proud of them but it makes me sad that when they are supposed to be enjoying themselves as children, they now have to do adult work. (R5)

Giese (2002: 64) further suggests that if suitable caregivers are not available, some children may become responsible for the care of younger siblings, living in child-headed households. The problem of child-headed households is poorly understood and data on the number of children currently living in child-headed households is scant (Statistics South Africa 2001).

Support for Learners in Schools

With respect to their children's knowledge about AIDS, the mothers expressed the concern that schools are not playing a role in educating their children around issues of sexuality and HIV/AIDS. The women felt that there were deficiencies in the system around AIDS education.

The Department of Education has developed a National Policy on HIV/AIDS for Learners and Educators in Public Schools (Department of Education 1999). The policy states that learners and students must receive education about HIV/AIDS and abstinence in the context of life-skills education on an ongoing basis. The policy explains that the purpose of education about HIV/AIDS is 'to prevent the spread of HIV infection, to allay excessive fears of the epidemic, to reduce the stigma attached to it and to instil non-discriminatory attitudes towards persons with HIV/AIDS.' The policy states that programmes should include age and context appropriate knowledge and skills in order that learners may adopt and maintain behaviour that will protect them from HIV infection.

All the eight mothers indicated that they were unaware of support structures in schools for learners. There are no guidance counsellors or identified teachers that learners may confide in when in need of emotional support. Vally (2000) explains that loss of caregivers, either through prolonged illness or death, creates myriads of problems for the young children especially since children generally lose a stable care centre. The National Policy on HIV/AIDS for Learners and Educators in Public Schools (Department of Education 1999) states that in the primary grades, the regular educator should provide education about HIV/AIDS, while in secondary grades, the guidance counsellor would be the appropriate educator. The policy also stresses the need for the educators selected to offer this education to be specifically trained and supported by the support staff responsible for life-skills and HIV/AIDS education because of the sensitive nature of the learning content. The policy further states that the educators should feel at ease with the content and should be role models with whom learners and students can easily identify.

CONCLUSION

Both men and women are affected by AIDS, and in the context of this chapter, women particularly so, given how gender relations configure with sexual behaviour and economic security (Baylies 2000). AIDS also exposes women's vulnerability. From the data it can be said that in various ways, socio-economic position, gender, age and marital status 'intertwine to create a complex web of vulnerability' (Baylies 2000:13).

Ankrah (1991) describes women as a 'subordinate sector' in referring to their low status and powerlessness in connection with HIV. For Hamlin and Reid (1991: 3), it is precisely the link between powerlessness and risk of HIV which is the key to understanding the sources of women's vulnerability. From the voices of HIV+ women, it is evident that the context, content, nature and specificity of such powerlessness varies, and reflects a general failure in these womens' capacity to secure their needs and that of their children.

NOTES

1. An IsiZulu term used to describe whispering.
2. Premier of KwaZulu-Natal, State of the Province address on 25 February 2002, (Mtshali 2002).
3. KwaZulu-Natal is one of the nine provinces in South Africa.
4. IsiZulu is one of the official languages of the country and is the dominant language of the people in KwaZulu-Natal.
5. Gugu Dlamini (1962–1998) was a South African woman from KwaMancinza, a town in eastern KwaZulu-Natal province, who was stoned and stabbed to death after she had admitted in a Zulu language radio on World AIDS Day that she was HIV+. Retrieved from Wikipedia 2007.
6. An IsiZulu term for dirty.
7. R1, R2, R3, and so on, refers to Research Participants.
8. See South African Department of Health (Pembrey 1999) report on the relationship between STD and HIV prevalence.

REFERENCES AND SELECT BIBLIOGRAPHY

Ankrah, E.M. 1991. 'AIDS and the Social Side of Health', *Social Science and Medicine*, 32(9): 967–980.
Baylies, C. 2000. 'Perspectives on Gender and AIDS in Africa', in C. Baylies and J. Bujra (eds), *AIDS, Sexuality and Gender in Africa: Collective Strategies and Struggles in Tanzania and Zambia*, pp. 1–25. London and New York: Routledge.
Campbell, T. and M. Kelly. 1995. 'Women and AIDS in Zambia: A Review of the Psycho-social Factors Implicated in the Transmission of HIV', *AIDS Care*, 7(3): 365–373.
Carovano, K. 1991. 'More than Mothers and Whores: Redefining the AIDS Prevention Needs for Women', *International Journal of Health Services*, 21: 131–142.
Coombe, C. 2000. 'Managing the Impact of HIV/AIDS on Education in South Africa'. Presentation for the Centre for the study of AIDS, University of Pretoria.
Department of Education. 1999. *National Policy on HIV/AIDS, for Learners and Educators in Public Schools and Students and Educators in Further Education and Training Institutions*. Pretoria: Department of Education.

Dorrington, R. and L. Johnson. 2002. 'Epidemiological and Demographic', in J. Gow and C. Desmond (eds), *Impacts and Interventions: The HIV/AIDS Epidemic and the Children of South Africa*, pp. 111–14. Pietermaritzburg: University of Natal Press.

Eun Jung Cahill Che. 2002. 'Left Behind: AIDS Orphans by the Millions', *International Herald Tribune*, April 17.

Giese, S. 2002. 'Health', in J. Gow and C. Desmond (eds), *Impacts and Interventions: The HIV/AIDS Epidemic and the Children of South Africa*, pp. 59–77. Pietermaritzburg: University of Natal Press.

Gow, J. and C. Desmond (eds). 2002. *Impacts and Interventions, The HIV/AIDS Epidemic and the Children of South Africa*. Pietermaritzburg: University of Natal Press.

Halkett, R. 1999. *HIV/AIDS and the Care of Children*. Braamfontein: Republic of South Africa.

Hamlin, J. and E. Reid. 1991. 'Women, the HIV Epidemic and Human Rights: A Tragic Imperative', HIV and Development Programme. Issues paper #8, UNDP. Available online at http://www.undp.org/hiv/issues.htm (downloaded on December 2005).

Harber, M. 2000. 'Who will Care for the Children? Social Policy Implications for the Care and Welfare of Children Affected by HIV/AIDS in KwaZulu-Natal', Report No. 17, University of Natal.

Hirschowitz, R., W. Sekwati and D. Budlender. 2000. 'October Household Survey 1999', Statistical Release PO317, Statistics South Africa, Available online at http://www.statssa.gov.za (downloaded on 27 June 2006)

Kaiser Family Foundation. 2001. *Hot Prospects, Cold Facts: Portrait of a Young South Africa*. Johannesburg: Lovelife.

Karim, A. and Q. Karim. 2003. 'CAPRISA Researchers Discuss the Challenges and Options Facing South Africa in the Run-up to the Introduction of Antiretroviral Therapy in Resource Constrained Settings'. Available online at http://www.caprisa.org/Newsletters/November2003_Newsletter.pdf. (downloaded on 27 June 2006).

Lovelife. 2001. *Impending Catastrophe Revisited: An Update on the HIV/AIDS Epidemic in South Africa*. Cape Town: Remata Bureau and Printers.

Mtshali, L. 2002. 'State of the Province Address on 25 February 2002'. Available online at http://www.afrol.com/Countries/South_Africa/documents/mtshali_aids_2002.htm (downloaded on January 2007).

Noble, R. 2005. 'South Africa Needs to Face the Truth About HIV Mortality', *The Lancet*, 365(9459): 12–18.

———. R. 2007. 'South Africa HIV & AIDS Statistics', Available online at http://www.avert.org/safricastats.htm (downloaded on March 2007).

Patton, C. 1990. *Inventing AIDS*. New York: Routledge.

Pembrey, G. 1999. *HIV and AIDS in South Africa: Averting HIV and AIDS*. Department of Health, South Africa.

Schreedhar, J. 2000. India's Positive People (INP+) Unite against Discrimination: Building partnerships, impact on HIV *Family Health International Implementing AIDS Prevention and Care (Impact) Project*, 2(1): 11–23.

Sherr, L. 1993. 'The. Family and HIV Disease', *AIDS Care*, 5: 3–4.

Smart, R. 2000. 'Children Living with HIV/AIDS in South Africa: A Rapid Appraisal', *International Conference on AIDS*, July 9–14, Pretoria.

Sturm, A., D. Wilkinson, N. Ndovela, S. Bowen and C. Connolly. 1998. 'Pregnant Women as a Reservoir of Undetected Sexually Transmitted Diseases in Rural South

Africa: Implications for Disease Control', *American Journal of Public Health*, 88(8): 1243–1245.

Taylor, V. 1998. *HIV/AIDS and Human Development*. Pretoria: Amabhuka Publications.

Ulin, P. 1992. 'African Women and AIDS: Negotiating Behavioural Change', *Social Science and Medicine,* 34(1): 63–73.

UNAIDS. 2000. 'Report on the Global Epidemic'. Geneva: UNAIDS.

UNAIDS/WHO. 2004. 'Report on the Global AIDS Epidemic'. Available online at http://www.unaids.org/bagkok2004/GAR2004html/GAR2004_07_en.htm (downloaded on January 2007)

———. 2005. 'AIDS Epidemic Update'. Available online at http://www.unaids.org/epi/2005/doc/report_pdf.asp (downloaded on February 2007).

UNICEF. 1999. 'Children Orphaned by AIDS: Frontline Responses from Eastern and Southern Africa'. New York: UNICEF.

Vally, S. 2000. 'Reassessing Policy and Reviewing Implementation: A Maligned or Misarranged System?' *Quarterly Review of Education and Training in South Africa*, 7(2): 15–21.

Van Dijk, A. 2005. *HIV/AIDS Care and Counselling: A Multidisciplinary Approach*. 3rd edition. Cape Town: Pearson Education.

Webb, D. 1997. *HIV and AIDS in Africa*. Pietermaritzburg: University of Natal.

Wikipedia. 2007. 'List of HIV-positive People'. Available online at http://en.wikipedia.org/wiki/Gugu_Dlamini (downloaded on February 2007).

Whiteside, A. and C. Sunter. 2000. AIDS: *The Challenge for South Africa*. Cape Town: Human & Rousseau Tafelburg.

PART FOUR
Having Faith: Religious and Spiritual Journeys

It is remarkable how women hang on to their deep faith to overcome adversities in their lives. Religion and spirituality are among the deep roots of culture (Samovar and Porter 2004: 31) and they affect every aspect of cultural behaviour. This view is endorsed by Ishii, Klopf and Cooke (as cited in Samovar and Porter 2003: 31) who claim that religion 'is a deep and pervasive determinant of worldview' and that even 'those who reject religious faith still follow much of the religious heritage that influences their culture.' It is interesting to see how women's stories across diverse cultures nearly always touch on their spiritual and religious journeys.

In Part Four, stories highlight the role of spirituality as a source of courage. Sheila Chirkut's paper brings to the fore the culturally contextualised struggle that Hindu women in South Africa undergo in the workplace which does not recognise their multiple cultural roles and identities. Again, religion or worldview as one of the important elements of the deep structure of culture (Samovar and Porter 2004: 87) gives solace to those women who seek comfort in spirituality. Anniekie Ravhudzulo encourages women to take their rightful place in traditionally, male dominated careers such as the Church Ministry. Arlene Fester brings a grassroots perspective of a young 'coloured' women who was born during the Apartheid period in South Africa and who struggled against all odds (race, poverty, education, ethnicity, Apartheid) to find a place for herself in the new, democratic South Africa. The political landscape may have changed, but her continuing struggles exemplify the hefty burden of the Apartheid legacy. Fester's success is deeply embedded in her spirituality and faith.

REFERENCES

Ishlii, S., D. Klopf and P. Coooke. 2003. 'Our Locus in the Universe: Worldview and Intercultural Communication', cited in L.A. Samovar and R.E. Porter. (eds.), *Intercultural Communication: A Reader*, pp. 28–35. Belmong, California: Thomson Wadsworth.

Samovar, L.A. and R.E. Porter. 2004. *Communication Between Cultures*. 5th edition. Belmont, California: Thomson Wadsworth.

12

Cultural Identities of
South African Hindu Women*

Sheila Chirkut

INTRODUCTION

This study is premised with the recognition that most Hindu families
are gendered institutions and that the life experiences of working Hindu
married women are to a large extent influenced by their religio-cultural
contexts. My close interaction with working Hindu married women
in the Stanger area in the northern coast of KwaZulu-Natal in South
Africa provides the basis for the insights and understanding of the main-
tenance of their cultural identity through daily prayer and worship of
Goddess Lakshmi.[1]

Woven together in South Africa's diverse but rich religio-cultural
fabric, the Hindus try to express their set of beliefs, customs and traditions
in many ways such as through daily devotion and prayer to Goddess
Lakshmi. Hindus constitute a minority of the South African population
and they face many challenges in preserving their Hindu religious and
cultural identities within the content of the broader social, political,
educational and economic influences. This paper focuses on the role of
working Hindu married women whose lives centre around the religious
obligations of Hinduism. Women are charged with the responsibility of
helping to preserve the Hindu identity of their families and to transmit

*This paper was submitted by Sheila Chirkut prior to her sudden death in January 2008.
Her children, Subash and Shivani, gave permission to publish their mother's work
posthumously. Fay Patel assisted in preparing the paper for publication.

Hinduism to the next generation. Hindu married women attempt to strike a healthy balance among religious worship, family responsibilities and workplace commitments.

The multiple roles of Hindu women as wives, mothers and career women are a heavy burden. However, from an early age they are involved in various religio-cultural activities in the home and hence have internalised traditions, customs and rituals such as carrying out daily devotion in the home. The preliminary interviews revealed that working Hindu married women perceive themselves in a variety of ways in terms of dress, language, food, religion and culture because they are strongly influenced by their traditional value system.

Hindus believe in monotheism—the belief in the One Ultimate Reality. The One Ultimate reality is known as Brahman[2] who assumes various manifestations and forms because of His various functions and attributes. The different aspects are symbolised by many Gods and Goddesses. According to the scriptures, Trimurthi[3] is the three-fold diety—Brahma,[4] the Creater; Vishnu,[5] the Preserver; and Shiva,[6] the Destroyer. Hindus believe that on several occasions when the world is threatened by evil, in order to preserve the universe, Vishnu has been incarnated as a human being or in other forms (Kuppusami 1983). For many Hindus the Ultimate Divine Reality is personalised as either the Supreme Gods of the Trimurthi or the Supreme Goddess—Shakti.[7] Hinduism is unique among world religions in giving a significant place to the worship of the female aspect of God. Shakti can be regarded as manifesting Herself in a variety of forms, both as benign such as Lakshmi and Saraswati[8] or fierce such as Durga[9] and Kali[10] to name a few.

With reference to the interdependence of gender, Hindu religion and culture, many writers (Duley and Edwards 1986; Mohanlal 1998; Mukhopadhayay 1995; Sweetman 1995) claim that Hindu religion and culture are intertwined, interdependent and inseparable. Therefore, in Hinduism, there seems to be no absolute dividing line between religion and one's social activities. Mukhopadhayay (1995) further explains that religio-cultural practices reinforce the power of men by appealing to tradition. Mukhopadhayay further outlines that religion and culture are prescriptive about gender roles. Thus, this study further explores how power relations in patriarchal Hinduism is exercised during the daily prayer and provide explanations for the changing identities of Hindu married women.

Linking the culture, religion and gender discourse is the concept of patriarchy because Hinduism is largely patriarchal in its approach in human society, and is conducive to many social inequalities that most societies have suffered in the past and continue to suffer (Kumar 2000). Women had to be dependent on their fathers, then their husbands and after that on their sons. Bhopal (1997) explains that private patriarchy is within the household where women have to follow the cultural strands of acceptable behaviour such as modest dressing, being submissive and subordinate to mention a few. In public spheres, these ideas of culture are reinforced and are also replaced by the state and labour market.

THE COMING OF INDIANS TO SOUTH AFRICA

The experiences of the early indentured labour groups led to many different ways of expressing their identity. Rukmani (2005) points out that to which ever countries Hindus emigrated to, they had to find strategies to negotiate their identities. Many of the colonial era Hindu immigrants, who arrived 145 years ago, were illiterate and were from small villages. They brought with them to the South African Diaspora the memories and knowledge of their religio-cultural practices prevailing in their villages. In order to nurture these values, they prayed daily to Goddess Lakshmi and rigorously celebrated festivals. In the words of Rukmani (2005), many scholars of the diaspora and sociological studies have emphasised the preserving and nurturing nature of women. She further explains that it is the women who carry the traditions of religio-cultural practises and rituals to the places they move to and make their homes.

The indentured Indians were a highly heterogeneous population. Of these many Hindi[11] speaking Hindus came from the northern areas of India from the United Provinces of Agra, Oudh and Bihar who emigrated through the port of Calcutta (Dupelia-Mesthrie 2000). A large number of Tamil[12] and Telugu[13] speaking Hindus also came from southern India from the Madras Presidency, Mysore and the surrounding areas by way of Chennai (Chirkut 1993). From 1875 onwards, a second stream of immigrants, the 'Passenger Indians' or traders followed the indentured labourers. The passengers Indians were predominantly Gujarati[14] speaking Hindus and Urdu[15] speaking Muslims mainly from Bombay and Surat in western India.

RESEARCH STUDY

This section presents data from in-depth interviews with working Hindu married women in the Stanger area of KwaZulu-Natal that has a predominantly Indian population. Weedon (1987) argues that post-structuralist theory provides a suitable framework to understand and analyse the impact of culture on the cultural identity of Hindu married women. It also offered various mechanisms to understand the nature and relationship of gender roles and power relations to the religious and cultural identity of Hindu women.

Twenty-four working Hindu married women, in the age range of 25–60 years in the research made up a purposeful sample.

The study revealed that the role of Hindu married women as mothers is very important in the preservation and survival of the Hindu value system. In Hinduism, the essence of womanhood is concentrated in motherhood. She is trained from early childhood in participating in daily devotions in the home by her mother who was trained by her mother in exactly the same way by her mother and so on right down through history. The mother interacts with the children and imparts to them the culture, tradition and customs of the family unit and society (Singh 2004). South African Hindus have suffered greatly under Apartheid—in education, business, politics and religion. Amidst all this, it is the Hindu wife and mother who have solicitously maintained the customs and traditions brought from India such as daily prayer in the home.

Today the traditional role of the Hindu woman has definitely changed, not through disregard for religion, customs and beliefs, but increasingly from socio-economic factors.[16] Often wives are simply forced to work to supplement the family income. In doing so, she experiences independent self-worth and healthy self-assertiveness. This new found sense of independent worth does not imply the promotion of indifference to culture, and the Hindu woman's sacred role as wife and mother is not diminished but kept alive in many ways such as her daily prayer. Working wives and mothers have little time to relax because of the multiplicity of their roles. Despite their daily chores, many of the interviewees agreed that they achieved fulfilment and joy in their traditional roles as wives and mothers. They also indicated that prayer on a daily basis in Hindu homes is gender related. Worshiping Goddess Lakshmi, which they see as a component of their cultural identity, strengthens Hindu women's role as cultural custodians.

In many Hindu families, roles and responsibilities are gendered. Because of this, many of the women in the study believe that their forebears institutionalised gender roles and they see their expression in offering daily prayer with particular reference to Lakshmi as a way of maintaining their Hindu identity within the patriarchal system. However, the research revealed that some working Hindu married women, through empowerment and advancement in education are breaking away from the clutches of patriarchy and bringing about modifications in cultural practices. Another reason cited by many of the interviewees for modifications in cultural practices was the absence of the joint family system (Metha 1970).

An examination of the interviewee's narrations revealed that they perceived the construction of gender identity as a means of maintaining their cultural identity. The women in the study also revealed that cultural identification was not a gender role expectation of Hindu men. The general perception is that the construction of masculinity in Hinduism allows men to exempt themselves from certain cultural practices in the home such as lighting of the prayer lamp. Traditionally it was and still is the role of Hindu females to light the prayer lamp every evening.

DISCUSSION

The responses elicited from the interviewees revealed that religio-cultural activities such as daily prayer play significant roles in the lives of Hindu married women and are some of the most important sources of shaping and reinforcing their image and cultural identity (Bhopal 1997). As mothers, working Hindu married women have the innate feeling of motherly duty to pray for the prosperity and good health of their families.

Almost all Hindu homes have either a special room or a corner where puja[17] is performed. All the interviewees indicated that they either have a special room or a corner in which there is a family shrine. Pouring oil into and lighting the sacred lamp, decorating the deity and lamp with flowers, Hindu women render their prayer by bringing their hands together in front of the deity and uttering the *mantras*[18] or recite their prayers in either vernacular or English. Prabhakaran's (1994) research claims that it is traditional Hindu cultural habit and a priority for the majority of Hindus in the diaspora to have a small puja place in a separate specified place in the home. I observed this in the homes of all the interviewees for this study. The shrine contains images or *murti*s of their favourite deities. For interviewee A and all the women in the study, beginning the day with a definite routine of prayer sets the tone for the day. This indicates the acknowledgement of the Divine and the commitment towards maintaining the daily religious tradition. The striking feature that emerges is the sincerity and loyalty of these women in mothering, caring and praying for the welfare of their families. Findings of the study on daily prayer confirms, earlier cited findings by Mohanlal (1998), Prabhakaran (1994) and Singh (2004) who found that daily ritualistic worship by Hindu married women such as lighting the prayer lamp (dedicated to Goddess Lakshmi) serve to retain their cultural identity. Numerous studies (Barot et al. 1999; Bhadouria 1995; Ghadially 1998; Kumar 2000; Metha 1970) claim that motherhood is the greatest glory of Hindu women. In a patriarchal society like Hinduism, marriage and motherhood are considered mandatory for fulfilment and identity formation (Ghadially 1998), hence, the emphasis on prayer for the family's welfare.

From an early age, Hindu women are involved in various aspects of religious activities and are given a solid grounding in domestic rituals. This is congruent with Singh's (2004) research on Hindu women in South Africa which confirms that their mothers and grandmothers prepare them for motherhood, a role in which their identity finds completion.

This is also in keeping with the Zulu tradition where mothers and grandmothers prepare young females for motherhood. Modern working Hindu married women have after all been exposed to the teachings of their mothers and foremothers who had deeply internalised traditions such as ideas of ritualistic daily worship and relationships with God. In a bid to satisfy their inner urge of (tradition) motherly duty, the women in the study are constantly conscious of their religious responsibility. Thus Hindu married women in maintaining their status, see it as their religious duty as mothers to pray for the welfare of their families. In this context, the belief in the ideals of motherhood gives them inner peace, satisfaction and freedom within the bounds of duty towards their spouse and children. Ruddick (1994) argues that the peacefulness with which mothers are credited is usually a sweet and appeasing gentleness. She further explains that maternal peacefulness is a way of fighting as well as living, as angry as it is gentle. This trait is also reflected in the various female deities such as Mother Durga who is the goddess of warfare and destruction, yet protects the innocent.

Sokoya (2003) expresses the ideology of motherhood, as a mystique, which I believe is inherent in Hindu society because the trials and tribulations Hindu women go through as mothers, is indeed a mystery. Although the burdens of motherhood are most of the time heavy, for working Hindu married women, motherhood is still viewed as central to a woman's identity. Sokoya's (2003) research on Nigerian women reveals motherhood as a natural and unchanging aspect of being a woman, which is true in the Hindu context as well. An interesting inquiry would be to determine to what extent motherhood is embraced as a fulfilment of the women's personal identities or empowerment and how much is based on the expectations of family and society.

The narratives of the interviewees are congruent with Ghadially's (1998) argument and confirm her earlier findings that many religio-cultural practices in Hinduism focus on the prosperity and the well-being of families. She further maintains that woman's rights seek protection and general prosperity of their families. The religious practices of Hindu women are influenced largely by conceptions and perceptions of the family and society of her as a female which provides justification for her not being an active participant in the more significant powers exercised by men. Yet in the domestic sphere, women are vital religious practitioners who have developed a subsidiary religious realm of traditions. Moreover, Hindu women's rights relate to their dual roles as wives and mothers. The foregoing discussion demonstrates that rights and duties become synonymous.

Women conform to this, believing it to be an important determinant of female honour, status and identity. This remains true in South Africa today despite increasing westernisation and secularisation of the Hindu community. The embracing of wifehood and motherhood by Hindu women as a mark of status and respect coincides with the findings of Metha's (1970) and Mohanlal's (1998) researches on Hindu women, suggesting that wifehood and motherhood are viewed as central to their identity. Social practices based on religion and traditions have placed women as inferior and subordinate to men. It is believed that ideal Hindu wives are to be submissive and subservient, and must not question or debate such social practices. Each family conducts rituals in a manner that is appropriate and handed down by their ancestors. The Hindu woman is bound by marriage to respect and follow the family tradition. This in turn accords her respect and honour from her husband and his family for keeping and maintaining the tradition and inducing the children to follow the religio-cultural practices. I see Hindu women as the stereotype of the dutiful wife, maintaining the harmonious atmosphere in the home and remaining dependent on their husbands for their status of wifehood and motherhood to complete their identity. This is so because in Hindu tradition marriage is considered important in the life of a woman. In the course of time, matrimony is followed by maternity. Repeated childbearing makes her dependent on the husband for some time.

According to the laws of Manu, Hindu women are bound by marriage to be dependent on their husbands (Singh 2004).

Findings of the study revealed that religion and culture give Hindu women a positive sense of cultural and religious identity. However, the impact of factors such as the social structures of male dominance that oppress women is not clearly seen by many women. They do not realise that they are subjected to patriarchal exploitation because it is accepted naturally that they have to abide by the rules of male authority. Hindu women experience a form of patriarchy where the traditional ideology operates powerfully in the home, which is the private sphere. Patriarchy is exhibited by the internalised ideology of gender roles, entrenching the dominance of men and subordination of women. This ideology plays a strong influence in the continuation of the heritage of traditions such as the glory, respect and status of motherhood and wifehood. How long will Hindu women be the carriers of this patriarchal ideology? Will our daughters carry the torch of patriarchy? However, modern Hindu women, through empowerment and advancement in education are breaking away from the clutches of patriarchy. The balance could change if motherhood/wifehood were freed from the subordination aspect of gender relations, that wifehood/motherhood are positive and open doors to power rather than limiting them to these two roles. Then they will not have to resist alternatives of change (or emancipation) to maintain their honour and dignity.

The prayer room or shrine indicates that the homes of these Hindu women in many respects have been patterned according to the traditional Hindu way. But from a gender perspective, it is the wife and mother who propitiate the deity. However, women have to carry this tradition because women are seen as the custodians of socio-cultural and religio-cultural values. The question is why do women have to take on this responsibility and not the men? I assert that women believe in finding a positive meaning in doing this in terms of societal expectations, to maintain their respect through the role of wifehood and motherhood and the role of internal instinct, which is probably exploited by males. It is perhaps the only niche where they are given precedence, and within the confines of patriarchy they find their religio-cultural identity through exploiting the niche.

The lighting of the sacred lamp, which is usually conducted every evening by the women, is a pattern of tradition among the Hindu community handed down for generations. I maintain that it is the respectability of motherhood in the Hindu tradition that is socio-culturally constructed that expects Hindu women to light the lamp. The majority of the women echoed a common sentiment, 'I am the Lakshmi (meaning light and mother) of my home.' Goddess Lakshmi is the epitome of Hindu women and every home is the dwelling place of Mother Lakshmi (Sivananda 1987). Hinduism holds motherhood in high esteem

(Bhadouria 1995; Bhopal 1997; Ghadially 1998; Metha 1970). These women, being mothers, feel closer to Mother Lakshmi. It was evidenced during the interviews that all the women were in agreement with identifying themselves with Mother Lakshmi as all mothers want peace, prosperity and good health (which Goddess Lakshmi represents) for their families. What I think the women are saying is that, 'I am like Mother Lakshmi.' Hindu women believe that Mother Lakshmi cares in the same way as any mother does, giving eternal care, protection and nourishment. As stated by the women in this study, there are remarkable similarities with the findings of Mohanlal's (1998) research, which revealed Hindu women's identification with Goddess Lakshmi. My analysis is that as a child one's world is generally centred on a loving mother from whom one receives love and care. One turns to one's mother for comfort and cling to her for protection. She would sacrifice herself in the sense that she deprives herself of personal needs such as clothing, food, rest and sleep. Ruddick 1994 confirms that in many societies, the ideology of motherhood defines maternal work as a consuming identity requiring sacrifices of health, pleasure and ambitions for the well-being of children. Naturally one feels freer with one's mother than one's father. From a gender perspective, fathers are viewed as harsh disciplinarians and more forbidding and intimidating.

Mohanlal (1998) maintains that Goddess Lakshmi represents the fire in the home which is kept burning through the symbol of the God lamp which is a distinct feature of every Hindu household. This in more ways than one reflects the statements of Metha (1970) and Bhadouria (1995) when they point out that with all the restrictions placed on Hindu women, they enjoy a high status in the home because she is referred to as a Goddess and the most stable force in the home, making women's bondage sweeter and more appealing. But the practice dictates otherwise and it can be seen as the underlying ideology of female inferiority, which is disguised in an idealised image of wife and mother. According to Sivananda (1987), the Vedas[19] describe Mother Lakshmi as one of the most popular Deities in all Hindu homes. This assertion prompts me to say that the interviewees believe that identifying themselves with Mother Lakshmi, gives them a status in their homes. This belief reinforces the pattern of tradition, which has firmly established itself as transcendental reality. The extent to which the gender identity is forged within the social rules of motherhood to achieve this status is under the guise of culture and religion in a traditionally based, male dominated culture, and in wider society that for centuries has suppressed the rights of women. Thus, it can be said the religious expressions of the Hindu women which lead them to developing faith is strongly influenced by traditional values which treat the women differently from men. This is cause for concern in the context of this discourse on gender dynamics, wherein women are constrained to relish and thrive on the selected gender roles, mitigated by euphemisms, which are thrust on them. Further investigation into this phenomenon could contribute to the development of post-structuralist feminism and religio-cultural theory. It could also involve discussion on the inexorability of biological process versus gender dynamics.

Another major festival when Goddess Lakshmi is worshipped is *Navaratri*. Navaratri is observed in honour of the consorts of the Trimurthi, when the Universal Mother is worshipped in three ways—as Durga or Kali, the consort of Shiva who is the destroyer; as Lakshmi, the consort of Vishnu who is the preserver; as Saraswati the consort of Brahma who is the creator. In the context as the consorts of the Trimurthi, the Divine Mother is noted for her submission to the male principle, acting as an essential undercurrent of creation. She is gentle, erudite and wise, a perfect wife and mother—the ideal Hindu female. Yet as Durga or Kali she is strong and independent. Although the different Goddesses are the manifestations of one and the same energy, these different forms are conceived in order to elucidate and emphasise the different functions they have to discharge.

Navaratri is celebrated all over India and in the Hindu diaspora in different ways but the basic aim of the celebration is the worship of Shakti (power and strength), meaning the Divine Mother in Her aspect as power. It is Mother Shakti that works through all of us. The nine days of Navaratri are equally distributed among the three manifestations (Durga or Kali, Lakshmi and Saraswati) and the tenth day, *Vijaya Dasami*, meaning victory is taken as the day of victory when evil was overpowered and banished by the Supreme Mother for the welfare and the continuous prosperity of the world (Maharaj 1994). The second three days of Navaratri are spent in the worship of Mother Lakshmi, the bestower of wealth and prosperity. The spiritual seeker however, is interested mainly in spiritual wealth; meaning divine qualities like love, compassion, good health, generosity and calmness which are really priceless and cannot be exhausted. On the last three days, devotees pray to Mother Saraswati, the bestower of divine knowledge. This marks the conclusion of Navaratri. The celebration of Navaratri takes place with great devotion by the women in the study with cultivation of the idea that every woman without distinction of caste, creed, or religion is but Shakti herself like the Goddesses including Mother Lakshmi.

CONCLUSION

The findings of the study revealed that the characteristics of Durga, Lakshmi and Saraswati have left their impact on the lives of Hindu women. The post-structuralist perspective helps to understand the impact of the significance of Lakshmi puja and how Hindu women uplift their status to identify themselves with God female. Feminist post-structuralism helps to theorise the conscious and unconscious thoughts and emotions of Hindu women and how they shape their socio-cultural lives. Moreover, Mohanlal (1998) maintains that identification of Hindu women with the Goddess Lakshmi and their elevation to supremacy at ritual times gives them respite from patriarchal structures. This is an important feature of women's psychological well-being as well (Sokoya 2003). Whilst identifying with the Divine Mother motivates Hindu women, it also supports their trust in their own power and in the power of other women. Perhaps a realisation of their own innate power makes them silently acquiesce in the male domination, just to keep the peace. As discussed in previous studies (Prabhakaran 1994; Mohanlal 1998; Singh 2004) Hindu women identify themselves by worshipping Goddess Lakshmi.

NOTES

1. The Hindu Goddess of health, wealth and prosperity; consort of God Vishnu.
2. Brahman is believed to be God, the Supreme Reality.
3. Trimurthi is the three-fold Deity—Brahma, the Creator; Vishnu, the Preserver; and Shiva, the Destroyer.
4. Brahma, a Hindu God, unlike Vishnu and Shiva is seldom worshipped.
5. Vishnu is believed to be one of the great of Hinduism.
6. Shiva is believed to be one of the great deities of Hinduism
7. Literally meaning energy. A name for the Goddess (as consort or as supreme being), which can be used generically.
8. The Hindu Goddess of knowledge and learning.
9. A Hindu Goddess, the slayer of demons.
10. A Hindu Goddess with fierce and destructive characteristics also regarded as the benevolent Mother.
11. One of the four main languages brought to South Africa by the indentured labourers from north India.
12. Tamil is one of the languages spoken by south Indians.
13. Telugu is one of the four main languages brought to South Africa by the south Indian Hindus.
14. Gujarati is one of the languages spoken by Hindus who came from western India.
15. Urdu is related to Hindi but with many Persian words. It is mainly spoken by the Muslims.
16. Personal communication of the author with R. Sitaram, Senior Research Associate (Professor), Department of Language, Literature and Linguistics. University of KwaZulu-Natal
17. Puja is worship to a deity and/or its visible image in an atmosphere of devotion.
18. Sacred utterances of the Lord's name.
19. These are Hindu scriptures written during the Vedic period.

REFERENCES

Barot, R., H. Bradley and S. Fenton (eds). 1999. *Ethnicity, Gender and Social Change*. London: Macmillan Press.

Bhadouria, G.S. 1995. *Women in Art*. Delhi: Agamkala Press.

Bhopal, K. 1997. *Gender, Race and Patriarchy*. London: Ashgate Publishing Limited.

Chirkut, S. 1993. 'Hindi Instruction in the Indian Primary Schools in South Africa'. MA Thesis, University of Durban-Westville.

Duley, M.I. and M.I. Edwards (eds). 1986. *The Cross Cultural Study of Women. A Comprehensive Guide*. New York: The Feminist Press.

Dupelia-Mesthrie, U. 2000. *From Canefields to Freedom*. Cape Town: Kwela Books.

Ghadially, R.(ed.). 1998. *Women in Indian Society*. London: Sage Publications.

Kumar, P.P. 2000. *Hindus in South Africa: Their Traditions and Beliefs*. Durban: University of Durban-Westville.

Kuppusami, C. 1983. *Religions, Customs and Practices of South African Indians*. Durban: Sunray.

Maharaj, K.L. 1994. 'Shakti Worship: What it means?', *The Hindu Horizon*, 8(1): 1–2.

Metha, R. 1970. *The Western Educated Hindu Woman*. London: Asia Publishing House.

Mohanlal, S.N. 1998. 'The Emergent Hindu Women in a Changing South Africa'. MA Thesis, University of Durban-Westville.

Mukhopadhayay, M. 1995. 'Gender Relations, Development Practice and Culture'. In *Gender and Development*, 3(1): 13–18.

Prabhakaran, V. 1994. 'The Religio-Cultural Dynamics of the Hindu Andhras in the Diaspora'. PhD Thesis, University of Durban-Westville.

Ruddick, S. 1994. *Mother Troubles: Rethinking Contemporary Maternal Dilemmas*. Boston: Beacon Press.

Rukmani, T.S. 2005. 'Women as Cultural Ambassadors in the Montreal Hindu Diaspora', *Nidan—International Journal for the Study of Hinduism*, 17.

Singh, C. 2004. 'Symbolism and Patterns of Tradition of South African Hindu Women in the Greater Durban Area'. PhD Thesis, University of Durban-Westville.

Sivananda, Swami. 1987. *Hindu Fasts and Festivals: Yoga Lessons for Children*. Vol. 1. Durban: 7 Sivananda Press.

Sokoya, G.O. 2003. 'Socio-Cultural Constructions of Gender Roles and Psychological Wellbeing in Farm-Families of Ogun-State, Nigeria: Exploring the Complexities'. PhD Thesis, University of Natal.

Sweetman, C. (ed.). 1995. *Woman and Culture*. Oxfam: Oxford.

Weedon, C. 1987. *Feminist Practice and Poststructural Theory*. Cambridge: Blackwell Publishers.

13

Spiritual Strength in Overcoming Adversity

Anniekie Ravhudzulo

INTRODUCTION

During the past 10 years, South Africans witnessed dramatic changes in their government and as a result, in their daily lives. In general, as South Africans, we feel that our country is going in the right direction, but we must still face the most important challenges that the government is trying to address such as unemployment, crime, HIV/AIDS and housing. Many people are hungry for strong and moral leadership in all the sectors of our country. This hunger leads to pressures which most men are threatened by successful women. We have a problem.

BACKGROUND

My position as a Christian woman is supported by the International Religious Freedom Report (2002, 2003 and 2004) released by the Bureau of Democracy, Human Rights and Labor, which contends that the Bill of Rights prohibits the Government from unfairly discriminating directly or indirectly against anyone on the ground of religion, and it states that persons belonging to a religious community may not be denied the right to practice their religion and to form, join, and maintain religious associations with other members of that community. Cases of discrimination against a person on the grounds of religious freedom may be taken to the Constitutional Court.

With religious freedom comes responsibility and with responsibility, accountability. We are accountable to our fellow man and above all we are accountable to God. South Africa, a country that suffered from three centuries of colonialism and five decades of apartheid, is proudly celebrated its first decade of freedom in 2004.

Leaders like Mandela, whom apartheid rulers jailed for 27 years, Mbeki, Chris Hani, Winnie Mandela and several others sacrificed their youth and social life to fight against white minority rule. Ten years after the collapse of Apartheid, South Africa, under the able leadership of Mandela (1994–1999) and followed by Mbeki, is emerging not only as a model democracy for developing nations, but also a regional power in Africa. South Africa is an exceedingly complex nation. It is a nation of surreal contradiction, between urban and rural, wealth and poverty, between the absolute beauty of the countryside and impoverishment of rural labourers.

WHAT IS RELIGIOUS FREEDOM?

The basic idea of freedom of religion is that no one, especially the government, is allowed to force religion on anyone else or prohibit anyone from practicing a religion. To force others to support a church or profess belief in a church's tenets is as much a violation of their civil rights as is preventing them from practising their religion. Religious freedom is the notion that people of religion can freely partake of the practices of their religion without opposition. This would not only include private devotions, but also acts of religious significance within the realm of government. Again, if we as a people do not understand what freedom of religion means, and where it comes from, it can be taken away from us by our own Democratic Government, and we would not even know it.

According to the Annual International Religious Freedom Report (1999) and International Religious Freedom Report (2002 and 2003) released by the Bureau of Democracy, Human Rights and Labor the Constitution provides for freedom of religion, and the government generally respects this right in practice. This freedom extends mere *freedom of thought* by adding the freedom of *worship* and the freedom of religious congregation, and has become regarded in the 20th century as one of the basic *human rights*.

In conclusion, from my point of view regarding religious freedom, the Church in each place must be free to define the mission it believes it has received from God. Likewise, individual Christians and other believers must be free to practice their faith in whatever manner they believe necessary, commensurate with their not violating the same freedom of others. Every religious organisation, formed or maintained by action in accordance with the rights of individual persons, has the right to determine its policies and practices for the accomplishment of its chosen purposes.

STUDY METHODS

Of the various designs available for data collection, I have decided to combine aspects of both qualitative and quantitative designs in the study because of the nature of the problem being investigated (Leedy 1993: 139). For this research, I chose the qualitative approach because the research procedures are not as strictly formalised, while the scope is more likely to be undefined and a more philosophical mode of operation is adopted (De Vos 1998: 15).

The advantages inherent in the design selected are their helpfulness and flexibility with respect to the organisation, presentation, interpretation and analysis of data. How qualitative researchers proceed depends on theoretical assumption (meaning and process are crucial in understanding human behaviour, collection of descriptive data is important and analysis is best done inductively) and on data collection traditions (participant observation, unstructured interviewing, and document analysis). This view provides the parameters, the tools and the general guide of how to proceed.

The case study is one of the research methods used in this study. The typical case study is an intensive investigation of one individual or a single small social unit such as a family or a school (Ary, Jacobs and Razavieh 1972: 286). The emphasis is on understanding why individuals do what they do and how behaviour changes as they respond to the environment. This requires a detailed study over a considerable period of time. The mainline and charismatic churches are cases included in this study. The case study method is an in-depth multifaceted investigation that uses qualitative research methods. When researchers study two or more subjects and settings, they are doing multi-case studies or multi-site studies. This has been the case in this study.

GENDER AND LEADERSHIP

One of the hottest issues in many churches today is the role of men and women within the church. For much of church history, male leadership was assumed, not only in the church, but also within government, society and family. Since 1994, gender roles have shifted in society and in many churches. As a result, churches are being challenged to re-evaluate their historic positions.

From the interviews I conducted with a sample of 50 women concerning gender and leadership the following are the findings:

- Interviewees indicated that male pastors undermine female pastors with the reason that God first created man and there after a woman. They further indicated that men base their argument on Genesis1: 7 forgetting Genesis 1: 27.
- Another finding was that male pastors think that God cannot call a woman into ministry. The interviewees mentioned that where there are female pastors, they are addressed as assistant pastors.
- There is a strong feeling that women could make a difference in the world by preaching Christianity, establishing churches and nurturing churches if God called them.

Many within churches have asked why we have traditionally allowed only males to become pastors or deacons (board members). I want to encourage women by saying, 'Nothing lasts Forever,' the struggle is over.

Between 1994 and 2004 transformation regarding leadership took place in the government, organisations, churches and ministries. Men are fearful of losing their control and authority over the church if they delegate competent women to leadership roles in the congregation.

'So God created humankind (*adam*) in his image… male and female he created them' (Genesis 1.27). 'There is no longer male and female; for you all are one in Christ Jesus' (Galatians 3.28).

In the church we often quote such verses, but in practice we deny them. Gender stereotypes are still upheld by many Christian communities. In many congregations women outnumber men, but they are often excluded from decision-making and assigned 'jobs' which are seen as an extension of home life— flower-arranging, cleaning, preparing meals, teaching at Sunday school, fundraising and charity. Women are placed in a lower position to the sidelines. Their visions, voices and values, which emphasise compassion, caring, cooperation, economic justice, diversities among women and respect for human rights, are not referred to.

My other concern regarding the gender issue is the way in which single people are treated right in the church by pastors and married people. They are considered as if they do not exist. That is the reason why I published a book entitled *Can a Single Woman be in a Ministry: Time for a Change*. Again I want to challenge all the churches by asking two questions: Who created single people? and where should they go? In my ministry, 'Nothing Lasts Forever Ministries of Hope', I preach the message that there is life after singleness and hurting. The findings from the interviews with single people regarding their commitment with God's work is as follows:

'We really want to be involved in the church of God.'

We thank God for having people like Dr Anniekie Ravhudzulo the Director and Founding Pastor of Nothing Lasts Forever Ministries of Hope in Limpopo and Gauteng Provinces, Mrs Violet Liremi the President of Women of Destiny in the Limpopo Province and Pastor Lydia Monareng the President of You Are Not Alone (YANA) women Ministries in Gauteng Province who empower us with powerful teachings on how to deal with singleness, fear and sex.

WOMEN IN LEADERSHIP IN SOUTH AFRICA

In South Africa a high proportion of women MPs is largely as a result of the African National Congress adopting a one-third quota for lists. Other parties also included women, and the result is that South Africa has among the largest percentage of women parliamentarians in the world (30 per cent). There has been a steady increase in the number of women ministers and deputy ministers in the South African Cabinet since the first democratic elections. Post 1999 elections, the cabinet consists of nine women ministers from a total of 27 ministers and eight deputy ministers from a total of 16.

The picture at the provincial and government levels is not that positive. Only three of the nine provinces have over 30 per cent representation of women in their legislature: Gauteng, Northern Province and North–West Province (only one province has a women premier, the Free State). In our big metro cities we have only one mayor who is a woman, that is, Cape Town Metro Council.

Women are also senior office bearers in the parliament—speaker, deputy speaker, chairperson of the National Council of Provinces and a number of chairs of parliamentary committees in the National Assembly and National Council of Provinces are women. Chairs of parliamentary committees in the National Assembly are women. About 30 per cent of committee chairs in our parliament are women.

Women also chair national commissions such as the Independent Electoral Commission and the Commission for Gender Equality. Women are also represented in the Human Rights Commission, in the Public Services Commission as well as the Judicial Services Commission. We are excited when change is in place and women are taking their rightful positions.

The time for the healing of the wounds has come. The moment to bridge the chasms that divide us has come. The time to build is upon us. We have, at last, achieved our political emancipation. We pledge ourselves to liberate all our people from the continuing bondage of poverty, deprivation, suffering, gender and other kinds of discrimination.

Gender and Leadership in the Old Testament

In *Genesis* (1–2), the creation account does not teach that women should be subordinate to men. It teaches that both men and women were created in the image of God and are equal in personhood. Statements in Chapter 3 about the man ruling over the woman (3:16) are descriptive of the way things are, rather than the way they should be (like pain in childbirth or the weeds in your garden). Women in the Old Testament, in the context of a highly patriarchal society, are pictured as serving in some of the most significant leadership roles.

Gender and Leadership in the New Testament

Jesus called 12 men to be his disciples. Some argue that this sets a pattern for the leadership of the church. However, this group was called for a specific purpose, and also had other unique characteristics that does not form a pattern for the church (for example, they were all Jewish). Jesus had women followers. He instructed women (Luke 10: 38–42), talked with women in public, allowed women to touch him (Luke 8: 45–46) and had women travel with him (Luke 8: 1–2).

In life, I went through difficulties at work, church and in the community I was residing so I know what is it to be hurt and suffer. In life, I have learnt that there is life after hurt and that life is like a game of tennis, you cannot win without serving.

Through God's grace the motivational talks and preaching I do touch the lives of those who have been hurt, wounded and are bleeding deep down their hearts.

Ravhudzulo (2004: 38) maintains that you do not underestimate your worth by comparing yourself with others. It is because we are different that each of us is special. Do not set your goals by what other people deem important; only you know what is best for you. Do not take for granted the things closest to your heart, cling to them as you would to your life, for without them life is meaningless.

Since 1994, women have an increasing role in the work of the church. Women not only lead women in 'women's ministries', but also lead men and women in music, prayer, teaching and speaking. Some people wonder why women should be allowed to do anything in church; others wonder why women cannot do everything in church.

To give Biblical and South African perspectives on this issue, let us look at evidence that God has used women to speak to his people. Women have spoken and who are still speaking the word of God, they have done so and they are still doing it with Divine approval and authority. Blessed be the name of the Lord, Oh! Hallelujah. Life has taught me that I must never sit down and mourn because the world would not stop for my mourning.

Old Testament Perspective of Women's Influence

Hagar

The Lord gave Hagar a promise similar to the promise given to Abraham (*Genesis* 16: 7–10). Hagar then 'gave this name to the Lord who spoke to her: "You are the God who sees me," for she said, "I have now seen the One who sees me"' (verse 11). What Hagar said is now in the word of God. She told us one of the names that tell us who God is. He is the God who sees us, and Hagar is the person who spoke that truth.

Miriam

After God brought the Israelites through the Red Sea, Miriam sang praises that are now part of the word of God: Miriam the prophetess, Aaron's sister, took a tambourine in her hand, and all the women followed her, with tambourines and dancing. Miriam was a prophetess, which means that she spoke the word of the Lord. A prophet is someone who speaks on behalf of God to the people, a prophetess had the same role. Miriam had a role of spiritual leadership.

Deborah

Deborah was a prophetess and a judge, and in both roles she spoke the word of God. Her role was not just a one-time event, but an ongoing responsibility. People came to her for leadership on a regular basis—and there is nothing in the Bible to suggest that anyone thought it was unusual for a woman to perform this role. She was simply the most qualified person, and people accepted that.

New Testament Perspective of Women's Influence

In the New Testament we learn of other women who spoke the word of God. Mary sang praises that are now in the Scripture (Luke 1: 46–55). Anna was a prophetess (Luke 2: 36–38). After Jesus was resurrected, he appeared to some women and gave them a message: 'The women hurried away from the tomb, afraid yet filled with joy, and ran to tell his disciples.'

Jesus had no problem with women delivering commands to men. There is nothing inherently wrong with that. He gave them that authority by giving them the message, and in doing so, these women were speaking the words of the Lord. Jesus expected men to listen to women and obey the commands delivered by them. God inspires both men and women to speak.

The women spoke like Esther: *If I perish, I shall perish.*

Gender is one of the universal dimensions on which status differences are based. Since the beginning of time, women have held a lower social status than men. And today, although much advancement have been made, many of the same inequalities in employment and salary still exist. In the letter of Peter (5: 6) we read that, 'Humble yourselves, therefore, under God's mighty hand that He may lift you up in his own good time.' God resists the proud but gives grace to the humble. We need to humble ourselves under God and He can complete His work within us. Women have been quiet for a long time. As a result God lifted us up at the right time.

Hardship

The people that come into our lives are teachers. They enter your lives to help you grow. You need to be willing to make healing a priority in your life if you are ever going to have a chance to have a healthy relationship. Life is constantly changing. There are always going to be endings and new beginnings. There is always going to be grief and pain and anger about what we have to let go of, and fear of what is to come. It is not because we are bad or wrong or shameful. It is just the way the game works.

When you do not let the past painful memories go, negative emotions take upper hand. Negative thought prevent this ability and focuses your thoughts elsewhere. Your mind holds on to beliefs that restrict your ability to love or trust.

When you know how to let them go, the invisible scars from past experiences will disappear. I remember very well the time I was healed from all the hurts I had, I confessed, admit to God, and to another person, my faults, I committed my life to God and was liberated from past experiences. The last thing I did was to forgive myself, this is usually not easy.

Struggles

Life has taught me how to stand in the word of God in the midst of tempting circumstances. Tempting circumstances arise when you begin to give and receive love in sharing the Body of Christ. God does not want you merely to learn how to stay out of sin; He wants to teach you how to be transformed into His image. You will realise that by coming to love each other as he loves us. I want to remind you to allow yourselves time to process whatever you need to feel from the situation you are in. Go ahead and be angry if you have to. But do allow yourselves to feel the feelings and be proactive in the process.

In my life experience I realised that reaching out and making impact on other people is important. This is a key to healing a broken heart. By reaching out, you can do yourself a favour. Phoning an old friend is a good idea. Or, perhaps, simply just do something kind for a stranger. One of the ways I reached out was to make trips to visit each of my family, in-laws and friends several times. I did this to let them know how important they were to me.

Let me tell you, your value does not come from who you are with. Your value comes from who we are. Did you know that your relationship with a significant other or life partner does not determine your happiness?

Your own thoughts determine your happiness. So, why not choose thinking that will support your highest celebration of yourself? Make yourself happy today. You can make it a point that even when you are alone you will reach out and find ways to connect with other people.

Why not start by becoming proactive, making a plan for our happiness, and reaching out to love and live again? The time is now!

If it had been not religious freedom I do not think that I would get this platform to say what women are going through. Through the grace and mercy of God the stone that has been rejected by the builders has become a corner stone. This is the right time for Christian women in the world and South Africa in particular to be heard, respected, and seen as wonderful servants of God who resembles Christ. 'No one can dim the light that is shining from within.'

REFERENCES

Apostle Paul. 1989. *KJV Bible: King James Version*, New York: American Bible Society, Thomas Nelson.

Ary, D., L.C. Jacobs and A. Razavieh. 1972. *Introduction to Research in Education*. New York: Holt, Rinehart and Winston.

De Vos, A.S. (eds). 1998. *Research at Grass Root: A Primer for the Caring Professions.* Pretoria: Van Schaik.

International Religious Freedom, South Africa. 1999. Report submitted to the Committee On Foreign Relations of The U.S. Senate and the Committee on International Relations of The U.S. House of Representatives by the Department of State. Released by the Bureau for Democracy, Human rights and Labor, Washington.

———. 2002. Report submitted to the Committee on Foreign Relations of The U.S. Senate and the Committee on International Relations of The U.S. House of Representatives by the Department of State. Released by the Bureau for Democracy, Human rights, and Labor Washington.

———. 2003. Report submitted to the Committee on Foreign Relations of The U.S. Senate and the Committee on International Relations of the U.S. House of Representatives by the Department of State. Released by the Bureau for Democracy, Human rights and Labor, Washington.

———. 2004. Report submitted to the Committee on Foreign Relations of the U.S. Senate and the Committee on International Relations of the U.S. House of Representatives by The Department of State. Released by the Bureau for Democracy, Human rights and Labor, Washington.

Leedy, P.D. 1993. *Practical Research: Planning and Design.* New York: Macmillan.

Moses.1989. *KJV Bible: King James Version.* New York: American Bible Society, Thomas Nelson.

Ravhudzulo, N.A. 2004. *Nothing Lasts Forever: Strategies to Cope with Pressures of Life in a Realistic, Responsible and Accountable way while Holding on to your Faith.* Meyerton: PCN Printers.

14

Finding Work in
the New Democracy

Arlene Fester

The first half of my story is about loosing my job within four months of moving from Cape Town to Gauteng and the next part is about witnessing the faithfulness of God and His provision. I was offered a job in Johannesburg and prayed about coming here as I did not have any family or friends and I said to the Lord that I could not afford to make a mistake at my age (38 years old at the time), so He must really speak *loud* and *clear*. One morning the Lord woke me up and said: 'Peter never knew he could walk on water until he got out of the boat, it's time to get out of the boat.' I then realised that I was in a comfort zone (living in my mum's house, being around all my family and having many friends). With that in mind, I made my way to Gauteng in February 2002.

Within four months of arriving in Johannesburg, I got retrenched from my job. At first all these doubts went through my mind, but then I reminded the Lord of what He said about walking on the water. I was seeking for a church and had just joined Rhema. They had a conference and Tim Storey was one of the speakers. My spirit was down and so I did not much feel like going that evening (Wednesday, 30 May 2002). I told the Lord I would go that night to hear what Tim Storey had to say, and in any case I only had R50 in the bank and did not have enough money for petrol for the whole week—travelling to work and going to church every evening. I went to the bank to withdraw the R50 and found R300 had been deposited into my account. I later discovered it was my friend Letanie and her husband. ...*OK Lord, so I guess you want me to go every evening*!

That evening there were about 8000 people in the auditorium, but it felt as if Tim Storey was preaching only to me. He said:

> God's favor is on your life; God dried up the one side so it can rain on another; to allow the new thing to happen let go of the old; God is taking you from Almost, to Most, to Utmost; God hasn't brought you this far to leave you; when you get a setback, don't step back, God has prepared your come back; mentality is a state of the mind, get a Miracle mentality.

Proverbs 3: 5–6: 'Trust in the Lord with all your heart and lean not on your own understanding. In all your ways acknowledge Him and He shall direct your paths.' Then Tim gave an Alter Call. He did not say do you need a job; do you need finances; are you going through a tough time right now; he said: 'Do you need a break-thru in 30 days?' (in 30 days I was going to be retrenched). Then Lionel Petersen and the Worship Team sang: 'because He lives, I can face tomorrow, because He lives, all fear is gone, because I know, yes I know He holds the future, and life is worth the living just because He lives' (it's also my mum's favourite chorus). I just stood there and the tears rolled down my cheeks… I couldn't sing.

One morning I was listening to TBN (Trinity Broadcasting Network). Pastor Haggie said: 'Our lives are made of various tests. Depending on how well we pass this test, determines whether we go to the next level. If we fail, we will have to do it all over again.' I said to the Lord: *He must please help me to pass this test first time, it's just too painful to do all over again…*

While looking for work I decided to go and teach Literacy at Rhema. I felt I wanted to do something for someone else who was in a less fortunate position than I was…I did not want to sit at home feeling sorry for myself. Those students taught me the power of being able to read and write; we often do not realise how privileged we are.

One evening I went to Fruit and Veg City and met Pauline. We met a couple of years ago at Cape Technikon, very briefly. She heard about my retrenchment and gave my CV to one of the ladies working on a pilot project at Technikon SA. The project was funded by an American company in Washington and ran for six months. Though I did not have the qualifications for the job, they took me on the basis that I had experience in counselling and that I had done missionary work in Botswana, Zimbabwe and Mozambique. I had the privilege of working with ex-combats (APLA & UMKHONTO WE SIZWE), giving them counselling and teaching them various Life Skills programmes. The contract ended in December and I then had to look for new work.

The following year I got a job at an attorneys company in Craighall Park working as a receptionist/typist. I was not very happy there. My boss and the candidate attorney would go to lunch and stay away for two hours. On returning he would give me stacks of files and told me I could not leave until all had been typed and faxed. On Valentines Day they took me and the other secretary to lunch. He have us each a G-string as gifts and made sexist remarks. I was totally disgusted because he was a married man. The final straw was when he wanted me to do typing for his wife. She is a psychologist and writes books. I did it the one time and told him that I was hired to work for the attorneys, not to do his wife's private typing. He was so angry and fired me. I prayed about whether to take him to court or not. I consulted a pastor friend of mine (also my ex boss). He sought advice from a friend, who worked at an attorneys company in Randburg. She put me in contact with the Associate Director of Du Plessis & Associates and Advocate Corné Goosen (we took him to CCMA). Hennie, my ex boss was so spiteful and withheld my last salary cheque (I had been working there for eight months).

It was a difficult three months after that. Being close to the end of the year and with most company's closing it was not easy to find work. During that time I have really seen the Hand of God on my life. I made friends with domestic workers and they were amazing. One afternoon Joyce came to me and gave me R100 and said she had just come from a part-time job and wanted to sow the money into my life. I had to fax my CV to a company and had R20 on me. My CV was 21 pages long. After it was sent, they charged me R99. I truly stand in Awe of this God that I serve. I would stand in my kitchen and pour the last milk in my tea and look up and say to the Lord, *you see this is my last milk.* Sarah then dropped by after work and brought me R20 to buy bread and milk. Isabel bought me airtime. One time I told the Lord I have no more sugar and rice and the toothpaste is also low; and my neighbour, Elfrede came by and brought me sugar, rice, toothpaste, shampoo and conditioner. Anne (Pauline's sister) called one evening and said she had a box of fruit and vegetables which I must fetch. Amazing!

I have friends in Klerksdorp and they phoned and said I should come through so that they could spoil me and they paid my petrol money.

Before I left to come back, Katryn called me into the room and gave me a cheque for R1000. I paid my bond. So many friends came and blessed me with money to pay my electricity and water or money for petrol. I never had any money or food in my cupboards, but I never went to sleep one night without food even if it was just jam and bread...

The court case was a long process, but my advocate was brilliant and I finally *won*! Normally I go home for Christmas, but December 2003 I could not because I did not have any money. My sisters and my cousin paid my air ticket to come home. The attorneys who assisted me in my court case phoned to ask me if I could come and help them out for two weeks (before the Christmas holidays). I telephoned my sister to tell her that I was offered a job for two weeks and I would rather work and earn something, than to come home without anything. When they closed on 19 December, the attorneys asked me to come back the following year and I was offered a permanent position in their company.

Have any of you ever felt that you have just come through a tough time and your head is just about coming out of the water when another big wave hit you and you feel you are going down again?

One Saturday morning, I got up early as it was the end of the month (had to pay all my accounts). When I got outside my car was gone (28 May 2005). Joyce slept over that weekend. I told her I have to go to the police station to report my stolen car. Joyce got a shock, screamed and started crying. She wanted to accompany me, but I told her that I would rather she stayed and intercede for me. I also phoned Isabel and Sarah and told them I do not want them to get a shock, I just needed them to intercede for me. When I arrived home about two hours later after giving my statement, Joyce shared a scripture the Lord had given her. Sarah arrived 30 minutes later to see if I was OK and also shared a scripture the Lord had given her. Isabel was in Pretoria when I called. She called me every two hours after that to see if I was OK and wanted to assure me that she was praying for me. The scripture I received was:

Psalms 33: 1–22: Let all of the joys of the godly well in Praise to the Lord, for it is right to Praise Him. For all God's words are right and everything He does is worthy of our Trust...But the eyes of the Lord are watching over those who fear Him, who rely upon His steady love...We depend upon the Lord alone to save us. Only He can help us; He protects us like a shield...

Isaiah 59: 19*:* 'When the enemy comes in like a flood, the Spirit of God shall raise up a standard against him.'

Psalms 115: 1–18: 'Glorify Your Name, not ours O Lord. All you His people trust the Lord. Jehovah is constantly thinking about us and He will surely bless us. Jehovah who made Heaven and earth will personally bless us.'

We later prayed together and the Lord gave me a scripture

Psalms 94: 16: Who will protect me from the wicked? Who will be my shield? Lord when doubts fill my mind, when my heart is in turmoil, quiet me and give me renewed hope and cheer. God has made the sins of evil men to boomerang upon them. He will destroy them by their own plans. Jehovah our God will cut them off.

On Sunday, Pastor Ray McCauley preached and said: 'the difference between Happiness and Joy is that happiness changes with the circumstances, but as Christians we live in Joy because we can rejoice amidst the circumstances.' ***Nehemiah 8: 10***: 'The Joy of the Lord is your strength.' He shared ***Psalms 125: 1–2***: 'Those who trust in the Lord are steady as Mount Zion, unmoved by any circumstance. Just as the mountains surround and protect Jerusalem, so the Lord surrounds and protects His people.'

Being without a car was tough. I got up at 03:30 a.m. in the morning to leave my house at 04:30. The walk to the station was about 30 minutes and my train was at 05:05 a.m. I got off at Princess Station, walked to Westgate Mall and got a bus at 06:00 a.m. which dropped me in Randburg, and then walked 15 minutes to work.

I thought travelling to church was going to be as easy; but I was sorely mistaken. On Sunday morning, I left at 07:45 a.m. and again walked to the station to catch a train. When I got to Westgate the guy sweeping told me there are no buses on Sundays, I will have to take a taxi. I have never taken a taxi before. The first taxi stopped and they were going to Johannesburg. I was walking all along Ontdekkers waiting on the next taxi. After the fourth taxi I discovered that there are no taxi's to Randburg on Ontdekkers. Since I came too far to turn back, I just kept walking. I stopped a guy on the road and asked him how I could get to Randburg. He told me to go to Checkers/Hyper in Weltevreden Park. When I got there the lady told me I would not find a taxi there I will have to walk down the road to the BP Garage. So I kept walking and on my way a white Mercedes car stopped to pick me up—it was my boss, Thea. The chances that she would be driving there was slim as she lives on the other side of the 'mountain'. She and her mum were on their way to Life Style and she dropped me off at church first. I came just-in-time for the 12 noon service. The 10:00 a.m. service was ending and Pastor Ray said: 'the devil came to steal from you, but God is going to restore it to you.'

A week later Inspector Lazarus called me from the Vehicle Pound in Chamdor to say they had found my car. My boss told me to fetch the car immediately and one of my colleagues, Zenobia took me. When I got there, the car was badly smashed. The police spotted the vehicle and they were in a high speed chase and collided with each other. That evening as I was travelling home in the bus I said to the Lord: 'I don't understand. I got so excited when they told me my car was found; but look what it looks like. In all of the 11 years that I've had the car, it never looked like that.' Then the Lord reminded me of the scripture He gave me the evening I prayed: 'He will cause the sins of evil men to boomerang upon them, He will destroy them by their own plans...' Hallelujah!

One day my friend Cheryl called me and said she and her husband wants to sow R2000 into my life so that I can go and buy myself a washing machine and whatever else I needed. I never told anyone how it was always an issue for me to stand Saturday after Saturday over my bath doing my washing. My blow-dryer also packed up in that week. That weekend the washing machine was on special and I could buy myself a blow dyer as well. *Prys die Here op dy Spot—Is die Here nie Amazing nie, julle!* I was crying as I put down the phone and everyone at work asked whether I received bad news about my mum (everyone knew my mum was ill).

My cellphone was also stolen and I told the Lord I do not have money to buy a new one now. I felt bad because Prudence had given me the phone when I moved to Gauteng. On my birthday, Cindy-Lou (Pastor Jaco's wife) took her SIM card out of her phone and gave me her phone. After the battery packed up on that phone, the friends who blessed me with the monies for the washing machine called to say they were posting a brand new Samsung cellphone to me. I have no words except: 'The Lord really loves me...!!!'

One of my friends, Zien, whom I met while working at Technikon SA, was going to visit her family in Klerksdorp for the weekend and offered me a lift (6 November 2005). She knew I often visited Pastor Jaco and the Vosloo's. I and Liezel were in the kitchen preparing for supper that evening. Katryn came in and asked whether I could spare five minutes, she wanted to show me something outside. Liezel followed and said she also wanted to see. Vossie and Rudi were standing outside and Urshela and Clayton also joined the 'party'. (Vossie and Katryn are married and they have two daughters Liezel and Urshela. Rudi and Clayton are their husbands.) Vossie teased me about getting a new car because I visit too seldom. Then he told me that they decided to bless me with the car standing there (Daewoo, golden colour). I screamed and started crying and Katryn hugged me and started crying with me.

A friend sent me an SMS that day which read: 'only God can turn a mess into a Message; a test into a Testimony; a trial into a Triumph; a victim into a Victory.' The song that came to mind then was: 'He's all I need, He's all I need, Jesus He's all I need. He satisfies my need supplies, Jesus He's all I need.'

I later realised when one hears so many things happening in taxi's or trains, that God had really protected me and kept His hand over me. *His eye was on this sparrow…*

REFERENCE

Veerman, David, R. (ed.). 1992. *Life Application Bible for Students*. Wheaton, Illinois: Tyndale House Publishers Inc.

PART FIVE
Finding Spaces:
Women's Empowerment

Over the centuries women have attempted to raise their status through various mechanisms such as women's groups and clubs, through forums that aim to empower women and to liberate them. Most of the women try to influence policy and practice that recognise their contributions in the workplace. However, in the 21st century, while women have come a long way in claiming their identities there is yet much to do. Empowerment is a concept that is loosely used in the developing and developed world contexts. Can there be true empowerment of women in the workplace if all workplace policies and practices are designed to disempower them by creating barriers and obstacles to their progress at every turn?

In Part Five, we see the resourcefulness of successful women who struggle through pain and suffering caused by health and wellness barriers. Another strong message of hope and comfort comes through Robyn Andrews' paper of women like Jane in Calcutta who display a deep sense of positive spiritedness and overcome disability. Diane Saarinen reminds us once again that the world is a harsh place to live in. It is more harsh if you are a woman and disabled. Disability continues to guarantee you a place outside the mainstream of society and puts you at a higher risk of being exploited, even by women. Vivian Ojong claims that 'gendered spaces become less significant in transnational contexts when survival is the key factor.' Sita Venkateswar brings forth hope and suggests that some women who are slightly more advantaged in one way or another can make a positive difference in other women's lives. They act as catalysts for change and pave the way for less fortunate women to progress.

15

Living and Working in Calcutta: Jane's Story

Robyn Andrews

INTRODUCTION

Jane[1] is in her mid-thirties, lives in her own well-appointed apartment in central Calcutta,[2] and has full-time employment as secretarial assistant to an influential and highly respected public figure. This outcome would have seemed unbelievable to anyone who witnessed Jane more than three decades ago—when she was handed over to a welfare officer by her poverty-stricken parents as a tiny handicapped infant.

Jane's life history was recorded as part of a larger project focussing on Calcutta's Anglo-Indians. Her story, presented here largely in her own words, is one of physical and emotional suffering overcome by the combination of good luck, the goodness of others, fierce determination and a deep commitment to God. Jane views her experiences positively. There is no question that she is successful in all her undertakings and her story is inspirational.

The first time I saw Jane was just before midday in Kyd Street, central Calcutta. My attention had been drawn to a black-haired woman who was taking some time to emerge from her taxi. She was elbowing her way out of her seat while the driver stood patiently waiting. Once she worked her way to the edge of the seat she took the crutches he held for her, thanked him and then used the crutches to support herself as she got out. She made her way across the busy, potholed street close to where she was meeting us for lunch. The fact that the street was uneven certainly did not help, but it was not enough to stop her. Life for Jane, as I was to discover, was very much like that street: bumpy, uneven but never enough to stop her.

When I first met Jane I was in Calcutta carrying out research on Anglo-Indians. I was interested in meeting people and recording their life stories. Anglo-Indians are a mixed-descent, minority community which came to exist through European explorations of India, particularly through British colonisation. Anglo-Indian cultural practices, which are relatively western (for example, they speak English as their mother tongue and are practicing Christians) distinguish them to some extent from others in India. As part of my research I was interested in capturing the experience of what it means to be an Anglo-Indian living in Hindu, and in some areas, Muslim dominated Calcutta.

I met Jane through a woman whom she and many others I met call 'Aunty'. One day when I visited her she was meeting Jane for lunch and suggested I join them. We lunched in a Chinese restaurant where I sat next to Jane and soon learned that this tiny Anglo-Indian woman in her mid-thirties was intelligent, articulate and very independent. I was delighted to meet her, not least because she contradicted some negative stereotyping I had come across.[3] She exudes life and energy and optimism. She has a very good job as secretarial assistant to a high profile man with considerable public influence, and is highly regarded by him. She lives in a flat that she owns and is able to take an overseas holiday most years. Given the circumstances of her early life, it is remarkable that she is able to live such a life.

After that initial lunchtime meeting, when I told Jane about my research and she agreed that I could record her life story, I arranged to see her again a few days later at her flat. To get there I took a taxi from my accommodation in central Calcutta—getting into the taxi only after throwing off the unwelcome 'assistance' of a Bengali gentleman by assuring him that I was quite capable of getting where I wanted to on my own! This prelude to visiting Jane highlighted the necessity for a woman, especially one with the disabilities she has, to have secure living arrangements and be confident about transportation. On the evening of the first interview session, Jane answered my knock on her door with a smile and the affectionate, typically Anglo-Indian, kiss on each cheek as she welcomed me in. Her flat was spacious and bright in contrast to the dingy, grubby entrance and lift I had used to get there. After sitting down and briefly chatting about our days since we last met, we settled into the work; she told me about her life and I taped her story. While I have not included all of her story here, the details of her early life and her enormous faith, effort and determination are obvious and account to a large extent for the life she leads today.

Jane was struck by polio when she was a child but this was only one of a number of blows that she has had to contend with. I will let her tell her story from those times. I have lightly edited her words but it is very close to the way I heard it.[5]

JANE'S STORY

It Was Difficult for My Parents to Take Care of Me because I Have Polio

'When I was one year old suddenly I contracted polio. My parents didn't give me the vaccine. But there were five of us in the family.'

'*You were the youngest?*'[6]

'I am in the middle (of four sisters and one brother) so it was very difficult for my parents to take care of me because I had polio, and they are from a very, very poor family.'

'They were facing a lot of problems and during our childhood my parents separated. They have both remarried. So, looking at all this poverty they wanted to discard me as a handicapped child. My mother thought that, "In the future how am I going to support this girl when I also have others to take care of ?" So then she took me to a lady who works [as a Welfare Officer at a Hill Station boarding school]. I never saw my parents again.'

Being born into an extremely poor family was her first disadvantage; contracting polio was another and as she says:

'But I had another disadvantage… To be born a girl… is like a sin.'

'My main problem is that I had polio, but also it's because I'm a girl child. We face discrimination from there itself. To be a girl is a big boon[7] here in India and being handicapped people think that it's because your parents have sinned, and that the sin has fallen on the child. That's why people don't want to take such a child out into society or expose them to friends and family.'

'*So they looked at your polio…?*'

'Yes.'

'*Looked at the effect of that, and say that that's a result of their sin. Is that what you mean?*'

'Yes, sort of. They feel like that in the Indian society.'

'*Is that a Hindu belief?*'

'It's more a Hindu belief, yes. So that's why… for me to come out and walk on the streets… They look at me and people think, "How could she walk on the streets like that?" Yes, but, I'll come back to that.[8] And this lady, the Welfare Officer, said, "Okay if this case is genuine, and if it's so that her parents don't want her, maybe the school could try to take care of her."'

But I Always Say That God Has Been so Good to Me

'*Did you have to be Anglo-Indian to go to the school?*'

'No.'

'*Did your family have to be Christian?*'

'My parents are Roman Catholic, but [admission] was based on the situation, not on being Christian. So because I had polio, and I was in a critical condition; I was very thin, and very weak… It was a blessing in disguise. You can see children like that being used here, by their mothers, to beg. They even break their bones to put them on their hips and then take them around to beg. But I always say that God has been so good to me.'

'When they took me to the school I was very weak and really needed some attention. I was loved by all of them. They did exercises for me. They made special parallel bars so that I could practice walking, and I had massages every day. I would always cry because my legs used to pain quite a lot. But they really took good care of me, gave me vitamin pills and every day I used to have exercises. I didn't much like to do the exercises. Of course, as I started growing up I realised that I have to do things for myself and have to try to be optimistic in life and see what I can do with these legs.'

'I'm also a human being and I have feelings and it's not easy when you have parents, and yet you don't have them at the same time. Here in India, to get an education is very difficult. My mother approached that same lady and said, "Maybe this handicapped girl would like somebody to help her, so why don't you take my elder daughter into the school as well?" And so my elder sister was admitted into the school with me.'

'*How much older is she?*'

'She's one year older to me. But the sad part was, as we started growing up, she never recognised me as her sister because I was handicapped and excelled in the class.'

'I was always a fun-loving kid. I loved to get attention, and… so what if I'm handicapped? I've got my hands. I've got my brains. But the growing up was not easy, because being a child you want to play, run and swim, do it all, try to take part in all the activities in the school. But I just had to sit and look at them and I really felt that I was missing something in life. The girls would get parcels and letters from their parents and I have this younger sister who used to write to me only.'

'*She used to write to you when you were at school?*'

'Yes. They studied in a Catholic school here in Cal. As we started growing up we were taught about Christianity, and that was a very important aspect in my life then. I said to the Lord, "If I don't have anyone, at least I have you." And that was a big source of inspiration to me. I came to the understanding that He was asking, "What are you going to do in this dark world?" And it was then that I really gave my life to the Lord and said, "You take over my life. You have brought me to this world and now it's up to you to break me, mould and make me into what you want." So after I gave my life to the Lord I really felt that things started moving positively for me.'

'*How old were you then?*'

'I was eight years old.'

'*Quite young.*'

'Yeah, I was quite young.'

If I'm Going to Sit Back and Just Cry Over My Polio It's Not Going to Help

'I always felt that if I'm going to sit back and just cry over my polio it's not going to help. So I tried to take part in as many events as I could in my school and I discovered my singing, drawing and handicraft talents—stitching and sewing. So I really felt that I should put more emphasis on that and give some more importance to that. We had singing competitions and dramas that I used to take part in. My school friends never ever treated me like a handicap and that was really one plus point for me. They'd say, "Come on Jane, let's go here" or "let's go there". So I thought, "Yeah, why not?"'

'*How did you get around? Did you use crutches?*'

'Yes, from the age of three I started using crutches and calipers. And since we have three months of holiday during the wintertime, my school would pay for me to go to a very big Christian medical college in South India to have full physiotherapy, muscle assessment and to see if I was improving. But the doctors made me aware that calipers and crutches would always be a part of my life. So I knew from an early age that there was no chance of improvement. Since I was slowly growing, I had to have new caliper and crutch measurements, and I would be there for practically all the winter holidays. Every year I had to go back and forth.'

'Initially I did feel a bit lonely because I was just a child. I didn't know the patients because they were changing all the time. I spoke English so I would talk to all the medical students and sometimes one would say, "Why don't you come and sing to us? Bring the guitar, and we can have a singsong. Or read the Bible and pray with us. I'm sure the patients would love that."'

They Say It Is Very Difficult to Get One Certificate... I Had Seven!

Jane completed her secondary schooling and then was given the option of staying on at the school while she completed further training as a secretary.

'I did a secretarial course through the Pitman's Board in London. They say it's very difficult to get *one* certificate. And it was a correspondence course so the question paper comes from England. When I got the results, I had seven certificates and I did the highest examination! I got a first class advanced certificate and I did all the other examinations. So that really gave me a big boost and I thought, "This is something for me to go out with into the dark world." And what occurred to me was that, especially because I'm from a poor background, I really had my mind set on working for poor people. So I thought if I take this secretarial training I could sit in an office and do some correspondence and be a secretary, and that became my aim in life. So after I did my training at school I came back down to Calcutta. This was a shock to me at first, to be living in such a vast and crowded cosmopolitan city after the calm and serenity of the school in Darjeeling district—which is up close to the Himalayas.'

But I Had One Problem, and That Was Transport

'It was Aunty who helped me to find a place to stay as a paying guest. It was not easy. I think they must have turned her down quite a lot of times because nobody wants the risk of taking care of a handicapped person. But finally she did get a nice Anglo-Indian family and I stayed there for three years.'

'As a boarder, a paying guest?'

'As a paying guest, yes. It means you pay for the month, and they give you just one bed, and maybe some food. It depends on their household situation. So there were times when I had to depend on the shop food.'

'When I came down to Calcutta I had to look for work. Even though I knew that finding employment was not going to be easy, because of my disability, I had to support myself financially to survive. I went for many interviews to all these NGOs,[9] because these are the ones who are supporting poor people. They would ask if I was willing to sit for a test. I always said, "Of course". I didn't want to be taken because I'm handicapped. I knew I had the ability. I have a sharp brain and definitely I can pick up the skills. I can pick up things very fast. I did sit for a lot of examinations and they would say, "Yes, you've got the job" immediately. But I had one problem, and that was transport. I can't depend on the buses or even waiting for a taxi. It's too hard for me. Also, it's expensive, and it's difficult to get a taxi everyday to come and go. So I asked these companies, "What about giving me transport?" "Oh, I'm very sorry, we don't give transport to staff." I said, "But you have to make an exception. You are the ones who are helping people in need. We are the ones in need. I mean you have to make an exception somewhere." So opportunities would arise, but then not materialise because they couldn't offer me transport. I had to turn down a number of offers of work because they weren't in a position to offer me transport to and from my residence.'

'I was starting to feel really rejected but then an opportunity came up for me to go back and do a year's 'service' at my old school. This turned out to be a blessing in disguise because just as I was about to finish the year I heard about a job with an International Christian NGO. I was excited but half expecting that even if I was successful it would meet with the same fate of "no transport". It took some of the seniors at school to talk me into applying, and then I was selected.'

'And this time I managed to get through to the organisation about transport. They said "We will give you transport but we will take a part of your salary—60 rupees." So I joined this organisation and I was there for 19 years. I really feel that it's so rewarding when you give your whole life for the cause of poor people. Especially when I didn't get it from my parents... This organisation offered help to deprived and poverty-stricken people of our country but it also offered hope to people like me, for my self-improvement. I have since left this NGO and have joined another religious firm, to date, holding a prestigious post for the top-most boss.

I asked Jane about the flat she lived in. It is a beautiful, spacious, well-maintained and well-furnished home: one of the most pleasant homes I visited in Calcutta, or anywhere else for that matter. The difference between this and her earlier accommodation must have been striking. I can only speculate about how it affected her well-being and ability to work. While she may have been pleased to leave her previous shared accommodation each day to go to work, the lack of comfort and privacy must have begun to take a toll on her: physically, mentally and emotionally.

'A handicapped friend from Holland bought this flat for me as a gift. He saw that I was going through such a bad time. I was staying as a paying guest at first but then I moved into a hostel. It's not always easy to be a paying guest. You have to be very obligated to the person you stay with.'

'Did they not trust you in the house?'

'No, it's not that. It's just that they feel it's not nice that a girl stays alone over there, especially when she's like this... Or they think people will take advantage of you. In that protective way. Wherever I've stayed, they have always been very loving to me. And they were all Anglo-Indian people. But for the last six years before I got this flat, I stayed in the hostel which is just outside my office gate. It was quite difficult for me because I had to climb three floors every day. It was a real olden-day building. I had to share this room about the size of my bathroom with three old people.

It's Been so Wonderful Just to Feel That I Have a Place of My Own

She told me of the visit to Calcutta made by her Dutch director.

'He was interested in me because I was handicapped. He would always try to help me and he would take me out to the clubs and parties. One time the Dutch director's friend paid us a visit and when he came to see me he said, "Jane, where are you living? I'm really interested to get to know you better because you and I have something in common. We both have polio."

Jane offered to show him where she had been living for the last six years, sharing the little room with three others who were all over 60 years old.

I said: 'I am living in that room.'
And he said: 'I can't believe it. I can't see how you can climb up all those steps.'
I said: 'It's so difficult to get accommodation in Calcutta and even if you get the accommodation, it's so expensive.'

'So this friend didn't even really know me, and he's got his own family abroad. But when I was away in Norway that year he said to my Dutch director, "I am so upset about Jane living in that condition I want to buy her a flat. No matter what the cost is I just want to buy her a flat." So my friend said, "What are you saying? It's so expensive." But he responded, "I just want to see that this girl gets rehabilitated and she has something of her own."

So he bought the flat that I visited her in and gave it to Jane. Accommodation in Calcutta has become expensive which has led to many Anglo-Indians who once lived in the central areas moving to outlying regions. Jane's flat is comparatively close to the central part of town and was very convenient to her place of work.

'And now I'm living here from '96. Friends keep visiting me and it's been so wonderful just to feel that I have a place of my own.

I didn't have even a spoon to my name when I was in that hostel. I just had this one suitcase with all my clothes for the office. In the hostel, they just gave us one bed and a small table and a chair—for 400 rupees per month. It wasn't much, but at the same time...'

'You didn't get much for it either?'

'They put on the water pump only three times a day and if I missed the water in the morning...because the next two times it would get turned on I was in the office. So if I missed that one...'

'I would fill up on water first, because there were the other three who had to fill the water also, and they just put it on for one hour, and so we had a lot of problems...If I come back from work very late and I wanted to eat something hot or drink some hot beverage, I couldn't because they wouldn't allow us to keep a stove. They were very strict and at the same time accommodation is so difficult, so I really...'

'How did you eat then, how did you manage?'

'They gave us the food. They brought it in a tiffin carrier and they kept it on the table. But when I came back at nine o'clock or ten o'clock it was so cold. It was all I had so I had to eat that cold tasteless food.'

You Should Try to be Optimistic and Go Out and Reach Your Goals and Try to Touch Others' Lives

As well as making her way through each busy day and becoming an extremely valuable employee, she does all she can for others, especially those she identifies with. I asked her about the organisations she works with.

'Mostly, I'm involved with the handicapped, because I myself am a handicap, I really like to help these type of children. There is this centre started by one lady from England who got the calling from God to work for these children. Because there're so many handicapped kids on the streets and everywhere in India but nobody to take care of them. So she started this home and my devotion to them is, well... Just because I am a handicap I feel that, okay, I didn't get love from my parents so I know what it is for them to just be lying and crawling around without getting any affection, except from the servants who just like, treat them like a doll—they just lift them up and dump them somewhere else and you know I really feel sad about that.'

'So this is one of the organisations I work for, and I take a lot of visitors over there and they donate quite a lot. And even if they don't they go back and they collect money to send to the children. The other one I work with is a place for the juvenile children and their mothers who have been thrown in prison because of no fault of theirs. These women, they sleep on the pavements and sometimes a man just wants to have a fling or sex or they want to have some fun with women so they go and they take them to the backyard or somewhere...and they rape these mothers, then the mother gets pregnant and then for no reason they are put into prison. Then they give birth and have the child. They literally are growing up in the jail. So a missionary from Norway started a centre for these types of women.'

This is Amazing, that Somebody from Another Country Does This!

'He already knew that there's so much poverty here they don't have enough time and money to look to somebody else's needs like. So many are poor and they are just scraping to look after themselves, and if they take on somebody else it's a burden to them. So it had to come from an outside source, to see the need for these types of children. I go and visit them quite often. I take visitors over there and, but you know they are such talented children. I mean you just have to give them a little push and they sing, dance, draw, they do so many different things and they make beautiful embroidery, art and everything. Once in a year they have an exhibition. They get a lot of sales and whatever money they get, it goes back to the girls because then they need to be taken care of.'

Jane does all she does out of a deep sense of compassion for others. She, more than most, knows about the impediments that can be part of one's lot. Her life could have been very different from what it is and she does what she can to make a positive difference to others. She is appreciative of what she sees as the primary source of all that is good in her life.

'God has taken away my legs but He's given me ten gifts in their place, and I really feel like... I can be so proud of my achievements and what I have done today for people, and many people have said that I have been a great example to them.'

It's just that I'm very positive and I always feel that if you sit and brood over things that will not help. You should try to be optimistic and go out and reach your goals and try to touch others' lives. And I know that God is with me and He's really using me through my singing or through even just talking to people. That is a strong testimony for Him as well. I have been so lucky because my friends have sponsored me abroad eight times to Norway and Holland, and I have travelled to thirteen countries in the world. I even studied in Norway for one year. Where could you get all these opportunities if it were not for the love of God?'

Jane's story is so varied and complex. One cannot but marvel at its path: its highways, its dips, its dead ends. But always there seems to be a beacon at the end of the road: a benefactor, a kind word, a solution to a problem. How does Jane see it all? Her final comment to me was to implore readers 'not to look at the disability but at the ability instead'.

ACKNOWLEDGEMENT

I would like to acknowledge with thanks the part that 'Jane' has played in the construction of this work.

NOTES

1. I have used a pseudonym to protect 'Jane's' identity.
2. Calcutta is now known in India as Kolkata but I will refer to it by the old name as most Anglo-Indians, including Jane, use this name, and because people living outside India know the city by this name.
3. Anglo-Indian women are negatively depicted in literature and film as being promiscuous, dishonest and living the high life without thinking of the future, for example, see Nirad Chaudhuri's *The Continent of Circe* (1965) and the Merchant Ivory film *Cotton Mary* (1999). Megan Mills discusses Anglo-Indian stereotypes in her works (1996, 1998).
4. He was very keen to get into the taxi with me saying he would make sure I got to my destination. I was suspicious of his real intentions and felt much safer without his assistance.
5. Jane has reviewed this slight reworking of her interview and has given her permission for its inclusion in this form.
6. While this interview is primarily in Jane's words I have included my questions and comments and indicated where these occur in the interview by the use of italics.
7. I presume Jane is being ironic in saying this.
8. Later in the interview she added:

   'And literally people they just stop me on the street as though, "My God, how can you just walk on the street. How can you...?"'
   'Is this in India (She's visited thirteen other countries in the world)? Who are the people who stop and...?'
   'Mostly Hindus.'
   'Is it children?'
   'No, the parents. Because most of them have handicapped children in their homes... so they feel that I am a living example to them. Some of them are so positive, and some of them just want to know how I have progressed in life.'
9. Non-governmental organisations.

REFERENCES

Chaudhuri, Nirad. 1965. *The Continent of Circe*. London: Chatto and Windus.

Merchant, Ismail (Director). 1999. *Cotton Mary*. Produced by Nayeem Hafizka and Richard Hawley. A Merchant Ivory Production. Universal Studios.

Mills, Megan, 1996. 'Some Comments on stereotypes of the Anglo-Indians', *The International Journal of Anglo-Indian Studies*, 1:1. Available online at http://alphalink. com.au/~agilbert/jmills1.html (downloaded on February 2, 2005).

————. Unpublished. *Ethnic Myth and Ethnic Survival: The Case of India's Anglo-Indian (Eurasian) Minority*. PhD Thesis, York University, 1998.

16

Surviving with a Disability in New York City

Diane Saarinen

When I first became disabled by an inner ear disorder two decades ago at the age of 21, my future career was not my immediate concern. I was just finishing up my junior year of college, was on the dean's list, had a part time job and was considering which archaeological dig I would embark on—the one to Mexico or the one to England? Living in New York City, I can say that was the last time I would think of such long distance travel for a long time to come.

What I first experienced was a headache that was the worst of my life. It lasted three days. One side of the room looked higher than the other side. When I tentatively journeyed outdoors, one side of the sidewalk also looked higher than the other side. Seemingly overnight, my world had gone out of focus and out of balance.

It turned out that I did indeed have a balance disorder, called variably (over the years) Meniere's disease, autoimmune disease of the inner ear or just disequilibrium. I was first told I had migraines, mainly because I was a woman and I was under stress. Never mind that I explained to the doctors that the constant state of having these so-called migraines was causing me stress. Little by little, my life became more and more dismantled, as I was no longer able to work part-time, the subway trips caused intolerable nausea, and I even had to drop my classes I felt dizzy even just sitting in a chair in the classroom. Going through the medical system with a mystery illness and no medical insurance further complicated the situation. By the time I found the specialist—an otoneurologist—who was able to tell me my problems stemmed from my inner ear, I had stumbled upon him by sheer hit-or-miss.

I was in my early 20s, and I found myself on welfare, mainly so I could receive the medicaid that would pay for my medical expenses. At least in *theory* it would pay for my medical expenses. My doctor was a top research doctor in New York City, and his office did not accept medicaid. My father, never a wealthy man to begin with, paid for my visits, treatments and drugs out of his pocket at first, with the few remaining dollars he had managed to stash away for his old age.

Time passed, and the research doctor did not have a cure for my illness. However, he was busy writing papers on us patients and trying us on one drug after another. The quality of my life was zilch. I had no social life; my symptoms had turned me into a young invalid. Missing school, and looking for a way to keep my mind active, I began exploring the possibilities of attending classes in some way without actually having to travel to campus. This was in the late 1980s when we did not have the Internet for what is now called distance learning.

I came across a programme in New York City called External Education for the Homebound. This was unique in that the students at home attended the same courses that the students on campus did, only via speaker phone. Proctors who came to your home administered tests. While I did not particularly like being called 'homebound', my symptoms had pretty much forced me into fitting that description.

When I first called the programme's director, I explained that I just wanted to take some courses to keep myself busy. She, however, had other plans. The director explained to me that the Homebound programme was working with some employers who would be willing to give jobs to disabled students once they completed training. She suggested the two year Word Processing Certificate programme to me. I remember thinking I did not want to type for a living, in addition to being on the dean's list in college; I had gone to a high school for intellectually gifted students. Secretarial work had never entered my mind as a career choice. And I also did not think this kind of work could be possible; I did not even know how to type, other than the hunt-and-peck method I used on an old Smith Corona. Not only that, I did not have a computer! Computers routinely cost US$4000 in those days.

The director gently laughed, and assured me that computers would be given out on loan to each student for the duration of the studies.

I could not believe it and with an offer that generous, I did sign up. In addition, I was now poor enough that the state would pay for my education. I did, however, tell the director I probably would not need to work from home forever anyway, as my specialist was diligently working on a way to cure me of the inner ear disorder that had curtailed my life so. I suppose the director had heard stories like that before because she said, in a way so as not to upset me, that she was sure that would indeed be the case, but just in the event things did not turn out as expected, it might be a good idea to be prepared. Besides, it would always be a good skill to fall back on.

I was fairly gung-ho about my new Homebound programme once I enrolled, though my friends and family were a bit puzzled by it. To be honest, they were a bit puzzled by my whole illness. An inner ear disorder is an invisible disability in many ways: the sufferer can appear to be quite normal, while internally experiencing vertigo. And usually, when the inner ear attacks are so bad as to be accompanied by headache, vomiting and nausea, that the sufferer is usually flat on his or her back in bed and certainly not taking visitors or even phone calls, so who is around to see that? So not only is it a type of invisible disability, it ultimately renders the victim invisible: not seen in the world at large, existing in the shadows.

With very little encouragement and sometimes abject discouragement from people such as my brother-in-law who gave me sage bits of advice such as, 'Don't be a sick person; no one likes to be around sick people,' as if this were something in my control. I approached my Secretarial Sciences with the same enthusiasm that I had once reserved for my history and archaeology classes before I became ill. And I did learn to type, although the process was an onerous and slow one. On a daily basis, I began to visualise what it would be like to be self-sufficient, to be off of welfare, and to move out of my father's apartment and into one of my very own. I felt as if I was approaching these goals closer and closer each day.

You can imagine how disappointed I became when I began to realise that the Homebound programme really did not have the employers waiting for us at the end of our certification process. The one job I had been offered in the interim while completing my studies was that of booking entertainment parties for a psychic who needed someone who spent a lot of time at home—she would forward her business phone to me when she was out on a job. Needless to say, this did not pay well, but I accepted the work because at that point, I would do any kind of work that came to me. I should mention that in addition to booking psychics for parties, this same woman also had a stripping agency, with herself being one of the strippers as well. She had her very own schtick where, apparently skilled as a magician, her clothes would magically come off through a series of tricks! I felt ridiculous describing this to callers on the phone and trying to sell her act.

Another part-time job that I did during the time I was in my early 20s and still in the Word Processing programme was to baby-sit my older sister's infant son while she was off at work and, after work, pursuing her PhD. I did this despite having avoided the experience of babysitting as a teenager altogether. It seemed that, as I became a work-at-home type, a shut-in, only the most menial jobs were being offered to me.

Still concerned because the Homebound programme had no potential employers for me, I began to look in the newspaper. Even so, I could not understand why the programme could offer me no job prospects since companies receive tax breaks for employing those with disabilities and I could just as easily work from home with the help of faxes and modems, even though this was before the internet. I saw an advertisement in the *New York Times* that asked for something called a medical transcriptionist, and it clearly stated that there was an option to work from home. Bingo! I felt like I had hit the lottery. I knew that medical transcription had something to do with transcribing doctors' dictations, and even though my typing skills were still not up to par, was confident that they would improve with practice. I made an appointment for the interview and honestly told the potential employer that I had absolutely no experience whatsoever, but by being practically a professional patient by now, felt as if I had absorbed a lot of medical lingo by osmosis!

The interviewer, of course, did not hire me. However, she did give me the sound advice that I should pursue this line of work if I wanted to work from home since the opportunity was there, and medical transcriptionists were scarce and hard to find. I went home, and looked in my college course book. I found a class called 'Medical Office Procedures' which spent a few weeks out of the semester on transcribing. Once again, the school lent me the equipment I would need this time: a transcriber and practice tapes (spoken by actors). I would eventually find out in short order what a real doctor sounded like!

I actually landed my first job as a medical transcriptionist a few weeks shy of completing my word processing certificate. I would be typing Social Security Disability reports and the irony was not lost on me. I had never applied for social security since becoming disabled because I did not want to rule out the possibility of working while still only in my early 20s. I did accept welfare because I needed to survive, and had hoped that the medicaid would cover my medical bills, which were enormous. By this time, I had tried so many different treatments with my research doctor, yet none of them had worked. I was determined to be self-sufficient despite my disability, and if that meant working from home, I was ready to do it.

When I started medical transcription, I felt ready to cry every night. There was no training. I was just given tapes, which I picked up, brought home and listened to, while I tore through pages in medical dictionaries trying to understand what the doctors were saying. I must have done all right since the company that hired me to type the reports kept me. I was never praised for my work, and never saw the doctors that I transcribed for. I was once wrongly given back a page that had been transcribed by another transcriptionist with my same initials here a doctor had scrawled 'give this typist a dictionary!' Also, I technically was not an employee and I had no benefits from this job. I was working as an independent contractor responsible for my own self-employment taxes, health insurance, and, of course, I would never be able to get benefits such as unemployment. I was on my own. It was scary but it was the only choice I had.

As I became more experienced, I grew weary of the subway rides (which still induced nausea) that I needed to take to pick up tapes of transcription. I had heard about a company where you could type hospital reports and do this completely from home, by plugging in an audio device in a telephone line. This was for a very large and busy hospital, and I would be learning a lot in a short period of time: more medical jargon and new doctors' accents. Once again, I devoted my time to listening to the dictations, rewinding and searching for words in the medical dictionary. I did not have much of a social life, since in addition to not feeling well most of the time, it seemed that *all* of my life was spent transcribing or recovering from transcribing. It was cerebral work and very monotonous work. By this point, though I had moved into my own apartment and was completely self-sufficient, albeit living pay cheque to pay cheque, disabled and without health insurance.

The hospital, which was the ultimate recipient of my work, had no contact with me. I only heard comments through the agency with which I had the account, and then only if work was piling up because they had a 24-hour turnaround time. The hospitals were saving a fortune using transcription services instead of hiring individual transcriptionists, and the agency was profiting off of my work by holding the contract with the hospital and from my status as an independent contractor.

I worked for the same agency for 14 years and never met the woman who ran the agency face-to-face even once during the entire time. There was no office to go to. If she had a machine to lend me, it came via messenger. She and I had phone calls, but these were short and to the point. Corrections in my work usually came in the form of printed out copies mailed to me, with the incorrectly spelled words crossed out and the correctly spelled words written above them. It all seemed a perversion of the adage that children should be seen and not heard. Only I, an adult, was not even seen or heard from. I just silently plugged away at my work, and when a file was finished, sent it out through cyberspace on an old 2400 baud modem.

Meanwhile, *this* was considered one of the better transcription agencies to work for! There were tales of other at-home transcriptionists who were questioned about the hours they set aside for work, whereas I was basically free to accomplish my quota anytime during the space of that my 24 hour turnaround period allowed. Working in isolation took its toll on me, and I took to becoming a night owl, typing when no phone calls would disturb me, in the wee hours of the morning.

Needless to say, being self-employed meant not receiving vacation days or sick days. Truthfully, I felt sick most days working anyway, but this was the bargain I made with myself way back in my early 20s. Being *really* sick, where I could not function, that is, *work*, meant that I was racked with guilt as well as worry, knowing I was losing money for the day because I was not producing my transcription. And then I would fall behind, and would ruin it for *everybody*...

As the Internet became popular, the face of medical transcription began to change. Now national companies could bid on local hospitals, as they would not have to worry about long-distance telephone charges while hooked up to dictation machines. New York City is an expensive place to live, but at least the rates to transcribe for an agency that held a city hospital as an account were not as bad as the rates I began to see for the national companies. What might be a good wage in, say, the Midwest, was definitely not a good wage for me! Even the owner of the agency I had been with for 14 years had said, before the advent of the national companies, 'I hate to say it, but we just aren't paid enough. I think if there were more men in the field, we would be getting paid more.' I absolutely agree with that.

Going on with the idea of the Internet transcription companies, I began to take a look at their ads to see what they were offering. One company had an ad with a woman, presumably a transcriptionist, sitting at her work desk with her infant child! The idea, apparently, was that you could be a mother *and* work at home, earning income, at the same time. I had heard from mothers who were transcriptionists that it was quite impossible to get work done, and the child still needed to go into daycare.

Eventually a national company took over the account I had for 14 years and it was time to bid *adieu* to the agency owner that I had never once met in person. I moved on to transcribing X-rays for a company that actually had a storefront I had travelled to and where I was able to meet the people working there. Since they had met me, and I was about 35 years old at the time, it never made sense to me that I was referred to by the much younger male manager of my account as 'the girl'. I knew I was 'the girl' because although he also seldom telephoned me, he did so in times of emergency when it would usually be to tell me that 'the other girl' was not going to working that day, or 'the other girl' would be transferred to another account temporarily and would I fill in?

Technology is also catching up in the field of medical transcription and voice recognition software is gaining popularity with some doctors and hospitals. This is speech recognition software where the doctor speaks and the text appears directly on the computer. This takes the medical transcriptionist completely out of the equation of compiling medical records, something I suspect the powers that we are giddy with, since it saves them the cost of using an agency for transcription services, and what do transcriptionists *do* anyway? It is not like anyone ever sees them.

Well, at the present time, I am still a medical transcriptionist and still have the inner ear disability. I do have a feeling of pride about my entrepreneurship in the sense that I know for a fact that in the external education for the Homebound programme university programme, I am considered one of their 'success stories' in that I did become self-sufficient. However, I can chalk that up to my own stubbornness and perhaps even a sense of denial over what my limits truly were. I can also say that the inner ear disorder has calmed down to a degree where I am able to pursue something that I really do enjoy doing—writing—and I am able to get out and about with much less difficulty than before.

There is also another component to my life that is different these days. Despite having a severely constricted social life while supporting myself, working all the time in the wee hours of the morning, I did meet a man in my neighbourhood who I later fell in love with and married. This would have to be a whole other discussion—the economics of marriage—but on a purely practical level, by moving in with Peter, the costs of supporting myself lessened, and I received the all-important health insurance through his company employer that makes my getting treatment easier. I am certainly able to work fewer hours, as Peter is willing to support me more and more, which makes it easier for me to feel well and thus I have a much better quality of life than I had previously.

So is it possible to be disabled, a woman and an entrepreneur? I hesitate to even use the word 'entrepreneur' since even though technically I was self-employed and a business owner, it appears that as a medical transcriptionist I was more of an unofficial employee without any benefits. I did work for myself, though, but not without the experience leaving scars on me. However, the desire to be self-sufficient was stronger than any of the deterrents I encountered while pursing this lifestyle. I suppose, when I was younger, I could have applied for Social Security

Disability (realising that I would still have a great deal of difficulty getting by on their meagre payments). I suppose, particularly as a young woman, that I could have played the helpless ingénue and tried to find a man to support me.

Instead, I made my choices with a clear conscience, and do not fret about mistakes I made or time I may have wasted. What is important is that I have made it through my experiences, have hopefully learned from them and have a better life today.

17

Gendered Spaces: Men in Women's Places

Vivian Besem Ojong

INTRODUCTION

At different levels amongst women entrepreneurs in South Africa, efforts have been made to include and empower women in decision-making positions, but men are covertly and openly sidestepping women and denying them the opportunity of reaping the benefits of their entrepreneurial endeavours. The data used for this paper is based on ethnographic research conducted cross-culturally among women entrepreneurs in KwaZulu-Natal from 2001 to 2005. A majority of the women were Ghanaian migrant professional hairdressers (50).[1] Seven South African women who were Zulu speaking, two Nigerian women who ran bakeries and two others who ran clothing shops and 10 Ghanaian male hairdressers.

WOMEN'S POSITIONING VIS-À-VIS CULTURE

Societies have been structured in a way that roles are attributed to different sexes. If you are a woman, it is accepted that you should freely perform the reproductive and catering role that reflects the needs of the family. However, roles change with changes in social life. In a patrilineal society such as in KwaZulu-Natal, most men fail to recognise these changes in the status and roles of women. Writing about western culture, Biddle and Thomas (1966) highlight that women were long pictured as naturally more stupid, delicate and emotional which justified their exclusion from better occupations and subordination to men generally. However, with changing gender constructions and women ascending to positions of business ownership, the balance of power as far as entrepreneurship is concerned, is changing with women-led businesses.

Entrepreneurship is still a contested space for women because of cultural practices which still expect them to be subordinate to men. Although women are establishing themselves in the area of business ownership, certain cultural practices are still a hindrance to their advancement, based on their gender. In KwaZulu-Natal like most societies in the world, men dominate in all spheres of life. According to the Zulu culture, a man is seen as superior to a woman and should be respected. However, amongst the matrilineal Akan of Ghana, women are taught through the socialisation process to be strong, motivated and strive for success (Ojong 2005). Ashanti women from matrilineal Akan in Ghana have a great deal of economic independence and are capable of pooling resources for business ventures. The Akan culture encourages women to 'reach out and take opportunities for entrepreneurship'. All the Ghanaian women who were included in our study were Akan and were permanently residing in KwaZulu-Natal and contributing to the local economy. Some Akan women had migrated to South Africa where they were running businesses in KwaZulu-Natal.

OBSTACLES THEY FACE
AND HOW THEY OVERCOME THEM

Entrepreneurship has enabled women to be self-reliant and non-dependent on their husbands for economic survival. The old power centres have shifted, and the women of power have not only shifted with them: they have helped this shift; indeed, they have been responsible for it by silently putting the weight of their ability where it will count, instead of just being counted (Miles 1985). Despite the obstacles they face, women are not prepared to lay down their economic independence simply to boost their husbands' masculine pride (Ojong and Moodley 2005). The obstacles come about as a result of the fact that they are women and have employed men to work in their businesses. For women, being in positions of authority brings a change in the balance of power between men and women because the position of women does not exist in a vacuum. It exists only in relation to the position of men (Davies 1994).

Davies (1994) remarked that male domination in patrilineal societies is built into the social and cultural systems and that even if a woman is brave enough to challenge these and tries to step out beyond the traditional female role, her husband can still exercise his ultimate control through force and re-establish the status quo, at least for that moment. In the study, it was found that it is not only the husbands who tended to exercise male control; boyfriends and even male employees often tried to renegotiate the status quo. The end result of this power struggle is often violence against the women entrepreneurs. Violence is experienced both at the workplace and at home, which impacts on their productivity as women, as leaders and as entrepreneurs.

A 44-year-old widow, Makhosi a South African businesswoman in KwaZulu-Natal owned a hair salon, 'Salon Makhosi', which was one of the biggest and oldest salons in Empangeni. Established in 1993, just before the first democratic elections in South Africa, she had six employees: four women and two men. She said that it was much easier for her female employees to take instructions and learn from her than it was for her male employees. As the owner of the business, she demanded that her employees arrive at work on time and that they explain any absence from work. She said it was 'a tough road' as far as her male employees were concerned. The men came to work whenever they wanted to and if they were absent from work, they refused to give reasons. When asked why she employed men, she said that she was obliged to employ men for two reasons. First, some male customers refused to be attended to by women and expected men to shave their hair. Second, because female owned businesses were easy targets for burglary, she employed men to act as security for her business. Makhosi's predicament was common across cultures for all female owned businesses.

Angela, a 42-year-old Nigerian woman owned a bakery in Richards Bay. She had been a secondary school teacher, teaching science until 2003, when she decided that she had had enough working under the leadership of men and started her own business. She went into this business jointly with her husband but she was the one managing the business on a daily basis. She had 11 employees: four men and six women. She said that as a woman running a business, she encountered many problems, from both Zulu men whom she employed, who expected not to take instructions from women and her Nigerian husband who expected to have total control of all income despite the fact that they jointly owned the business which she ran.

Women face obstacles which range from access to financial assistance to violence, which impact on their productivity. Women face violence perpetrated by men at the workplace and in the home. In most of the female led businesses, male employees attempt to invade women's space and tell them how the business is to be run. For instance, in Angela's bakery, when she asked the men to bake bread, they told her they were busy making buns. Sometimes she would start baking the bread and when she did so the men would join her. At other times, she would take over what they were busy with in order to emphasise her expectations of them.

Any attempt to dismiss a male employee can easily lead to violence towards the woman concerned. When dismissing a male employee, it is mostly done openly in the presence or vicinity of other employees because of the vulnerability to attacks. However, this is no guarantee that violence will be prevented because once fired, men often organise with their friends, who steal money and other valuables. Even those who are still employed may be involved in breaking into the business and stealing money and equipment. The question arises: how is a woman expected to perform at her maximum potential in the economy when she is being violated at the domestic and business environments?

Power struggles often occur as men fail to draw the lines between being husbands at home and being partners in business with their wives. They believe that women are incapable of taking the right decisions, despite the fact that they are running the business. Men who are in joint businesses with their wives, often expect that all daily sales be given to them or be deposited into their personal accounts despite the fact that the businesses have separate accounts. The African perspective is that a woman is subordinate (Krige 1962) and the informants believed that joint business ventures were used as strategies to maintain male dominance. Like Abner when a woman went into business alone, it was difficult for a man to subdue her economic independence.

A common problem that women who own businesses jointly with their husbands face, is verbal abuse. When the woman refuses to deposit all the money earned from the business into her husband's account, she is addressed as a thief in the presence of her children. As entrepreneurs, women feel like stopping at times since their husbands are only interested in using them to make profit. To be able to succeed under such circumstances, some women have decided to ignore their husbands and do what they believe is right for the well-being of the business and their future.

At home, women face violence because their husbands or boyfriends are intimidated by their financial independence and become aggressive. This happens often in situations where the women earn higher incomes than the men. Such men feel that whatever they give the women is insignificant. They feel threatened and resent other men talking to these women, even physically abusing the women if they see them talking to other men.

On 12 March 2005, Makhosi was seriously beaten by her boyfriend because she decided to take control over her finances. She had scars on her mouth and face from the abuse. She was scared of being involved with a man because she believed she could be violated again. When men approach her 'for love', she asked them whether they wanted her or the 'Makhosi salon'.

WHAT SPACE IS RESERVED FOR GENDER?

Gender is one of the oldest forces shaping human life. It distinguishes between male and female activities (Glen 1999). In the past decades, gender spaces have been fixed not fluid as was elutriated by the apprenticeship system in Ghana. Under this system, skills are taught for specificity and technicality (Fluitman 1992). Thus in Ghana, under the influence of the colonial type of education with the introduction of separate education for the different sexes, boys learnt to become carpenters, bricklayers, electricians, plumbers and so on, while girls learnt hairdressing, catering, dressmaking and so forth.

An apprentice is someone who works with another person with the aim of acquiring similar skills. With the increasing presence of Ghanaians in South Africa, the above mentioned gender stereotype activities seem to have become unimportant. This was observed during several months of fieldwork which initially was intended to investigate the reasons why the Ghanaian women were succeeding as hairdressers in South Africa.

In locating informants for the study, it was realised that gender spaces were becoming reconstructed as far as transnational activities were concerned. More Ghanaian men than women were found actively involved in hairdressing in South Africa. In Ghana, a woman and not a man is expected to learn hairdressing. According to the informants, girls who dropped out of school or whose parents could not afford school fees were sent to learn hairdressing. On the other hand, boys whose parents could not afford school fees were sent to acquire skills prescribed for men. In the past 15 years in South Africa, there seems to be a reconstruction of gender spaces especially with the encroachment by the Ghanaian men of women's spaces. This 'hijacking' of the Ghanaian women's social space has now led to competition of public spaces as men and women have to make similar choices in business.

Finding many men owning hair salons in Durban, a space which is supposed to be occupied by women, a decision, though unintended, was taken to investigate the new occurrence. An interest in finding out why men were now taking up careers as hairdressers was developed and whether from local to cross-border their decision would be the same. Most of the men, however, indicated that it was because of migration that they are involved in hairdressing. Among the men interviewed were carpenters, electricians, shoe-menders, bricklayers, plumbers. Upon arrival in South Africa, some of them realised that their skills could not be utilised because they all came in as refugees and could not be given employment. Asumang Isaac, one of the informants said that, 'if you go to look for a job, they would ask you for your identity book but in the salon, I do not need an identity book to work because I am working for a fellow Ghanaian.'[2] On the other hand, some of them decided to learn hairdressing before leaving Ghana. Some had been hairdressers in countries like Cameroon and Nigeria before coming to South Africa.

When asked whether they were proud of their new careers and whether they would feel the same way should they go back to Ghana, their feelings portrayed that it was only in transnationalism that gender spaces become unimportant. They indicated that they were respected in South Africa, but should they decide to go home, they could not remain in hairdressing, but would return to their original careers or open shops to sell different goods. They believed that at old age it would be difficult for them to continue dressing women's since women were attracted to them and came to their salons because they were young. Some said that South African women came to their salons because they believed that men had patience for them. What was observed during the fieldwork was that, when girls came to the salons (owned and ran by men) the Ghanaian men joked with them, which they enjoyed. They all saw hairdressing as a neat job and as a quick means of earning an income. Apart from those who came from other countries with capital to start their businesses, most of them worked for others for about a year or two before opening their own salons. During that period, they looked for means of regularising their stay in South Africa. A very popular means of doing this was to get involved in a marriage of convenience with a South African, or opening a shop using someone's identity.

Thus, from domestic to cross-border, the borderlines of gender spaces become fluid in nature. Looking at the fluidity in gender construction of spaces across borders, it is obvious that such spaces cannot be constructed in a vacuum, since transnational forces tend to affect peoples choices of activities.

THE EMBEDDED SPACE OF FAMILY LIFE AND BUSINESS ACTIVITY BY GENDER

The gender space in terms of decision-making in the household is also being affected by women's involvement in entrepreneurial activities in transnational spaces. One major observation which was made as far as gender representativity in hairdressing in Durban was concerned, was that although the Ghanaian men were assuming the activities of the other as far as financial survival was concerned, they were still tied to the traditional Ghanaian stereotype of a woman being responsible for the upkeep of the household (washing of clothes, cooking, taking care of children).

Thus, although women are involved in similar business activities like men, the Ghanaian women have integrated their entrepreneurial activities with their family or home responsibilities and sometimes, struggle to find a balance. Restaurants run by fellow Ghanaian women have lessened the burden of preparing lunch for other families as they all have resorted to buying from the restaurants for lunch. This is particular with those who are married. When lunch is bought, some is kept for the children who, as a daily routine, pass by the salons from school to eat before heading for home.

Although gender activities were changing because of transnationalism for the Ghanaian Diaspora in Durban, gender roles in the home had maintained its stance. This, however, was having a negative impact on the Ghanaian women since both the men and women were in the same type of business, taking cognisance of the fact that business is about competition.

Most of the women indicated with annoyance that while they woke up in the morning to prepare the children for school and breakfast for the entire family, their husbands remain on the bed and have enough rest. When they woke up, their only chore was to have a bath and eat and afterwards head for their workplaces. Most of the times, the women were the ones to wait for their domestic servants to come before they could leave for the hair salons. On some occasions, should the domestic servant fail to pitch for work, it was the responsibility of the women to clean the house as well. When they all went home after each day's work, the woman still had to cook while the men might relax and watch television.

As a result of the above, while hair salons run by men were opened as early as 7:30 a.m., those run by women could only be opened by 8 a.m. or earlier if they have managed to employ a Ghanaian man who was given the responsibility of opening the salon early. Most of the married women often went to their business sites after 9 a.m. or by 8:30 a.m. at peak periods of business.

It would be an overstatement to say that these women enjoyed absolute independence as the migration experience did not oust one's cultural practices as has been demonstrated above. Their culture stipulates that a man is supposed to take care of his household. Although the same culture also expects a woman, through specialisation to be engaged in a profitable employment, it is the responsibility of the man to provide for his household. The men are still the heads of their households, especially as seen in the eyes of outsiders (Ghanaians in Durban). This is especially demonstrated in public gatherings when such men take all the decisions and the women submit to them.

CONCLUSION

The findings in the study demonstrate that gendered spaces become unimportant or insignificant when people are involved in transnational spaces. This is because across borders, survival becomes the essential factor and ego or machismo is given the 'back seat'. Culture seems to be losing its place in the negotiation of gender activities across national boundaries. As more Ghanaian men become hairdressers across borders, there seems to be a renegotiation of gender spaces. In Ghana, the culture stipulates different types of socialisation for both girls and boys, which are very distinct. This new trend demonstrates the fact that culture is not static but subject to change with global forces. This change not only affects their economic power but also their decision-making authority at home with their husbands.

The old stereotype is for the Ghanaian men to provide for their families. On the contrary, especially in the case of those women entrepreneurs who were already established as entrepreneurs in South Africa before marriage, the women are now providing for their families. As the women owned several salons and in most cases, encouraged their husbands to run one of them, it could be said that 'the tides had turned'.

As the family becomes rich in terms of their increase in assets (a house back in Ghana, a flat in South Africa), and the woman's financial contribution in the building or purchasing of these assets, is acknowledged and the women are no longer subordinate to their husbands in earning capacity.

NOTES

1. This was the initial group I had set out to investigate before expanding my sample to include women from other cultures to see the commonalities and differences with respect to gender spaces and women's positioning.
2. Interview of a Ghanaian male hairdresser called John Kwesi, Durban, South Africa, 20 July 2004.

REFERENCES

Biddle, B.J. and E.J. Thomas. 1966. *Role Theory*. New York: John Wiley.

Davies, M. 1994. *Women and Violence*. New Jersey: Zed Books.

Fluitman, F. 1992. *Traditional Apprenticeship in West Africa: Recent Evidence and Policy Options*. Geneva: International Labour Organisation.

Glen, E.N. 1999. *The Social Construction and Institutionalisation of Gender and Race: An Integrative Framework*. London: Sage publications.

Krige. J. 1962. *The Social System of The Zulus*. Pietermaritzburg: Shuter and Shooter.

Miles, R. 1985. *Women and Power*. London: MacDonald.

Ojong. V.B. 2005. 'Entrepreneurship and Identity among a Group of Ghanaian Women in Durban'. PhD thesis, Department of Anthropology and Development studies, University of Zululand.

Ojong, V.B. and V. Moodley. 2005. 'Leadership and Issues Affecting the Productivity of Women Entrepreneurs in KwaZulu-Natal', *Agenda*, 65: 65–82.

18

Poverty, Empowerment and Grass-roots Democracy: Defining Participatory Approaches

Sita Venkateswar

'Words do not signify things but intimate relations.'
Martin Buber, *I and Thou.*

'I wanted to develop a style of writing which would be consonant with lived experience, in all its variety and ambiguity.'
Michael Jackson, *At Home in the World.*

And thus begins this paper, which is not really a paper as much as an experiment in form. Through this writing, I seek a mode of expression that is appropriate to the relationships that we are attempting to forge while delineating the process of engaging in this research and writing about it. The inspiration for this endeavour comes from Bochner and Ellis (2002) innovative text, which instructs and illustrates these entwined processes. While the content of this paper is broadly about the research that we are involved in Kolkata, it is also about the collaborative and participatory modes in which we aspire to engage with each other and the participants in this research. Hence, the pronouns in this essay move fluidly between the singular and the collective, the various voices appear and merge with each other or stand apart marking an individual and separate presence. And to be faithful to the spirit of this endeavour, the form of this paper as manifest here marks the first expression of a longer process of collaborative writing that will occur over a period of time during subsequent fieldwork stages over the next few years.

In my view it is suggestive of excessive *hubris* to assume a point of origin for the process when we appeared on the scene in September 2004, so, we begin with Amina and her discussion of her work in Howrah since 1998.[1]

Amina:

Assalaam Aleykum.

I am Amina Khatoon, and have come from Howrah's Shibpur locality. There is an organisation there, whose name is Howrah Pilot Project. I have been associated with this organisation since 1998. Through this organisation, a school is run, called Talimi Haq School. This is a non-formal school. About 70 children come to this school to learn. The children who come to this school have never attended a school before, nor have their families ever thought that the children should go to school. These children start working from the time they are seven and start earning money. We bring such children to our school. We teach them. We do not give them any degree or certificate but we try to make them into good human beings. We try to instill in them a sense of good and bad, right and wrong. After giving them a rudimentary education we admit them to the local formal primary school.

Because this is quite a poor basti, where mainly mill workers and their families live, illiteracy is high and because of lack of education there are more children in families. Having many children, women's health is poor. In association with the Marie Stopes clinic, we also started working for family planning. In the beginning, it was difficult to do this work. In a Muslim basti, doing family planning work was seen negatively. Slowly, after counselling them about their health, we started organising ligations for the women. For this I had to say that I myself was a mother of two children. They did not like it that an unmarried girl spoke about such things with them. So I had to adopt this ruse that I too was married and had gone in for an operation and was well.

Apart from these activities, we are also involved in another work. This is making masalas. We started this work in 1999. Because we are Muslims, our food is distinct and tasty, especially biryani, champ, etc. At that time we did not have any shop nor anyone to sell this through.

We took our masalas to meetings, conferences and exhibitions. Thus our masalas started getting sold. Though cheaper masalas were available in the market, nonetheless people who took our masalas wanted to buy more again. During this time we came in contact with SASHA, a livelihood enterprises support shop in Calcutta. After 3 years of trying to interest them in our products, they started ordering masalas from us. Initially they used to buy 30 packets at a time. Now they are exporting our masalas.

For the women here, it is good that they can earn something from this. And now we want to directly export our masalas ourselves. The surplus from this can also support our school. We want this to become an independent enterprise without any support. We want to convert the organisation into one that can support itself from its own income. We are planning to start a small factory in a nearby area. Definitely this is impossible without your help and blessings. Such a factory will itself be an exemplary achievement. Through such an enterprise women will gain an income and our work will also get financial support. And simultaneously the future of the children will also be brightened, whose future is lost in today's darkness.

Tabassum:

My name is Tabassum Sidikur, and first, I will tell you one thing, I am not comfortable in English, but I will try my best to give you some points about my work and the area where I stay. The name of our organisation in Narkeldanga is Rehnuma-e-Niswaan. This is a woman's organisation committed to the cause of social welfare in the basti area of Narkeldanga and its immediate neighbourhood. The area is an all Muslim dominated basti spread over approximately three square kilometres. It is a thickly populated Muslim area belonging to economically disadvantaged sections with impaired or no access to basic services of life. With increasing population and concentration in small pockets, a large number of illegal constructions are taking place in the basti resulting in very high levels of congregations and public health hazards. Most of the people are daily wage earners with low wage levels and irregular income. Again, the closure of large numbers of factories led to wide-scale unemployment and also that has resulted in people adopting illegal ways to support their families. There are two government aided schools in the area, one secondary for girls and one secondary for boys. However, considering the population, the capacity of the schools is not adequate. The level of education is also very low, very poor especially among the women, making them very vulnerable to social and economic exploitation. The problems range from poor health conditions consequent on early marriages and having large numbers of children, to having very little means to earn a livelihood for themselves, leading to a situation of total disenfranchisement of the women in the community. The objective of the organisation is empowerment of the women by provision of means to acquire some skills to earn a decent livelihood to support themselves. Improvement of livelihood is conceivably the most important entry point in a low income settlement or community, and through this a variety of their social concerns like education, primary healthcare and hygiene. Empowerment of women and the community as a whole can be addressed through these means.

Sita:

I am now going to talk about the research that I am undertaking in the city. It started quite recently, in January 2003, and I am working with some grassroots women's organisations in really poor parts of the city. This research is located in Howrah and Narkeldanga. For residents of Kolkata, these names would immediately signal various categories of information about these areas, the demographics and socio-economic condition of that population. I am exploring the various initiatives by small, grassroots women's organisations which have emerged in these areas led by young, Muslim women like Amina or Tabassum, and others like them, who challenge and subvert the many stereotypes that are made about poor, Muslim women. We have young women here, who are articulate, reflective and proactive. Who have taken the initiative to change not only the course of their own lives, but the lives of those around them. These women have a vision for the future, an aspiration for themselves and their community, which does not conform to any of the images that are disseminated in the media. The work that I have started attempts to understand what these women are doing in the neglected parts of the city, the process by which these have come about, the impact it is having on the women themselves, their individual lives and circumstances, on their families and the larger community. The premise that I am using is that, if these initiatives are a manifestation of empowerment (and here I define empowerment as the ability to take action to make some change in one's life), then how does empowerment actually impact on that particular individual's life? In what ways does it manifest over the course of their lifetime? Therefore, my research is envisaged as a long-term process that will track these people's lives, the lives of the community, recording and documenting the changes that have ensued since their activities commenced.

My research also has a corresponding applied dimension to it. I cannot appear on this scene with a research interest, without involving myself in the activities that these women undertake. My role then, is also to facilitate, to support, to assist in obtaining funding, to construct networks, to open doors, create access that in various ways will enable them to do what they want to do better. One of the distinctions that I note between myself and what I can achieve and what Amina or Tabassum can accomplish is my cultural capital, my social capital and the access that I thereby have to various resources within the larger society which remains closed to them. Thus, my role is also to strategically manoeuvre through these various sectors of the society and open doors through which they can also pass.

Lorena:

I have mostly questions at this stage. I want to identify the conditions under which hope is constructed at both individual and collective levels. The relationship between hope, agency and empowerment is what I want to explore, and the role that local NGO activism plays in the facilitation of hope. What is the process by which hope is created and how is it shared by these women and their families? How is hope tempered? And what strategies are in place to deal with the constraints imposed on these communities by other forces (for example the state)? What is the role of pessimism under these circumstances?

You may start to wonder at this point, the context in which these voices were speaking and who they were addressing. Amina, Tabassum and my voice, as they are heard here speaking about poverty and empowerment, are addressing an audience at an international conference in Kolkata in December 2004. Lorena's voice, on the other hand was inserted into the paper that developed after our return to New Zealand,

and as a PhD student commencing her research, aptly, only has queries at this stage. The voices as constructed here mark an inter-subjective encounter and an emerging collective understanding of the context. But we also occupy our singular spaces which are never erased even if we sometimes speak with one voice. Despite appearing to conform to a Habermasian ideal speech situation we must not elide the micro politics of power that traverses the spaces between us, though we all seem to be equally enabled to speak. But that is the subject of a different paper, and I will not dwell on it here.

These voices have been brought together to address a very different forum, and I am certain that there would be consensus among all to lending their speech to the trajectory of the text that follows on from here.

Te haro o te kahu
(Look beyond the horizon to the expansive views seen through the eyes of the hawk—A *Māori* proverb)

And so, I step away from my immediate field of vision in Howrah or Narkeldanga and try to discern larger spaces. And in doing so, I arrive at a clearer view of my own location in these proceedings. I firmly position myself as a public anthropologist. I see that role as offering the potential to transcend the limits of our mandate as a merely academic enterprise, challenging us as anthropologists to consider forms of action and intervention as *the* ethical course within the current global conjuncture. But who or what is a public anthropologist? I borrow Borofsky's definition as it appears in his Public Anthropology site:

> Public Anthropology demonstrates the ability of anthropology and anthropologists to effectively address problems beyond the discipline— illuminating the larger social issues of our times as well as encouraging broad, public conversations about them with the explicit goal of fostering social change. It affirms our responsibility, as scholars and citizens, to meaningfully contribute to communities beyond the academy—both local and global, that make the study of anthropology possible.
> (www.publicanthropology.org/Defining/definingpa/htm<http://www. publicanthropology.org/Defining/definingpa/htm)

I want to trace a genealogy for the word 'scholar' as used here, which seems to have its origins in a mode of engagement first seen in Aristotle's writings. In his discussion of the 'intellectual virtues', Aristotle named the virtue that dealt with 'context, practice, experience, common sense, intuition and practical wisdom' as *phronesis*. In Aristotle's view, *phronesis* is the basis for an embodied, ethico-political existence which is explicitly tied to the goal of human flourishing. It is in the richness of Aristotle's vision of our humanness, an encompassing holism which includes our senses, our passions and attachments, as well as our life among friends and in communities that Aristotle seems to foreshadow a distinctly contemporary anthropological ethos. And it is anthropology more than any other discipline that brings to bear the various facets of knowing contained within Aristotle's conceptualisation of *phronesis*. Anthropology's sensitivity to multiple values, its emphasis on the particular together with the significance of emotions to reflection and understanding of the world, all of which have traditionally marked its tension with the 'hard' sciences, are integral components of *phronesis* or practical wisdom (cf. Polkingthorne 2002: 108.). Although conceived as an individual virtue, it is also integrally implicated within wider political concerns. As Flyvbjerg (2001) concisely summarizes, 'Aristotle, in discussing *phronesis*, is mainly talking about ethics in relation to social and political praxis, that is, the relationship you have to society when you act' (Bent 2001: 55).

It becomes immediately evident how seamlessly Borofsky's conceptualisation of Public Anthropology articulates with an Aristotelian rendering of *phronesis* as a basis for intellectual action. It emerges from a long and hallowed tradition of the role of the public intellectual in any society which has its roots among the ancient Greeks and acquired greater clarity with Gramsci's writing on the subject. But a puzzling omission in that call to action is the lack of mention of the objective of social change, that is, towards what end are we advancing social change? The inclusion of 'social justice' or, better yet, 'human flourishing', would firmly ground it as a 'good' that is derived from an ethico-moral framework that is more likely to generate widespread consensus as an appropriate utopian hope.

Exploring now what the above caption implies for us as 'citizens', is the 'citizen' referred to above bound to a specific nation? Or is it more of a transnational citizenship that is being conceptualised here, reflecting the diversity of our allegiances as anthropologists straddling varied field sites, or shifting between 'home' and the 'field'? These are not merely rhetorical questions I pose them as expressions of a dilemma that I am certain most anthropologists will acknowledge, as we struggle to define the field of our actions and interventions. My concern here is to define a legitimate field of action for us as public anthropologists, which extends beyond the scope of our territorially constituted citizenship and spans the globe. That, to my mind, is the landscape in which the public anthropologist is positioned. Notwithstanding the critics of the 'global citizen', whose arguments are based on interrogating the sphere of *rights* which can be legally conferred on such a person, suffice it to say that for the public anthropologist, it is as an active global citizen impelled by the 'ideal of public spiritedness and ethico-political concern' (Mouffe 1992: 238) that she responds to her allegiances to numerous communities across the world.

All this suggests that I have extended the scope of our 'ability as anthropologists to effectively address problems beyond the discipline...' in ways that denote more than 'encouraging, broad, public conversations' although that too is a significant part of our contribution as anthropologists. I am alluding to *other* interventions here, that draw on our uniquely anthropological mode of appraising any situation, to explicitly engender forms of action that are directly implicated in various radical emancipatory projects underway in many parts of the world. Therefore, our task as public anthropologists on the global stage, is to work in tandem with citizens elsewhere, towards a vision of a more plural and equitable social order.

But how are we to respond to the many situations that compel our attention and demand a response? As anthropologists, we are already interpellated within a variety of contexts through our research and our personal lives. Therefore, the forms of intervention emerge from those circumstances, and will vary according to what is demanded at a particular point in time. They require to be addressed alongside of the various communities whom we ally within the 'publicscape'[2] of our interventions as public anthropologists.

Pertinent to the context of my current research in Kolkata with Amina, Tabassum and others are the discourses related to decentralisation and local governance in India. They include the developments regarding citizen's access to information, with the potential to advance transparency and accountability in structures of governance. They are augmented by the expanded and empowered role of civilian groups as an outcome of these processes. The 'broad, public conversations' that I can generate which derive from my awareness of these possibilities is an illustration of how I can contribute as a public anthropologist in this context. Or the various models of intervention which follow on from these developments elsewhere in the world, which the activists and NGOs in my network can usefully explore within the context of their own actions within local communities. My ability to explore funding options to augment the outreach of some of these NGOs, to mobilise wider awareness and discussion on these matters among the larger population is another illustration of intervention that conceivably addresses issues of social justice.

In the current global conjuncture, the public anthropologist, both within the academy and beyond, can assist in mobilising social change. Harnessing an array of skills and resources that have accumulated in that capacity, she can contribute towards eventual human flourishing however distant that utopian hope may appear.

Kahohi ki te kanohi, pokuhiwi ki te pokuhiwi, ka whawhai tonu atu
(Face to face, shoulder to shoulder we will strive together without end—*Māori* proverb)

NOTES

1. This speech was originally delivered in Urdu and has been translated into English.
2. Following Arjun Appadurai's (1992) discussion of 'scapes'.

REFERENCES

Appadurai, Arjun. 1992. 'Disjuncture and Difference in the Global Cultural Economy', in M. Featherstone (ed.), *Global Culture: Nationalism, Globalization and Modernity*, pp. 295–310. London: Sage Publications.

Bent, Flyvbjerg. 2001. *Making Social Science Matter: Why Social Inquiry Fails and How It Can Succeed*. Cambridge: Cambridge University Press.

Bochner, Arthur and Carolyn Ellis. 2002. *Ethnographically Speaking: Autoethnography, Literature and Aesthetics*. Walnut Creek, CA: AltaMira Press.

Borofsky, Robert. 2006. *Public Anthropology*. Available online at www.publicanthropology. org/Defining/definingpa/htm < http://www.publicanthropology.org/Defining/definingpa/htm (downloaded on 8 August 2006).

Flyvbjerg, Bent. 2001. *Making Social Science Matter: Why Social Inquiry Fails and How It Can Succeed*. Cambridge: Cambridge University Press.

Mouffe, Chantal. 1992. 'Democratic Citizenship and the Political Community', in Chantal Mouffe (ed.), *Dimensions of Radical Democracy*, pp. 225–239. London: Verso.

Polkingthorne, E. Donald. 2002. *Practice and the Human Sciences: The Case for a Judgement Based Practice of Care*. Albany: State University of New York Press.

PART SIX
Conclusion

The concluding chapter focuses on the significance of women's cultural perspectives and identities as inspiring contributions to the workplace and recommends that global organisations make concerted efforts to integrate women's perspectives into workplace policy and practice. Fay Patel frames the struggle of women within a cultural context and encourages a multi-perspective approach across global organisational frameworks. She appeals for the recognition, respect and appreciation of women's multiple cultural contexts and rejects the continued negative judgements that women receive based on the dominant Western worldviews.

19

Locating Women's Struggles in a Cultural Context

Fay Patel

INTRODUCTION

Women's roles in organisations continue to be complex and ill-defined in the 21st century. Yet over the centuries there has been a wide range of women's movements that attempted to inform the policies and practices of organisations so that women's ways of working, knowing and doing could be acknowledged and respected. Organisations have evolved in a number of ways over the years, but it seems that women's cultural contexts have been overlooked. We need to place women's struggles within a cultural context in order to understand why women's perspectives conflict with workplace politics and practices that are designed according to Western norms.

Women's place in society has been the subject of debate over many centuries because women's social and professional roles are intrinsically woven into the web of values and beliefs of that society. This discussion provides a broad overview of the dilemmas facing working women in a new era and raises questions about women's continued marginalised status in national and global organisational contexts.

Are All Women the Same?

Unless we begin to recognise and respect women and their roles in society from their respective cultural standpoints, it is a senseless exercise to attempt to understand women's ways of working, knowing and doing. Wood (2001) uses the term essentialising to describe the inappropriateness of reducing women's and men's characteristics to a few generalisations. According to Wood (2001: 18), 'essentializing obscures the range of characteristics possessed by individual women and men and conceals differences among members of each sex.' We should exercise caution in essentialising women across cultures. Women are not a homogeneous group. Many Western workplace conventions were established on the basis that women are a homogenous group thus blatantly disregarding their unique cultural perspectives and knowledge, for example. These generalisations may have met the need for women in Western cultures to uplift themselves from the humiliating positions that they held for centuries in the Western society. Perhaps, it was an attempt to be seen as a united group and to present one voice.

Western Cultural Contexts

Women are frequently judged by their appearances, affiliations or non-affiliations to social groups, by their level of education and accomplishments in accordance with Western cultural contexts. A good example of this is in Audrey Shalinsky's chapter on 'Gender Issues in the Afghanistan Diaspora' in Hart, Weathermon and Armitage (2006: 134) where Nadia's accomplishments are judged and praised from an American cultural perspective. 'Since then she has lived in Wyoming and Washington DC, has learned to drive in rush hour like a native East Coast resident, and has been the first in her family to become a U.S. citizen.' As a result of similar judgements, women are often confined to their visible and invisible spaces. The use of the term 'Western' and 'West' in the context of this chapter refers to ideologies, structures, and practices that are associated with the United States of America (USA) as a culture and as a super power and one that influences global culture and communication through its economic and political policies. It also includes other economically powerful nations that share similar cultural values and beliefs as the USA. 'West' and 'Western' also refer to those countries that were once colonial powers, that promoted English as universal language, and European values and culture through various means.

The dominant culture that many women are acculturated into is the Western culture. According to Samovar and Porter (2005: 43–44), acculturation is an adaptation to a new culture while hanging onto the norms and values of a primary culture. There are women who may have lived and are living between the dominant Western culture and a suppressed other culture. This second or third culture has its own set of values and beliefs that may differ somewhat from Western culture resulting in cultural conflict in the workplace. Judy Yung's reconstruction of 'The Life and Times of Flora Belle Jan' a young Chinese immigrant who failed to assimilate into the American culture clearly illustrates the cultural conflicts that many women experience even today (Hart, Weathermon and Armitage 2006: 259). Yung articulates the essence of women's struggle by focusing on how 'the transformation of identity at different points in one's life (is) due to the interplay of history, culture, power, and personality.' Furthermore, Yung contends that Flora Belle Jan's story serves as a reminder of 'the high costs that women of colour have to pay for the racial and gender inequities of our society.' On the other hand, for some women, Western culture may be the only cultural context that they know. In these cases, these women may be totally immersed in Western culture because they have undergone the 'total process of learning (their own) culture' (Samovar, Porter and McDaniel 2007: 20–21).

Julia Wood (2001: 6) contextualises her communication, gender and cultural experiences within a Western framework based on living and working in America. From her lived experience, she claims that 'Western culture discounts your experiences and limits your opportunities.' Furthermore, Wood (2001: 8) contends that 'Western culture as a whole has constructed inequalities between men and women, and this continues in our era.' When women speak, they are expected to speak with authority (according to their class, education, wealth and language ability, for example). However, when women do not identify a source of authority, what they say is often either disregarded as significant or discarded altogether.

In this chapter, concepts such as 'women, culture and communication', 'workplace, work space, and organisational culture and communication,' 'empowerment of women' and 'women as catalysts for change' are reviewed to encourage comparison and examination from Western and non-Western perspectives. These terms of reference are briefly clarified within the discussion. Questions that are not addressed and that remain outside the discussion of this chapter include reasons why women in organisational settings take on the bullying patterns of behaviour over other women in an organisation; why feminist research continues to use women subjects mostly located in a Western culture; and why we, the 'educated, privileged women' continue to be the media through which other women have to be heard and seen?

Women are where they are today because of numerous factors that continue to obscure their value and worth as significant contributors to society. The irony is that various attempts to improve the condition of women in the West have brought us to a point where women are stuck with workplace policies and practices that belong to past decades. This discourse is framed within a multidisciplinary context because it is necessary to acknowledge the relevant aspects of the different approaches to women's struggles from a broad perspective.

Feminisms

It is hoped that the multidisciplinary approach provides a more in-depth understanding into how cultural contexts enhance and/or hinder women's full participation in organisations that are modelled on Western values and norms. Wood (2001: 5) defines feminism 'as an active commitment to equality and respect for life. Commitment to equality and respect for all people, as Wood (2001) claims, is our fundamental responsibility. She offers a good overview of the different feminisms that have emerged over the years in order to respond to a range of social inequalities in Western culture. No single feminism is of greater or lesser value than the other. One may embrace a number of qualities from different feminisms either consciously or subconsciously. It is important to acknowledge that there are other feminisms which embrace the struggles of non-Western women with strong commitment to equality and justice but these are not as well recognised in mainstream Western society. Therefore, women who are born and/or educated in the West continue to draw on Western models of feminism.

Which feminism gains prominence has everything to do with power and privilege. Which women are regarded as constructors of knowledge and whose knowledge is more important depends on the power and priviledge that they hold on society.

Many aspects of the multiple feminist approaches may easily justify the means one uses to overcome a particular situation whether it is dealing with an oppressive male manager in the workplace or trying to ignore subtle forms of harassment. For example, standpoint theory, (Wood 2001: 57) places emphasis on the influence of gender, race and class on a person's life, position in society and the experience that results from being placed in that position. A person's way of life and position in society reflects certain values, beliefs, behaviours and norms that are acceptable cultural practices within the structure of that society.

Locating women's struggle within a cultural context will contribute to a better understanding of the large number of cultural challenges that women face in a given situation. For example, cultural feminism acknowledges that women and men have different ways of knowing but this fact is often overlooked in an organisation. On the other hand, if one subscribes to socialist feminism one finds that women's struggles in the workplace are often a result of the extension of the stifling patriarchal structure within the family in many different societies. Wood (2005: 29) claims that Western culture is patriarchal as are some other cultures. We should pause for a moment to acknowledge the fact that stifling patriarchal structures are widespread across Western communities that are part of the 'developed world'.

Women in 'Developing Communities'

We have to acknowledge a different set of priorities, values, and norms that women's cultural contexts bring to the foreground when we situate women's struggle within a cultural content. For example, women in developing communities experience challenges that may be more intense than the challenges that women in developed communities experience. It is important to examine and compare the nature of empowerment of women in a developing community context with that of a developed community context in order to assess if empowerment really enhances the quality of life for all women in a specific context. For purposes of this discussion, the term 'developing community' is preferred instead of terms such as 'developing country and nation', the 'South' and 'Third World' which according to Melkote and Steeves (2001) are geographically defined and limited.

Communication for development experts often use these terms when they frame concerns of development among communities that are less advantaged, have little or no access to basic human rights, who live in poverty and under oppression because of their race, class and gender. Developing communities is a not geographically defined nor limited and includes communities that are disadvantaged by class, race and gender (among other categories) and who have been denied access to basic human rights in one form or another. It makes little sense to use geographically limited classifications in the 21st century when we find that there is an increasing migration of communities to the developed, industrialised, economically powerful countries and that there already exists a large number of people within the developed countries who have limited or no access to basic human rights because of race, class, and gender.

In reviewing women's roles in development, one may gain additional insights into challenges presented to women in a developing context and this would better inform feminist agendas and permit us to observe the distinctions between the developing and developed context. Melkote and Steeves (2001) contend that women's role in development was sidelined and ignored over the decades in terms of their contributions to the rural and agrarian communities in which they lived. They note from their extensive research into the dominant paradigm of develop-ment that it was biased towards men. According to Melkote and Steeves (2001: 100), the dominant paradigm of development in the 1950s to 1970s focused on modernisation and it was 'mainly concerned with economic growth…and encouragement of all factors and institutions that accelerated and maintained high growth in areas such as capital-intensive industrialisation, high technology, private ownership of factors of productivity, free trade, and the principle of laissez faire.' Under the dominant paradigm of development, Melkote and Steeves (2001: 186) found that 'the benefits of the modernization process had accrued exclusively to men who derived greater opportunities and resources, while women were confined to the welfare sector.' Furthermore, 'women were denied access to technical training, education, rights to land, and modernizing technology.' It is important to reflect on this event of the mid-twentieth century and identify the perpetrators of this gross injustice against women. It comes as no surprise that the modernisation package that originated in America was based on Western cultural values and norms and was exported to developing communities as an attractive package that guaranteed a 'desired level of development.' Women's significant role in development only began to gain recognition and momentum towards the end of the last century.

On a global scale, we find that many organisations (in both developing and developed community contexts) continue to resemble the male dominated organisational culture of the past centuries. Conrad and Poole (2005: 343) claim that the 'dominant perspective on organizations focuses on homogeneity and separation. Managers are separated from workers; organizations are separated from their environments; and employees are separated from their families and members of other organizations.' It is imperative that organisations revisit their culture and communication policies with a view to making them more inclusive of women's ways of knowing and doing.

WOMEN, CULTURE AND COMMUNICATION

The concepts of culture and communication have been defined and explained in numerous ways over the years. Culture in the context of this discussion is a combination of the values, beliefs, and norms that are embedded in the way of life of an individual or a group of people. According to Wood (2005: 19), 'gender is embedded within culture and reflects and shapes the values and assumptions of its cultural context.' How women communicate their cultural perspectives will be quite different from the way men communicate their cultural perspectives. For the purposes of this discussion, communication is defined as a dynamic, multi-channelled process through which we convey what we think we mean to those who then receive and interpret the message as best as they can by making meaning of it from their respective cultural contexts.

Women's and Men's Cultural Roles within Organisations

Women and men's roles in society are socially constructed and more frequently referred to as gendered roles. Wood (2001: 23) states that 'socially endorsed views of masculinity and femininity are taught to individuals through a variety of cultural means.' How women and men behave in an organisation, for example, is an outcome of how women and men have been groomed for their role within their individual social and cultural contexts. Each will communicate within that organisational context from their cultural vantage points. A women's cultural perspective is communicated in a number of ways that may not be acknowledged respected nor in the workplace. Culture and communication are intrinsically entwined and women's and men's way of communicating their cultural values and practices may vastly differ. Wood (2001: 35) asserts that to 'understand what gender means and how meanings of gender change, we must explore cultural values and the institutions and activities through which those are expressed and promoted.' Wood (2001: 61) suggests that gender is 'culturally constructed and that the meanings a culture assigns to femininity and masculinity are expressed and sustained through communication.' Other considerations that affect cultural context, according to Punnett (2004) are language and religion. These become even more important when an organisation conducts business on an international level. Punnett (2004) advocates that international managers need to understand the linguistic and religious variations among diverse cultures and the relationship between language, religion and cultural values in order to respond appropriately to workplace issues. Religious and linguistics considerations in the workplace are important for all communities because of the increased migration of diverse cultural communities. How gender is understood and received or rejected (and particularly how women are placed within the diverse cultures) in an international context is one of the many important considerations for all organisations if they wish to participate effectively in the global economy. Conrad and Poole (2005: 5) claim that organisational communication is complex in that the interpersonal and the organisational dimensions require constant negotiation. This is an area of effective communication that is often overlooked and underestimated among organisational managers in many parts of the world. Another important issue Conrad and Poole (2005) raise is that organisations are not mere 'containers' and are made up of people and therefore need to respond to their human needs.

WORKPLACE, WORK-SPACE AND ORGANISATIONAL CULTURAL CONTEXTS

This discussion focuses on organisational contexts that are mainly Western because that is a common and familiar scenario for many women who come from either Western cultures or have been educated in Western cultural contexts. This is done to illustrate that the dominant organisational culture and communication framework in the 21st century remains Western and that employees from diverse non-Western cultures remain on the periphery. Workplaces have evolved over the years in terms of a diverse workforce and working environments. However, many organisations ignore the changes and continue to operate as usual.

Workplace generally refers to the physical space where women and men work outside and inside the home. 'Work space' is a little more ambiguous. It could mean physical space but more recently it refers to the 'hidden' and silent spaces where women and men find themselves at work. Some of them are threatened because what was originally and traditionally women's or men's space is now being taken over by the other gender. Whatever the form of the organisational structure, physical workplace or work space, women are subjected to various forms of gender discrimination on an ongoing basis.

Glass Ceilings, Glass Walls and Fluid Floors

Gender discrimination occurs in verbal and non-verbal forms. Often, subtle forms of discrimination remain disguised in the workplace. Among the labels used to describe the subtle forms of discrimination against women are *glass ceilings* and *glass walls*. Wood (2001: 266–67) states that glass ceilings refer to 'the invisible barrier that limits the advancement of women and minorities' while glass walls refer to 'sex segregation on the job'. The latter is associated with ascribing traditionally feminine roles (such as secretary, typing of meeting minutes, and so forth) to menial tasks at the lower levels of the corporate ladder. Many women, depending on their race, class and culture have been subjected to such discrimination at some point of their working lives in an organisation. Women often share their frustration with trying to work between a given set of goals and time frames and new or modified requirements that emerge at short notice. This makes them feel highly stressed and anxious and sometimes results in them looking bad and incompetent in the workplace. The term 'fluid floors' may be used to describe such forms of subtle discriminatory practices. 'Fluid floors' refers to the unsteady surface on which the employee stands when the supervisor or team leader constantly expands and contracts the timelines and nature of the task. It makes the employee look unreliable and disorganised, but the condition for instability and disorganisation is created by the supervisor or team leader (a woman or a man) who constantly shifts the parameters. This is done through the modification of existing goals and introduction of new policies at short notice. This means that women have to struggle to achieve their primary goals as first set out by their supervisor and at the same time to accomodate the new directives.

The following scenario may be familiar to women in different contexts. For example, when one is given an assignment, one is required to fulfil several criteria. However, as the employee moves towards completion of the task and/or becomes fully engaged in the activity after spending a fair amount of energy and time, supervisors modify goals and directions. In other words, the floor covering changes and becomes fluid leaving the employee uncertain as to exactly how she is progressing.

The term 'fluid floors' is best described as having the rug pulled from under your feet leaving you unsteady and unsure of yourself. This may also explains why women's opportunities are hindered in the workplace. However, it is imperative that women's ways of working or wormen's work behaviour is given recognition and respect. It must be integrated into workplace performance reviews.

Women's Work and Ways of Working

What constitutes 'women's work?' This is a question that remains at the centre of the debate in an international context. It becomes more complex when one accepts that cultural norms define 'work' in different ways. If we continue to ignore this and to use only the Western definitions and understanding of 'work', this may result in cultural conflict. Women's traditional roles have changed in the same way that women's and (men's) carefully delineated career roles and paths of the past century have evolved. In addition to this, how women work, what patterns and behaviours women manifest in their working role and 'women's ways of working,' provide another dimension to placing women's roles within a cultural context. Research on 'woman's ways of working' is available but organisations are not integrating it in their policies and practices. Much of the gender inequity and discrimination that working women experience on a day-to-day basis is also unaccounted for within organisations. Dunn (1997: 161) focuses on women's working habits and highlights some of the important considerations that remain absent in the organisational culture and communication practices of most organisations. She contends that while it is abundantly clear that women differ from men in their work habits, this is often not considered in workplace performance reviews and evaluations. An organisational culture is built on a patriarch model of delivery. Women including those who hold important, higher level positions in an organisation are either ignored or overlooked. Communication researchers have categorised this as dysfunctional communication pattern that inhibit progress for women in the workplace.

Dysfunctional Communication Patterns

Women make references to negative workplace behaviour that intimidates them and hampers their success but these conversations are nearly always off the record. These behaviour patterns were examined by Reardon (in Dunn, 1997:165) who found that the 'Dysfunctional Communication Patterns' (DCPs) include categories such as dismissive, retaliatory, patronising, and exclusionary. She highlights some of the negative messages that women receive verbally and non-verbally on a regular basis but remain powerless to deal with. Among the dismissive DCPs that women experience are interruptions, ignoring and talking above women. In addition, Reardon (ibid: 179) cites the practice of being overlooked for promotion, having ideas stolen, and being underpaid and undermined, as reasons why women choose to leave organisations to move on. Clearly, workplaces, work-spaces and organisational culture and communication have diversified at a rapid rate over the last few decades. Unfortunately, although 'attitudes about a diverse workplace also have improved but still serve as barriers to change,' according to Conrad and Poole (2005: 377). However, various attempts are made to facilitate women's empowerment to enable them to challenge oppressive organisational policies and practices.

EMPOWERMENT OF WOMEN

Parpart, Rai and Straudt (2002: 15) provide a fresh perspective on empowerment in their text 'Rethinking Empowerment'. Most importantly, they reject the dichotomised definition of empowerment that distinguishes between those who hold power over and those who do not. In line with their view, it becomes necessary to view empowerment as a process and an outcome that will encourage women to behave in empowered ways because the (organisational) culture and communication is supportive and provides an environment that nurtures empowerment. Unless a work environment provides support for empowered women, they will quickly become frustrated. More than that 'gender balance alone cannot be the process or outcome in a world ridden with poverty and in class inequality' (Parpart, Rai and Straudt 2002: 244). In many instances, women's empowerment is judged by the visibility of women in the workplace. It is wrong to assume that if more women are seen in the workplace then women are empowered and that unequal status among women and men workers has been eliminated.

Empowerment as a Liberation Strategy

The concept of empowerment is misconstrued and used incorrectly in a number of local, national and global forums. Often, new and young democracies (and a few of the older ones) measure their empowerment record and successes in terms of the number of women in senior positions in corporate organisations and in government. Yet these same democracies have not altered the rules of engagement to nurture the empowered groups and individuals. Policies and practices to further develop the wider organisational community to recognise and accept women's contributions are either absent or hardly visible. So simply placing more women in senior positions does not necessarily mean that women in that organisation and society are empowered and liberated. While this chapter approaches issues of power and powerlessness in accordance with Western culture, it is important to note that other communities place power and powerlessness in different perspectives. For example, Bonvillain (1997: 337) drawing on research (Erickson 1978; Wetzel 1988 as cited by Bonvillain) on the concept of power and powerlessness in Japanese culture alerts us to the fact that in Japanese culture the powerless style is valued by all Japanese speakers. Powerlessness is considered as an 'indicator of the speaker's basic humanness'. As this example illustrates, powerlessness in a non-Western content is regarded as a strength.

In recent years empowerment has emerged as a concept that would liberate women from their enslaved states and provide them with an opportunity to embrace that promised freedom to make choices and to contribute fully to their societies. Empowerment is regarded as a desired result across the globe, but several questions emerge: why are women still confined to a state of disempowerment? why are they disempowered in Western democracies? why do they remain 'disenfranchised' even though they are more visible? does higher or equal representation of women in all areas of society mean that they are empowered? and what policies and practices are in place to support women's empowerment in a democracy, for example?

Gender and Access to Power

As mentioned earlier, the dominant paradigm of development favoured men over women. While the Women in Development (WID) movements in the mid-20th century called for greater participation of women, they were criticised for their focus on 'greater equality between the sexes' (Melkote and Steeves 2001: 189) instead of 'access to resources and power'. The WID movements were countered by Gender and Development (GAD) groups that called for integrating the 'assumptions of the dominant social, economic, and political structures that accord and perpetuate an inferior status to women relative to men,' according to Melkote and Steeves (2001: 189).

The absence or presence of power is an important factor in determining the potential or barrier to accomplish one's goals in a situation and in an organisation. Melkote and Steeves (2001: 356) argue that 'individuals are impoverished or sick or often are slow to adopt useful practices, not because they lack knowledge or reason, but because they do not have access to appropriate or sustainable opportunities to improve their lives. This is an issue of power.' They further contend that empowerment (ibid: 365) 'provides individuals, communities, and organizations with the necessary skills, confidence, and countervailing power to deal effectively with social change...' Colwill (in Dunn 1997: 186) in her study of women in management in the US and Canadian cultural context provides a very interesting analysis of power and powerlessness in organisations. She approaches the subject from three perspectives: personal power (power to control); interpersonal power (power to influence) and organisational power (power to access resources). Colwill (ibid: 100) found that in terms of personal power, women managers share the same control of their environment as men. With regard to interpersonal power, women were less able to influence others than men have, and with regard to organisational power, current research point to the fact that women are more effective business mangers than men. Marian Court (in Dunn 1997: 216) investigates the role of men and women in management in the field of education in New Zealand and concludes that 'what must change is the hegemony that reinforces ideas and structures that maintain certain kinds of male individuals as the leaders of society and the definers of culture.'

WOMEN AS CATALYSTS FOR CHANGE

Living and experiencing life in a developing community context presents many additional challenges to women. In developing communities, women's struggle is intensified several times in relation to their lived realities. However, in both developed and developing communities, women are not recognised as catalysts for change outside of their homes, in the mainstream of society and particularly in organisations in which they work. Yet over the centuries in many cultures women have been considered as the more significant advocates for change. When it came to their roles as mothers in a household, they have been responsible for discipline, the transmission of oral history, provision of nurturing and nourishment to their families, and for the social and religious education of their children. They have been regarded as the mothers of nations imparting knowledge and transmitting cultural norms and values to future generations. In the workplace however, women have been denied their right to become active participants in the creation and dissemination of knowledge, and to continue in their role as catalysts for change.

CONCLUSION

The preceding discussion briefly reviews concerns related to women's workplace dilemmas and it raises many important questions for further critical reflection. If we are committed to social equality and justice for all people, then we are obligated to take responsibility and action to create a fair and just working environment. Commitment to a social

responsibility ethic in the workplace is a precondition for the promotion
of social justice. Locating women's struggles within a cultural context
in an organisation recognises that women have a more complex but an
equally important role within an organisation. Acknowledgement and
recognition of women's struggles in a cultural context is a necessary first
step in organisational restructuring. Organisations must reshape their
organisation's cultural profiles; revisit their communication perspectives;
and rewrite their human resource portfolios in order to meaningfully
embrace and reflect women's cultural perspectvies.

REFERENCES

Bonvillain, N. 1997. *Language, Culture, and Communication: The Meaning of Messages*. 2nd
    edition. Upper Saddle River, NJ: Prentice Hall.
Conrad, C. and M.S. Poole. 2005. *Organizational Communication*. Belmont, California:
    Thomson Wadsworth.
Dunn, D. 1997. *Workplace/Women's Place*. Los Angles, California: Roxbury Publishing
    Company.
Hart, P., K. Weathermon and S. Armitage. 2006. *Women Writing Women: The Frontier Reader*.
    Lincoln, Nebaska: University of Nebraska Press.
Melkote, S.R. and L. Steeves. 2001. *Communication for Development in the Third World Theory
    and Practice for Empowerment*, New Delhi: Sage Publishers.
Parpart, J.L., S. Rai and K. Staudt. 2002. *Rethinking Empowerment Gender and Development
    in a Global/Local World*. London: Routledge.
Punnett, B.J. 2004. *International Perspectives on Organizational Behaviour and Human Resources
    Management*. New York: M.E.Sharpe, Inc.
Samovar, L.A. and E.R. Porter. 2005. *Communication between Cultures*. 4th edition. Toronto:
    Wadsworth, Thomson Learning Inc.
Samovar, L.A., E.R. Porter and E. McDaniel. 2007. *Communication between Cultures*.
    6th edition. Toronto: Wadsworth, Thomson Learning Inc.
Wood, J. 2001. *Gendered Lives: Communication, Gender and Culture*. 4th edition. Belmont,
    California: Thomson Wadsworth.
———. 2005. *Gendered Lives: Communication, Gender, and Culture*. 6th edition. Toronto,
    Ontario: Thomson Wadsworth.

About the Editors and Contributors

THE EDITORS

Kogi Naidoo is Deputy Director and Associate Professor at the Centre for Learning and Professional Development, University of Adelaide, Australia. Kogi Naidoo was born in South Africa and has worked in South Africa, New Zealand and Australia. She is a HERDSA Fellow (Higher Education Research and Development Society of Australasia) and has extensive work experience lecturing in English and Education, worked in the areas of academic development, research and quality assurance in South Africa and New Zealand. Her postgraduate research included designing evaluation programmes for staff development and quality assurance mechanisms for academic programmes. She has presented and published her work nationally and internationally, and has received numerous prestigious academic awards and fellowships, including the South African Junior Technikon Fellowship Award, the Ernest Oppenheimer Gold Medal and the South African Association for Research and Development in Higher Education (SAARDHE) Young Achiever Award. At Massey University she led a mentoring programme for women and is presently leading a national research project investigating the impact of academic development on first year student learning in New Zealand. Kogi has maintained a healthy work life balance and owes her success to her supportive family, her husband and two children, who are themselves now pursuing successful careers.

Fay Patel was born in South Africa. She is a new immigrant in Canada and a migrant worker in New Zealand. Fay has over 25 years of international experience in higher education in Canada, the USA, New Zealand and South Africa as a professor, researcher and programme manager across several disciplines.

Fay coordinates the teaching and learning programme at Massey University in New Zealand. Fay (then known by her maiden name of Gangat) began her higher education career at the University of Durban-Westville during the Apartheid years. The University was regarded as an Indian university which provided segregated education for Indian students only taught by white professors. During the early 1990s, she moved to Vista University and this was an African University in Pretoria with an Afrikaans and English speaking management and teaching staff.

Fay received several awards and scholarships to study in the United States of America between 1988 and 1998. This included a Fulbright Scholarship in 1994 and a doctoral study scholarship in 1998. Her areas of interest and expertise include international development, intercultural communication, teaching English as a second language, organisational communication, the diffusion of innovations in organisations, and promoting and managing academic development initiatives in higher educational institutions. Current research includes enhancing student learning, the integration of women's cultural perspectives and identities in the workplace, and building a global community.

THE CONTRIBUTORS

Robyn Andrews is a lecturer in social anthropology at Massey University, New Zealand. She has recently completed her doctoral thesis titled 'Being Anglo-Indian: Practices and Stories from Calcutta' (2005). This work is based on research over a three and a half year period from 2001 through 2004. In that time she spent prolonged periods of time in Calcutta where, among other fieldwork practices, she collected life stories of Anglo-Indians. She is particularly interested in the dynamics that are enabling the Anglo-Indian community to continue to exist as a distinct minority community despite the prognosis of decline and demise of the community due to eroding factors such as mass migration since Indian Independence. She is also interested in portraying what it means to be Anglo-Indian, living in Calcutta in the 21st century.

Sheila Chirkut passed away after a sudden, short illness early January 2008. Her children, both medical professionals, gave permission to publish her paper posthumously. Sheila Chirkut was a post-doctoral fellow at the University of KwaZulu-Natal. She taught courses in gender studies, social institutions, sociological analysis and social research, and social change in a global context. She has presented papers at conferences, both local and international, and has published articles on the cultural identity on Hindu women in South Africa.

Millicent Daweti is an education consultant at the University of South Africa. She is a mother of two and has worked as a school teacher, advisor and manager. She is currently pursuing doctoral studies in educational leadership and management. Her research interests include adult learning and organisational development.

Shelda Debowski directs the organisational and staff development unit at the University of Western Australia. She worked as an academic in library and information science for many years and later, in management. She has published widely in the areas of teaching and learning and organisational development. Her recent book, *Knowledge Management* (Wiley Press, 2006), explores the ways in which knowledge communities are evolving and adapting. She is active in the wider higher education community, and is currently the President of the Higher Education Research and Development Society of Australasia. She also has extensive experience as a leadership and development consultant to industry and educational enterprises.

Arlene Fester was born on the 19 August 1964 in Kraaifontein, Bellville, South Africa. Her father died of cancer when she was seven and her mother taught her to cook when she was 12. She has two sisters. They had a very big house in Kraaifontein, which her father built himself on 496sq metres of property. In 1975 they were forced off their property by the Apartheid government and then moved to Greenhaven. Arlene matriculated at Cathkin High School. In 1997 she completed her Diploma in Counselling and also a Beginners and Advance Course in Sign Language (for the Deaf). She started a ministry dance group

'Worship through Signing' using sign language and incorporated it with worship music and illustrating it through dance.

Dennis Francis is Associate Professor and currently, the Head of School of Social Science Education at the University of KwaZulu-Natal. He holds a PhD in sociology. He has written extensively in the areas of race, education for social justice, youth, sexuality and HIV/AIDS.

Nirmala Gopal is a researcher and lecturer at the University of Kwa-Zulu Natal. She has been working with children and women issues over a number of years. She has completed a doctorate in education where she examined the experiences of AIDS orphans. In her masters degree she focused on the way in which child sexual abuse is managed by educators at Indian schools. She has written about human rights, democracy and social justice. Her interest in children also led her to research and write about a group of refugee learners and the way in which they are treated in their host country. She has also looked at women in prison and the issues of power in lesbian relationships. She has presented several papers at both national and international conferences. She strongly believes that women's voices in research continues to be marginalised and advocates strongly against this practice.

Lynne Hunt is Pro Vice-Chancellor (Learning and Teaching) and Director, Learning and Teaching Support Unit, at the University of Southern Queensland. She has taught at all levels of higher education from transition to university to doctoral supervision. In the past decade, she has focused on change leadership to promote tertiary teaching and transitions in the student learning journey, in particular the first year experience, work-based university learning and postgraduate mentoring. She is the recipient of three university-level awards for teaching excellence and she is a nationally acknowledged teacher. She received the 2002 Australian Award for University Teaching in the Social Science category and the 2002 Prime Minister's Award for Australian University Teacher of the Year.

She publishes in the fields of health, sociology and tertiary teaching and received the 2002 Merit Award for Best Paper on Authentic Learning from the Higher Education Research and Development Society of

Australasia (HERDSA). She also co-edited the book, *The Realities of Change in Higher Education: Interventions to Promote Learning and Teaching* (2006). She was a member of the Board of the Australian Learning and Teaching Council (ALTC) from its inception until March 2008, and remains a member of two of its sub-committees. She has also served as a HERDSA Fellow and mentor, a member of the Academic Committee of the Batchelor Institute of Indigenous Tertiary Education (2005–2006) and as examination moderator for the University of Botswana (2003–2005).

Heide Kaminski is a single mother of three children and lives in South East Michigan. She was born and raised in Germany, but moved to the USA permanently in 1984. She is a preschool art teacher, freelance reporter/photographer and a published author. She also has stories included in more than 15 anthologies and has articles published in print magazines as well as online magazines. On the side, she does a little acting, with credits in three indie movies. On Sundays, she teaches Sunday school at the local Interfaith Center. Her dream is to break out of the low-income world by making her writing known to the world. Even though she is twice divorced, she has not given up hope that there is still someone out there who would represent a good husband.

Check out her books at www.thewriterslife.net/Kaminski.html; www. milliondollarghost.homestead.com; www.shadowbooks.homestead. com/homepage.html

Maureen Lewis began her higher education teaching career in South Africa where she taught art and history of art methodology for nine years. Maureen moved to New Zealand in 1994 and taught secondary school art until she was hired as a staff development lecturer at Manikau Institute for Technology for the past 11 years. She worked as a staff development programme leader for a teacher training programme. Maureen was involved in the induction of new staff and this included migrant staff who were introduced to a mentoring and support programme during their induction.

Thenjiwe Magwaza is Programme Director at the University of KwaZulu-Natal in the Gender Studies Department. She holds a doctoral degree in oral studies from the same university. Her area of research is cultural constructions of gender; with a special focus on the Zulu language and culture, and the impact of HIV/AIDS on women and home care givers. She has published papers and book chapters in these areas. Her recent publication is a co-edited book (2006) entitled 'Freedom Sown in Blood: Memories of the Impi Yamakhanda'.

Shirley Mthethwa-Sommers is presently an independent consultant. Her work focuses on social justice issues. She has taught in higher educational institutions in the USA and in South Africa and serves the boards of numerous feminism-centred organisations.

Nokujabula Myeza holds a masters degree in social justice education from the University of KwaZulu-Natal. She has taught for 20 years at a primary school in Lamontville, a township south of Durban. She serves as the regional gender convenor of the South African Democratic Teachers Union (SADTU) where she has worked with educators infected and affected by HIV. Nokujabula is currently the Deputy Chief Education Specialist in the province of KwaZulu-Natal, Department of Education and Culture.

Vivian Besem Ojong holds a PhD in anthropology and teaches at the University of KwaZulu-Natal, Howard college campus. Her research interests are in the fields of migration, gender, identity, inter-cultural mixing, entrepreneurship and livelihoods. Currently she is the deputy president for Anthropology Southern Africa and co-edits the newsletter of the association.

Anniekie Ravhudzulo is married to Dr Aaron; she is a loving wife, a woman of courage and a busy mother of four sons Hangwani, Hulisani, Thendo and Ndamulelo, a grand daughter Muanza-Zwivhuya and a daughter-in-law, Sara. Presently she is a research coordinator. She completed Master Doctorate in education. She published several motivational books.

Diane Saarinen is a freelance writer, and a regular contributor to *New World Finn* journal and *Finlandia Weekly* newspaper. Her work has appeared in numerous publications including *Quiet Mountain: New Feminist Essays, Women's eNews Daily* and *Her Circle Ezine*. She lives in Brooklyn, New York, with her husband, Peter, and their 18 pound cat. She is the book reviewer for www.newagejournal.com. She still works, albeit part-time now, as a home-based medical transcriptionist.

Kay Sexton was nominated by Pushcart and spent more than a decade as a house writer for charitable/environmental organisations worldwide. Her publication credits range from *H&E International* to *France Today* to the World Water Forum Annual Report and she works regularly with Jonathan Porritt, Chair of the UK Sustainability Commission. In addition she is an Associate Editor for *Night Train* journal USA and a Jerry Jazz Fiction Award winner with a column at www.moondance. org. Her website www.charybdis.freeserve.co.uk gives details of her copywriting and journalism, she blogs about writing fiction at http:// writingneuroses.blogspot.com/. Her current focus is 'Green Thought in an Urban Shade', a collaboration with the painter Fion Gunn to explore and celebrate the parks and urban spaces of Beijing, Dublin, London and Paris in words and images. 'Green Thought' has exhibitions in London, Dublin and Beijing.

Reshma Sookrajh is Associate Professor of education in the Faculty of Education at the University of KwaZulu-Natal. In 2005, she was the Deputy Dean of the Faculty of Education during the period of the merger of higher institutions in KwaZulu-Natal. Some of the areas include rural education in South Africa, Quality in Teacher Education and Community Education projects in the different provinces of South Africa. She has supervised the research projects of several masters and doctoral students in the discipline of curriculum and two doctoral students in the area of migration research.

Sita Venkateswar is Senior Lecturer in the social anthropology programme at Massey University. Her current research in Kolkata, India, explores poverty, empowerment and grass-roots activism. She is part of a coalition of individuals, activists and non-governmental organisations seeking policy-driven solutions to the situation of indigenous groups in the Andaman and Nicobar Islands.